Get the eBooks FREE!

(PDF, ePub, Kindle, and liveBook all included)

We believe that once you buy a book from us, you should be able to read it in any format we have available. To get electronic versions of this book at no additional cost to you, purchase and then register this book at the Manning website.

Go to https://www.manning.com/freebook and follow the instructions to complete your pBook registration.

That's it!
Thanks from Manning!

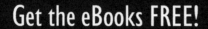

Redux in Action

Redux in Action

MARC GARREAU
WILL FAUROT
FOREWORD BY MARK ERIKSON

MANNING
SHELTER ISLAND

For online information and ordering of this and other Manning books, please visit
www.manning.com. The publisher offers discounts on this book when ordered in quantity.
For more information, please contact

> Special Sales Department
> Manning Publications Co.
> 20 Baldwin Road
> PO Box 761
> Shelter Island, NY 11964
> Email: orders@manning.com

Manning Publications Co.
20 Baldwin Road
PO Box 761
Shelter Island, NY 11964

Acquisitions editor:	Brian Sawyer
Development editor:	Toni Arritola
Technical development editor:	German Frigerio
Review editor:	Ivan Martinović
Project manager:	David Novak
Copy editor:	Katie Petito
Technical proofreader:	Ryan Burrows
Proofreader:	Alyson Brener
Typesetter:	Dennis Dalinnik
Cover designer:	Marija Tudor

ISBN: 9781617294976
Printed in the United States of America
1 2 3 4 5 6 7 8 9 10 – EBM – 23 22 21 20 19 18

To my wife for her dance moves, my family and friends for pretending to know what I'm on about, and the universe for plain good luck

—Marc Garreau

For M + D

—Will Faurot

brief contents

contents

foreword

Since its release in mid-2015, Redux has captured the attention of the JavaScript world. From its humble beginnings as a proof-of-concept for a conference demo and label as "just another Flux implementation," it's grown to become the most widely used state management solution for React applications. It's also been adopted for use by the Angular, Ember, and Vue communities and inspired dozens of imitations and spinoffs.

One of my favorite quotes is, "Redux is a generic framework that provides a balance of just enough structure and just enough flexibility. As such, it provides a platform for developers to build customized state management for their use-cases, while being able to reuse things like the graphical debugger or middleware."[1] Indeed, while Redux supplies a basic set of tools to work with and outlines a general pattern to follow for organizing your app's update logic, it's ultimately up to you to decide how to build your app around Redux. You lay out your app's file structures, write the reducer logic, connect the components, and determine how much abstraction you want to use on top of Redux.

The learning curve for Redux can be steep at times. Functional programming and immutability are unfamiliar concepts to most developers coming from object-oriented languages. Writing yet another TodoMVC example doesn't really showcase the benefits of Redux, or how to tackle building a "real" application. But the end benefits are worth it. The ability to clearly trace data flow in your application and understand

---

[1] Joseph Savona, Facebook engineer (https://github.com/reactjs/redux/issues/775#issuecomment-257923575).

where/when/why/how a particular piece of state changed is incredibly valuable, and good Redux usage ultimately leads to code that's more maintainable and predictable for the long term.

I've spent most of my time as a Redux maintainer helping people learn Redux by answering questions, improving the docs, and writing tutorial blog posts. In the process, I've seen hundreds of different Redux tutorials. With that in mind, I'm extremely happy to recommend *Redux in Action* as one of the best resources to learn Redux.

With *Redux in Action*, Marc Garreau and Will Faurot have written the Redux book I wish I'd written myself. It's comprehensive, it's practical, and it does a great job of teaching many key topics for real-world Redux apps. I especially appreciate the way this book covers areas that don't always have a single clear-cut answer, such as structuring a project, by laying out the pros and cons and letting the reader know this is an area where they may have to decide for themselves.

In today's fast-moving programming world, no one book can completely capture everything there is to know about a tool. But, *Redux in Action* will give you a solid foundation and understanding of the fundamentals of Redux, how the pieces fit together, how to use that knowledge for real-world apps, and where to look for more information. I'm excited to see this book released and look forward to having you join the Redux community!

MARK ERIKSON
Redux co-maintainer

preface

Redux is a curious little tool. As you'll discover, there's not all that much to it. You can familiarize yourself with each of its methods before you finish a cup of coffee.

Not only is Redux well-contained, but it's also a finished product. How often do you hear that? There's no roadmap, project manager, or Kanban board. Commits are still added to the GitHub repository, but they're usually improvements to documentation or the official examples.

How's that possible? You may find it helpful to think of Redux as an architecture pattern. The package you install from npm is an implementation of that pattern and it provides you with enough functionality to get your application off the ground.

The real kicker is how much you can accomplish with only those few methods. The stark truth is that the Redux pattern can completely untangle a JavaScript application, leaving behind something more predictable, intuitive, and performant. Thanks to the same pattern, the developer tools also provide unprecedented insight into an application's state and the flow of data through it.

But what's the catch? All software choices come with tradeoffs, and Redux is no exception. The cost is tremendous flexibility. That may sound like another advantage, but it presents interesting challenges. The Redux pattern isn't strictly enforced by the library or any other tool, and the small package cannot hope to educate or guide the developer to use the pattern effectively itself.

In the end, it's up to the developer to find their own way. This explains why the lines of documentation in the GitHub repository dramatically outnumber the lines of implementation code. As excellent as the official documentation is, developers typically gather context and best practices from scattered resources on and off the web: blog posts, books, tweets, videos, online courses, and so on.

The flexibility allowed by Redux also results in a rich ecosystem of add-ons: libraries for selectors, enhancers, middleware, and more. You'll be hard-pressed to find two Redux applications using exactly the same toolset. While it's great that each project can tailor their tools to their unique needs, this can be a source of confusion for newly introduced developers. Newcomers to Redux often find themselves staring down a challenging learning curve when they're asked to absorb not only Redux, but also the complexity of supplemental packages layered on. This is the main reason we wanted to write the book: to distill our personal experience and knowledge from dozens of different sources into one neat, accessible package.

We believe the real value of this book will be measured by how well it guides you through the rich Redux ecosystem, one bite-sized piece at a time. This won't be an exhaustive look at all the supplemental tooling. Instead, we've chosen a handful of the most popular add-ons that you're likely to see in the wild and are robust enough to tackle any client project. With that, happy reading! We're grateful you've chosen to spend your time with us.

acknowledgments

Writing a book is quite the undertaking. There are so many people who were vital to the process, whether directly or indirectly, that naming them all here may require all of the 300+ pages left in the book. We stand on the shoulders of decades of giants.

A strong community is the foundation of all successful software. The Redux community is a particularly strong one, and we're indebted to everyone who shared an approach they liked in a blog post, helped a fellow Redux user on a GitHub issue, or answered a question on any of the many online platforms frequented by Redux users across the globe.

First and foremost, this book wouldn't be possible without the work of Dan Abramov and Andrew Clark, the creators of Redux. On top of spending the time to research and implement Redux, they've spent countless hours supporting developers over the past few years. We'd also like to thank the current maintainers of Redux, Mark Erikson and Tim Dorr. On top of regular maintenance, like responding to issues and merging code, they volunteer their time on several different platforms. Together, these folks contributed a substantial amount of research to this book, and it wouldn't have been possible without them. Whether its weighing in on best practices, writing documentation, or providing feedback to curious developers, none of it goes unnoticed. We appreciate you.

Thanks to the entire team at Manning, including all our editors, for their guidance and support. We'd like to extend a special thank you to Ryan Burrows for his valuable feedback that helped improve the code for this book, as well as Mark Erikson for taking the time to put together a wonderful foreword. We would also like to recognize the reviewers who took the time to read and comment on our book: Alex Chittock, Clay Harris, Fabrizio Cucci, Ferit Topcu, Ian Lovell, Jeremy Lange, John Hooks, Jorge Ezequiel Bo, Jose San Leandro, Joyce Echessa, Matej Strasek, Matthew Heck, Maura Wilder, Michael Stevens, Pardo David, Rebecca Peltz, Ryan Burrows, Ryan Huber, Thomas Overby Hansen, and Vasile Boris. Thanks to all of you.

An extra-special thank you goes to our MEAP readers and forum participants. Your feedback and encouragement were crucial to the development of the book.

MARC GARREAU

Thanks first to my wife, Becky, who made the ultimate sacrifice: living with someone who's writing a book. I promise that I will probably not write another. Thank you to my family for mirroring my excitement, even if I were writing a book about slugs. Thanks to my friends for inspiring me, helping me combat imposter syndrome, and providing healthy distractions. More thanks to Jeff Casimir, Jorge Téllez, Steve Kinney, Rachel Warbelow, Josh Cheek, and Horace Williams for opening doors for Will and me in this industry. Thank you to Ingrid Alongi and Chris McAvoy for modeling empathic technical leadership in my career. Finally, thank you to my early JavaScript mentors, and particularly Michael Phillips, for imparting not only tolerance, but also enthusiasm for the technology.

WILL FAUROT

Thank you first and foremost to my parents. I wouldn't have made it without your guidance, enthusiasm, and encouragement. You helped me realize that something like this was even possible. You taught me how to believe in myself. Thank you.

Thank you to my family for all your support and love.

Thanks to everyone at Instacart who helped by giving feedback or by talking over ideas. Special thanks to Dominic Cocchiarella and Jon Hsieh.

Finally, thanks to Lovisa Svallingson, Alan Smith, Allison Larson, Gray Gilmore, Tan Doan, Hilary Denton, Andrew Watkins, Krista Nelson, and Regan Kuchan, who all provided invaluable feedback and encouragement throughout the writing process. You're the best friends and software confidants I could ask for.

about this book

Redux is a state management library, designed to make building complicated user interfaces easier. It's most commonly used with React, which we pair it with in this book, but it's also becoming popular with other front end libraries such as Angular.

In 2015, the React ecosystem sorely needed Redux to come along. Predating Redux, the Flux architecture pattern was an exciting breakthrough, and React developers around the world tried their hand at an implementation. Dozens of libraries received noteworthy attention and use. Eventually, the excitement gave way to exhaustion. The number of choices for managing state in a React application was overwhelming.

Redux immediately started to pick up steam after its release, and soon became the most recommended Flux-inspired library. Its use of a single store, focus on immutability, and amazing developer experience proved Redux to be a more simple, elegant, and intuitive solution to most of the issues facing existing Flux libraries. You still have several options for managing state in complex applications, but for those who prefer a Flux-like pattern, Redux has become the default.

This book will walk you through the fundamentals of Redux before moving on to explore the powerful developer tools. Together, we'll work step-by-step through a task-management application, where we'll explore real-world Redux usage with a focus on best practices. Finally, we'll circle back to testing strategies and the various conventions for structuring your applications.

Who should read this book

Readers should be comfortable with JavaScript (including ES2015) and have at least basic proficiency with React. We understand, though, that many developers end up getting thrown into Redux at approximately the same moment they're being introduced to React. We've tried our best to accommodate those in this category, and we believe they can make their way through this book with a little extra effort. However, our official recommendation is to gain a strong foundation in React prior to reading this book. If you haven't done any React development, consider the Manning titles *React Quickly* (https://www.manning.com/books/react-quickly) or *React in Action* (https://www.manning.com/books/react-in-action).

How this book is organized: a roadmap

This book includes 12 chapters and an appendix.

Chapter 1 introduces the landscape that Redux was born into and why it was created. You'll learn what Redux is, what it's used for, and when not to use it. The chapter wraps up with several state management alternatives to Redux.

Chapter 2 jumps headlong into your first React and Redux application. It's a whirlwind tour of a typical workflow used to create new features. You'll get a good high-level view of each of the actors involved: actions, reducers, the store, and so on.

Chapter 3 takes a step back to introduce the high-powered Redux DevTools. The developer tools are one of the biggest selling points for using Redux, and this chapter demonstrates why.

Chapter 4 finally introduces side effects to the example started in chapter 2. You'll set up a local server and handle API requests within the Redux pattern.

Chapter 5 dives into a more advanced feature: middleware. You'll learn where middleware sits in the stack, what it's capable of, and how to build custom middleware of your own.

Chapter 6 explores an advanced pattern for handling more complex side effects. You'll learn how to leverage ES6 generator functions; then you'll learn how to use sagas to manage long-running processes.

Chapter 7 puts the spotlight on the connection between the Redux store and your views. You'll learn how selector functions work, then implement a robust solution using the reselect library.

Chapter 8 addresses the common question as to how best to structure data in a Redux store. You'll reflect on the strategy used up to this point in the book, then explore an alternative approach: normalization.

Chapter 9 circles back to cover all things testing. You'll learn about popular testing tools such as Jest and Enzyme, as well as strategies for testing Redux actions, reducers, selectors, and much more.

Chapter 10 is all about keeping your application lean and mean. It covers performance profiling tools, React best practices, and Redux-specific strategies for boosting performance.

Chapter 11 covers several strategies for organizing your Redux application. Redux doesn't mind where you put things, so you'll learn popular conventions that have been established.

Chapter 12 reminds you that Redux can manage the state of more than a React web application. You'll get a quick tour of the role Redux can play in mobile, desktop, and other web application environments.

The appendix provides instructions for environment setup and tool installation. The book will direct you to the appendix at appropriate points.

About the code

Most of the code examples are for Parsnip, the book's example application. These examples are included as numbered listings, many of which are annotated to provide clarity and reasoning behind certain code choices. Code examples directly in the text can be identified by a fixed-width typeface, `like this`.

Source code for the examples in the book can be downloaded from the publisher's website at https://www.manning.com/books/redux-in-action or at https://github.com/wfro/parsnip.

One-step install scripts are available for OSX, Linux, and Windows, and are available along with the rest of the book's source code. See the appendix for instructions on getting started.

Software requirements

Most of the code examples, especially those related to the example application, require a web browser. We recommend Chrome, which will work seamlessly with React and Redux developer tools.

We bootstrapped the example application with create-react-app, which isn't strictly required, but highly recommended. It's the most painless way to set up a modern React development environment.

We used the following Create React App and Redux versions:

- Redux: 3.7.2
- Create React App: 1.0.17

Book forum

Purchase of *Redux in Action* includes free access to a private web forum run by Manning Publications where you can make comments about the book, ask technical questions, and receive help from the authors and from other users. To access the forum, go to https://forums.manning.com/forums/redux-in-action. You can also learn more about Manning's forums and the rules of conduct at https://forums.manning.com/forums/about.

Manning's commitment to our readers is to provide a venue where a meaningful dialogue between individual readers and between readers and the authors can take place. It isn't a commitment to any specific amount of participation on the part of the authors, whose contribution to the forum remains voluntary (and unpaid). We suggest you try asking the authors challenging questions lest their interest stray! The forum and the archives of previous discussions will be accessible from the publisher's website as long as the book is in print.

Other online resources

The Redux community is incredibly active on several different platforms. We recommend all the following resources to learn more, help solidify concepts, and ask questions:

- Reactiflux, the major chatroom for discussing React and Redux, is located at https://www.reactiflux.com/.
- Glossary from the Redux docs. For all its benefits, Redux does require a fair amount of jargon. Especially for beginners, referencing back to the glossary is incredibly valuable. See https://github.com/reactjs/redux/blob/master/docs/Glossary.md for more information.
- The official Redux documentation is at https://redux.js.org/.
- Mark Erikson's "Practical Redux" blog series. This is better for intermediate to advanced Redux users, because it provides more of a deep dive into real-world Redux usage. For more information, see http://blog.isquaredsoftware.com/2016/10/practical-redux-part-0-introduction/.

about the authors

 MARC GARREAU is a developer at the Ethereum Foundation on the Mist core team, where he wrangles application state in the Mist browser. Previously, he architected and executed applications using Redux at consultancies Cognizant and Quick Left. He's written a number of popular Redux blog posts and has spoken at several JavaScript meetups in the Denver area.

 WILL FAUROT is a full stack developer at Instacart, where he works on various consumer-facing products. A lover of all things front end, he specializes in building complex user interfaces with React and Redux. In past lives he taught tennis professionally and recorded old-time and bluegrass music. If you listen closely on a quiet night in the Bay Area, you may hear him plucking a few banjo strings.

about the cover illustration

The figure on the cover of *Redux in Action* is captioned "Habit of a Moorish Woman in 1695." The illustration is taken from Thomas Jefferys' *A Collection of the Dresses of Different Nations, Ancient and Modern* (four volumes), London, published between 1757 and 1772. The title page states that these are hand-colored copperplate engravings, heightened with gum arabic. Thomas Jefferys (1719–1771) was called "Geographer to King George III." He was an English cartographer who was the leading map supplier of his day. He engraved and printed maps for government and other official bodies and produced a wide range of commercial maps and atlases, especially of North America. His work as a map maker sparked an interest in local dress customs of the lands he surveyed and mapped, which are brilliantly displayed in this collection.

Fascination with faraway lands and travel for pleasure were relatively new phenomena in the late 18th century and collections such as this one were popular, introducing both the tourist as well as the armchair traveler to the inhabitants of other countries. The diversity of the drawings in Jefferys' volumes speaks vividly of the uniqueness and individuality of the world's nations some 200 years ago. Dress codes have changed since then and the diversity by region and country, so rich at the time, has faded away. It is now often hard to tell the inhabitant of one continent from another. Perhaps, trying to view it optimistically, we have traded a cultural and visual diversity for a more varied personal life. Or a more varied and interesting intellectual and technical life.

At a time when it is hard to tell one computer book from another, Manning celebrates the inventiveness and initiative of the computer business with book covers based on the rich diversity of regional life of two centuries ago, brought back to life by Jeffreys' pictures.

Introducing Redux 1

This chapter covers

- Defining Redux
- Understanding the differences between Flux and Redux
- Using Redux with React
- Introducing actions, reducers, and the store
- Learning when to use Redux

If you hop into any React web application in 2018, there's a good chance you'll find Redux there to manage its state. It's remarkable that we reached this place so quickly, though. A few years ago, Redux had yet to be created and React enjoyed an excited and blossoming user base. Early adopters of React believed that they'd found the best solution yet to the view layer—the "V" of the MVC (Model-View-Controller) front-end framework puzzle. What they couldn't agree on was how to manage the state of those applications once they became the size and complexity that the real world demands. Eventually, Redux settled the debate.

Throughout the course of this book, we'll explore Redux and its ecosystem through the lens of a React application. As you'll learn, Redux can be plugged into JavaScript applications of all flavors, but React is an ideal playground for a few rea-

1

sons. Chief among those reasons: Redux was created in the context of React. You're most likely to encounter Redux within a React application, and React is agnostic about how you manage the data layer of your application. Without further ado, let's jump in.

1.1   *What is state?*

React components have the concept of local, or component, state. Within any given component, you can keep track of the value of an input field or whether a button has been toggled, for example. Local state makes easy work of managing a single component's behavior. However, today's single-page applications often require synchronizing a complex web of state. Nested levels of components may render a different user experience based on the pages a user has already visited, the status of an AJAX request, or whether a user is logged in.

Let's consider a use case involving the authentication status of a user. Your product manager tells you that when a user is logged into an ecommerce store, the navigation bar should display the user's avatar image, the store should display items nearest to the user's zip code first, and the newsletter signup form should be hidden. Within a vanilla React architecture, your options are limited for syncing state across each of the components. In the end, you'll likely end up passing the authentication status and additional user data from one top-level component down to each of these nested components.

This architecture has several disadvantages. Along the way, data may filter through components that have no use for it other than to pass the data on to their children. In a large application, this can result in tons of data moving through unrelated components, passed down via props or passed up using callbacks. It's likely that a small number of components at the top of the application end up with an awareness of most of the state used throughout the entire application. At a certain scale, maintaining and testing this code becomes untenable. Because React wasn't intended to solve the same breadth of problems that other MVC frameworks attempted to address, an opportunity existed to bridge those gaps.

With React in mind, Facebook eventually introduced Flux, an architecture pattern for web applications. Flux became tremendously influential in the world of front-end development and began a shift in how we thought about state management in client-side applications. Facebook offered its own implementation of this pattern, but soon more than a dozen Flux-inspired state management libraries emerged and competed for React developers' attention.

This was a tumultuous time for React developers looking to scale an application. We saw the light with Flux but continued to experiment to find more elegant ways to manage complex state in applications. For a time, newcomers encountered a paradox of choice; a divided community effort had produced so many options, it was anxiety-inducing. To our surprise and delight, though, the dust is already settling and Redux has emerged as a clear winner.

Redux took the React world by storm with a simple premise, a big payoff, and a memorable introduction. The premise is to store your entire application state in a single object using pure functions. The payoff is a totally predictable application state. The introduction, for most early users, came in Dan Abramov's 2015 React Europe conference talk, titled "Live React: Hot Reloading with Time Travel." Dan wowed attendees by demonstrating a Redux developer experience that blew established workflows out of the water. A technique called hot loading makes live application updates while maintaining existing state, and his nascent Redux developer tools enable you to time travel through application state—rewinding and replaying user actions with a single click. The combined effect offers developers debugging super powers, which we'll explain in detail in chapter 3.

To understand Redux, we'd first like to properly introduce you to Flux, the architecture pattern developed at Facebook and credited to Jing Chen. Redux and many of its alternatives are variations of this Flux architecture.

1.2 What is Flux?

Flux is foremost an architecture pattern. It was developed as an alternative to the prevailing MVC JavaScript patterns popularized by incumbent frameworks, such as Backbone, Angular, or Ember. Although each framework puts its own spin on the MVC pattern, many share similar frustrations: generally, the flow of data between models, views, and controllers can be difficult to follow.

Many of these frameworks use two-way data binding, in which changes to the views update corresponding models, and changes in the models update corresponding views. When any given view can update one or more models, which in turn can update more views, you can't be blamed for losing track of the expected outcome at a certain scale. Chen contested that although MVC frameworks work well for smaller applications, the two-way data-binding models that many of them employ don't scale well enough for the size of Facebook's application. Developers at the company became apprehensive of making changes, for fear of the tangled web of dependencies producing unintended consequences.

Flux sought to address the unpredictability of state and the fragility of a tightly coupled model and view architecture. Chen scrapped the two-way data-binding model in favor of a unidirectional data flow. Instead of permitting each view to interact with its corresponding models, Flux requires all changes to state to follow a single path. When a user clicks a Submit button on a form, for example, an action is sent to the application's one and only dispatcher. The dispatcher will then send the data through to the appropriate data stores for updating. Once updated, the views will become aware of the new data to render. Figure 1.1 illustrates this unidirectional data flow.

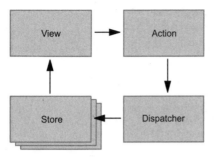

Figure 1.1   Flux specifies that data must flow in a single direction.

1.2.1   *Actions*

Every change to state starts with an action (figure 1.1). An action is a JavaScript object describing an event in your application. They're typically generated by either a user interaction or by a server event, such as an HTTP response.

1.2.2   *Dispatcher*

All data flow in a Flux application is funneled through a single dispatcher. The dispatcher itself has little functionality, because its purpose is to receive all actions and send them to each store that has been registered. Every action will be sent to every store.

1.2.3   *Stores*

Each store manages the state of one domain within an application. In an ecommerce site, you may expect to find a shopping cart store and a product store, for example. Once a store is registered with the dispatcher, it begins to receive actions. When it receives an action type that it cares about, the store updates accordingly. Once a change to the store is made, an event is broadcast to let the views know to update using the new state.

1.2.4   *Views*

Flux may have been designed with React in mind, but the views aren't required to be React components. For their part, the views need only subscribe to the stores from which they want to display data. The Flux documentation encourages the use of the controller-view pattern, whereby a top-level component handles communication with the stores and passes data to child components. Having both a parent and a nested child component communicating with stores can lead to extra renders and unintended side-effects.

Again, Flux is an architecture pattern first. The Facebook team maintains one simple implementation of this pattern, aptly (or confusingly, depending on your perspective) named Flux. Many alternative implementations have emerged since 2014, including Alt, Reflux, and Redux. A more comprehensive list of these alternative implementations can be found in section 1.6.

1.3 What is Redux?

We can't put it much better than the official docs: "Redux is a predictable state container for JavaScript applications" (https://redux.js.org/). It's a standalone library, but it's used most often as a state management layer with React. Like Flux, its major goal is to bring consistency and predictability to the data in applications. Redux divides the responsibilities of state management into a few separate units:

- The store holds all your application state in a single object. (We'll commonly refer to this object as the state tree.)
- The store can be updated only with actions, an object describing an event.
- Functions known as reducers specify how to transform application state. Reducers are functions that take the current state in the store and an action, then return the next state after applying any updates.

Technically speaking, Redux may not qualify as a Flux implementation. It nontrivially deviates from several of the components of the prescribed Flux architecture, such as the removal of the dispatcher altogether. Ultimately though, Redux is Flux-like and the distinction is a matter of semantics.

Redux enjoys the benefits of a predictable data flow from the Flux architecture, but it has also found ways to alleviate the uncertainty of store callback registrations. As alluded to in the previous section, it can be a pain to reconcile the state of multiple Flux stores. Redux, instead, prescribes a single store to manage the state of an entire application. You'll learn more about how this works and what the implications are in the coming sections.

1.3.1 React and Redux

Although Redux was designed and developed in the context of React, the two libraries are completely decoupled. React and Redux are connected using bindings, as shown in figure 1.2.

Figure 1.2   Redux isn't part of any existing framework or library, but additional tools called bindings connect Redux with React. Over the course of the book you'll use the react-redux package for this.

It turns out that the Redux paradigm for state management can be implemented alongside most JavaScript frameworks. Bindings exist for Angular, Backbone, Ember, and many more technologies.

Although this book is fundamentally about Redux, our treatment of it is closely tied to React. Redux is a small, standalone library, but it fits particularly well with

React components. Redux will help you define what your application does; React will handle how your application looks.

Most of the code we'll write over the course of the book, not to mention most of the React/Redux code you'll write period, will fall into a few categories:

- The application's state and behavior, handled by Redux
- Bindings, provided by the react-redux package, that connect the data in the Redux store with the view (React components)
- Stateless components that comprise much of your view layer

You'll find that React is a natural ecosystem for Redux. While React has mechanisms to manage state directly in components, the door is wide open for Redux to come in and manage the greater application state. If you're interested in an alternative ecosystem, chapter 12 explores the relationship between Redux and several other JavaScript frameworks.

1.3.2 *The three principles*

You have covered substantial ground by grokking that state in Redux is represented by a single source of truth, is read-only, and changes to it must be made with pure functions.

SINGLE SOURCE OF TRUTH

Unlike the various domain stores prescribed by the Flux architecture, Redux manages an entire application's state in one object, inside one store. The use of a single store has important implications. The ability to represent the entire application state in a single object simplifies the developer experience; it's dramatically easier to think through the application flow, predict the outcome of new actions, and debug issues produced by any given action. The potential for time-travel debugging, or the ability to flip back and forth through snapshots of application state, is what inspired the creation of Redux in the first place.

STATE IS READ-ONLY

Like Flux, actions are the only way to initiate changes in application state. No stray AJAX call can produce a change in state without being communicated via an action. Redux differs from many Flux implementations, though, in that these actions don't result in a mutation of the data in the store. Instead, each action results in a shiny, new instance of the state to replace the current one. More on that subject in the next section.

CHANGES ARE MADE WITH PURE FUNCTIONS

Actions are received by reducers. It's important that these reducers be pure functions. Pure functions are deterministic; they always produce the same output given the same inputs, and they don't mutate any data in the process. If a reducer mutates the existing state while producing the new one, you may end up with an erroneous new state, but you also lose the predictable transaction log that each new action should provide. The Redux developer tools and other features, such as undo and redo functionality, rely on application state being computed by pure functions.

1.3.3   *The workflow*

We've touched briefly upon topics such as actions, reducers, and the store, but in this section, we cover each in more depth. What's important to take away here is the role that each element plays and how they work together to produce a desired result. For now, don't worry about finer implementation details, because you'll have plenty of time in later chapters to apply the concepts you're about to explore.

Modern web applications are ultimately about handling events. They could be initiated by a user, such as navigating to a new page or submitting a form. Or they could be initiated by another external source, such as a server response. Responding to events usually involves updating state and re-rendering with that updated state. The more your application does, the more state you need to track and update. Combine this with the fact that most of these events occur asynchronously, and you suddenly have real obstacles to maintaining an application at scale.

Redux exists to create structure around how you handle events and manage state in your application, hopefully making you a more productive and happy human in the process.

Let's look at how to handle a single event in an application using Redux and React. Say you were tasked with implementing one of the core features of a social network—adding a post to your activity feed. Figure 1.3 shows a quick mockup of a user profile page, which may or may not take its inspiration from Twitter.

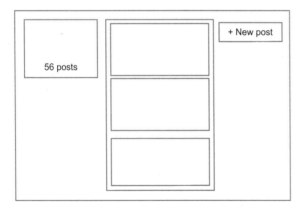

Figure 1.3   A simple mockup of a profile page. This page is backed by two main pieces of data: the total post count and the list of post objects in the user's activity feed.

The following distinct steps are involved in handling an event such as a new post:

- From the view, indicate that an event has occurred (a post submission) and pass along the necessary data (the content of the post to be created).
- Update state based on the type of event—add an item to the user's activity feed and increment the post count.
- Re-render the view to reflect the updated state.

Sounds reasonable, right? If you've used React before, you've likely implemented features similar to this directly in components. Redux takes a different approach. Code to satisfy the three tasks is moved out of React components into a few separate entities. You're already familiar with the View in figure 1.4, but we're excited to introduce a new cast of characters you'll hopefully learn to love.

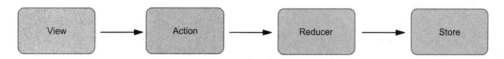

Figure 1.4   A look at how data flows through a React/Redux application. We've omitted a few common pieces such as middleware and selectors, which we'll cover in depth in later chapters.

ACTIONS

You want to do two things in response to a user submitting a new post: add the post to the user's activity feed and increment their total post count. After the user submits, you'll kick off the process by dispatching an action. Actions are plain old JavaScript objects that represent an event in your application, as follows:

```
{
  type: 'CREATE_POST',
  payload: {
    body: 'All that is gold does not glitter'
  }
}
```

Let's break that down. You have an object with two properties:

- `type`—A string that represents the category of action being performed. By convention, this property is capitalized and uses underscores as delimiters.
- `payload`—An object that provides the data necessary to perform the action. In your case, you only need one field: the contents of the message we want to post. The name "payload" is only a popular convention.

Actions have the advantage of serving as audits, which keep a historical record of everything happening in your application, including any data needed to complete a transaction. It's hard to understate how valuable this is in maintaining a grasp on a complex application. Once you get used to having a highly readable stream describing the behavior of your application in real time, you'll find it hard to live without.

Throughout the book, we'll frequently come back to this idea of *what* versus *how*. You can think of Redux as decoupling what happens in an application from how we respond to an event. Actions handle the what in this equation. They describe an event; they don't know and don't care what happens downstream. Somewhere down the road you'll eventually have to specify how to handle an action. Sounds like a job fit for a reducer!

REDUCERS

Reducers are functions responsible for updating your state in response to actions. They're simple functions that take your current state and an action as arguments, and return the next state. See figure 1.5.

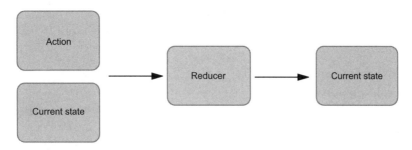

Figure 1.5 An abstract representation of a reducer's function signature. If this diagram looks simple, that's because it is! Reducers are meant to be simple functions that compute a result, making them easy to work with and test.

Reducers are typically easy to work with. Similar to all pure functions, they produce no side effects. They don't affect the outside world in any way, and they're referentially transparent. The same inputs will always yield the same return value. This makes them particularly easy to test. Given certain inputs, you can verify that you receive the expected result. Figure 1.6 shows how our reducer might update the list of posts and the total post count.

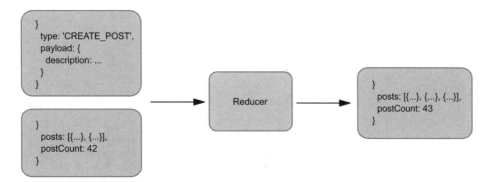

Figure 1.6 Visualizing a reducer hard at work. It accepts as input an action and the current state. The reducer's only responsibility is to calculate the next state based on these arguments. No mutations, no side-effects, no funny business. Data in, data out.

You're focusing on a single event in this example, which means you need only one reducer. However, you certainly aren't limited to only one. In fact, more sizable applications frequently implement several reducer functions, each concerned with a different slice of the state tree. These reducers are combined, or composed, into a single "root reducer."

STORE

Reducers describe how to update state in response to an action, but they can't modify state directly. That privilege rests solely with the store.

In Redux, application state is stored in a single object. The store has a few main roles, which follow:

- Hold application state.
- Provide a way to access state.
- Provide a way to specify updates to state. The store requires an action be dispatched to modify state.
- Allow other entities to subscribe to updates (React components in this case). View bindings provided by react-redux will allow you to receive updates from the store and respond to them in your components.

The reducer processed the action and computed the next state. Now it's time for the store to update itself and broadcast the new state to all registered listeners (you care specifically about the components that make up your profile page). See figure 1.7.

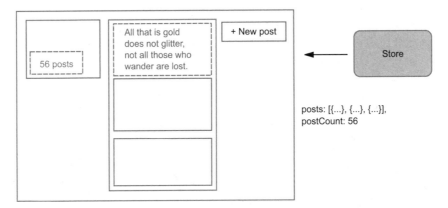

Figure 1.7   The store now completes the loop by providing the new state to our profile page. Notice that the post count has incremented, and the new post has been added to the activity feed. If your user adds another post, you'd follow the same exact flow. The view dispatches an action, reducers specify how to update state, and the store broadcasts the new state back to the view.

Now that you're familiar with several of the most important building blocks, let's look at a more comprehensive diagram of the Redux architecture. Several pieces will be unfamiliar now, but we'll revisit this diagram (figure 1.8) repeatedly throughout this book, and over time, we'll fill in each of those gaps.

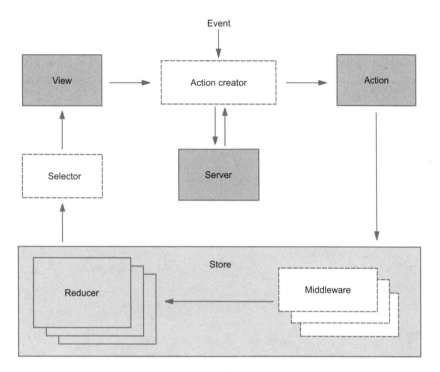

Figure 1.8 This diagram will anchor your understanding of the elements of Redux as you move forward. At this point, we've talked about actions, reducers, the store, and views.

To review, an interaction with a view may produce an action. That action will filter through one or more reducers and produce a new state tree within the store. Once the state updates, the views will be made aware that there's new data to render. That's the whole cycle! Items in figure 1.8 with a dashed border (action creators, middleware, and selectors) are optional, but powerful, tools in a Redux architecture. We cover each of these topics in future chapters.

If this feels like a lot, don't fret. If you're new to the kind of one-directional architecture that we're beginning to explore, it can be initially overwhelming (we certainly thought so at first). It takes time to let these concepts sink in. Developing a sense for what role they play and what type of code belongs where is as much art as it is science, and it's a skill you'll develop over time as you continue to get your hands dirty.

1.4   Why should I use Redux?

By this point, you've been exposed to many of the Redux talking points. If you have to pitch your boss on Redux by the time you finish the first chapter, let's consolidate those ideas into a highlight reel. In short, Redux is a small, easy-to-learn state management library that results in a highly predictable, testable, and debuggable application.

1.4.1   *Predictability*

The biggest selling point for Redux is the sanity it provides to applications juggling complex state. The Redux architecture offers a straightforward way to conceptualize and manage state, one action at a time. Regardless of application size, actions within the unidirectional data flow result in predictable changes to a single store.

1.4.2   *Developer experience*

Predictability enables world-class debugging tools. Hot-loading and time-travel debugging provide developers with wildly faster development cycles, whether building new features or hunting down bugs. Your boss will like that you're a happier developer, but she'll love that you're a faster one.

1.4.3   *Testability*

The Redux implementation code you'll write is primarily functions, many of them pure. Each piece of the puzzle can be broken out and unit-tested in isolation with ease. Official documentation uses Jest and Enzyme, but whichever JavaScript testing libraries your organization prefers will do the trick.

1.4.4   *Learning curve*

Redux is a natural step up from vanilla React. The library has a remarkably small footprint, exposing only a handful of APIs to get the job done. You can become familiar with all of it in a day. Writing Redux code also requires your team to become familiar with several functional programming patterns. This will be new territory for certain developers, but the concepts are straightforward. Once you understand that changes to state can be produced only by pure functions, you're most of the way there.

1.4.5   *Size*

If your boss is doing her job, one of the items on her checklist is dependency size. Redux is a tiny library—under 7KB when minified. Checkmate.

1.5   *When should I use Redux?*

We've hit you over the head with how great Redux is, but it's certainly no cure-all. We've argued in favor of why you should use Redux, but as we all know, nothing in life is free and no software pattern exists without tradeoffs.

The cost of Redux is a fair amount of boilerplate code and the added complexity of something more than React's local component state. It's important to realize that Redux, and the usage patterns you establish while using it, is one more thing for a new developer on your team to learn before they can contribute.

Redux co-creator Dan Abramov weighed in here, even publishing a blog post entitled "You Might Not Need Redux." He recommends starting without Redux and introducing the library only after you've reached enough state management pain points to justify including it. The recommendation is intentionally vague, because that turning point will be slightly different for every team. Smaller applications without complex data requirements are the most common scenario where it might be more appropriate to not use Redux in favor of plain React.

What might those pain points look like? Teams use a few common scenarios to justify bringing in Redux. The first is the passing of data through several layers of components that don't have any use for it. The second scenario deals with sharing and syncing data between unrelated parts of the application. We all have a tolerance for performing these tasks in React, but eventually you have a breaking point.

Redux is likely a good fit out of the gate if you know you'll want to build a specific feature that it excels at. If you know your application will have complex state and require undo and redo functionality, cut to the chase and pull in Redux. If server-side rendering is a requirement, consider Redux upfront.

1.6 Alternatives to Redux

As mentioned already, Redux entered a crowded state-management market and more options have appeared since. Let's run through the most popular alternatives for managing state in React applications.

1.6.1 Flux implementations

While researching, we stopped counting Flux implementation libraries somewhere in the low 20s. Astoundingly, at least 8 of them have received more than 1,000 stars on GitHub. This highlights an important era in React's history—the Flux architecture was a groundbreaking idea that spurred excitement in the community and, as a result, a great deal of experimentation and growth. During this period, libraries came and went at such an exhausting rate that the term JavaScript Fatigue was coined. With hindsight, it's clear that each of those experiments was an important stepping stone along the way. Over time, many of the alternative Flux implementation maintainers have graciously bowed out of the race in favor of Redux or one of the other popular options, but there are still several well-maintained options out there.

FLUX

Flux, of course, is the one that started it all. In the maintainers' own words, "Flux is more of a pattern than a framework." You'll find great documentation about the Flux architecture pattern in this repository, but a small API is exposed to facilitate building applications with the architecture. The Dispatcher is at the core of that API, and, in fact, several other Flux implementations have incorporated that Dispatcher into their libraries. Measured in GitHub stars, this library is about half as popular as Redux and continues to be actively maintained by the Facebook team.

REFLUX

Reflux was a fast follow to the original Flux library. The library introduces functional reactive programming ideas to the Flux architecture by ripping out the single Dispatcher in favor of giving each action the ability to dispatch itself. Callbacks can be registered with actions to update stores. Reflux is still maintained and about one-sixth as popular as Redux, measured by GitHub stars.

ALT

Unlike Reflux, Alt stays true to the original Flux ideas and uses the Flux Dispatcher. Alt's selling points are its adherence to the Flux architecture and a reduction in boilerplate code. Although it once enjoyed an enthusiastic community, at the time of writing, there have been no commits to the project in more than six months.

HONORABLE MENTIONS

To round out the bunch with greater than 1000 GitHub stars, you also have Fluxible, Fluxxor, NuclearJS, and Flummox. Fluxible continues to be well-maintained by the Yahoo team. Fluxxor, NuclearJS, and Flummox may be maintained, but are no longer active. To underscore the idea that these projects were important stepping stones, Flummox was created by Andrew Clark, who went on to co-create Redux with Dan Abramov.

1.6.2   *MobX*

MobX offers a functional reactive solution to state management. Like Flux, MobX uses actions to modify state, but components react to that mutated, or observable, state. Although part of the terminology in functional reactive programming can be intimidating, the features are approachable in practice. MobX also requires less boilerplate code than Redux but does more for you under the hood and is therefore less explicit. The first commits for MobX predate those of Redux by only a couple of months, in early 2015.

1.6.3   *GraphQL clients*

GraphQL is an exciting new technology, also being developed by the Facebook team. It's a query language that allows you to specify and receive exactly the data that is required by a component. This paradigm fits well with the intended modularity of React components; any data fetching that's required by the component is encapsulated within it. Queries to the API are optimized for the data needs of parent and children components.

Typically, GraphQL is used with a GraphQL client. The two most popular clients today are Relay and Apollo Client. Relay is another project developed and maintained by the Facebook team (and open source community). Apollo was originally implemented with Redux under the hood, but now offers additional configurability.

While it's possible to bring in both Redux and a GraphQL client to manage the same application's state, you may find the combination to be overly complex and unnecessary. Although GraphQL clients handle data fetching from a server and Redux is more general-purpose, there's overlap in usage between the packages.

Summary

This chapter introduced the Flux architecture pattern and where Redux ran with those ideas. You learned several practical details about the library.

Now you're ready to put the basic building blocks together and see a functioning Redux application end to end. In the next chapter, you'll build a task management application with React and Redux.

Key points you've learned

- Redux state is stored in a single object and is the product of pure functions.
- For the price of boilerplate code, Redux can introduce predictability, testability, and debuggability to your complex application.
- If you're experiencing pain points while syncing state across your application or passing data through multiple component layers, consider introducing Redux.

Your first Redux application

2

This chapter covers

- Configuring a Redux store
- Connecting Redux to React with the react-redux package
- Using actions and action creators
- Using reducers to update state
- Understanding container and presentational React components

By now, you're almost certainly itching to get started on a Redux application. You have more than enough context to begin, so let's scratch that itch. This chapter guides you through the set up and development of a simple task-management application using Redux to manage its state.

By the end of the chapter, you'll have walked through a complete application, but more importantly, you'll have learned enough of the fundamentals to leave the nest and create simple Redux applications of your own. Through the introduction of components that were strategically omitted in chapter 1, you'll develop a better understanding of the unidirectional data flow and how each piece of the puzzle contributes to that flow.

You may wonder if introducing Redux is overkill for the small application you'll build in this chapter. To iterate a point made in chapter 1, we encourage the use of vanilla React until you experience enough pain points to justify bringing in Redux.

If this chapter were the whole of it, Redux would indeed be overkill. It's not until you reach features introduced in later chapters that it really begins to make sense. As a matter of practicality, you'll head straight for Redux; that's why you're here, after all! As a thought experiment, you may enjoy rebuilding the application in React to determine when including Redux makes sense for yourself, once you become comfortable with the fundamentals.

2.1 Building a task-management application

The path you'll walk is a well-trodden one: building a project task-management application. In this chapter, you'll implement simple functionality, but you'll add increasingly complex features throughout the rest of the book as we cover each concept in more detail.

This app is lovingly named *Parsnip*. Why Parsnip? No good reason. It spoke to us in the moment, and we went with it. Specifically, Parsnip will be a Kanban board, a tool that allows users to organize and prioritize work (similar to Trello, Waffle, Asana, and a number of other tools). An app like this is highly interactive and requires complex state management—a perfect vehicle for us to apply Redux skills.

To see Redux in action without the bells and whistles, you'll start with one resource, a task. Your users should

- Create a new task with three properties: title, description, and status.
- See a list of all tasks.
- Change the status of a task. For example, a task may move from Unstarted, to In Progress, and finally to Completed.

By the end of the chapter, you'll have something similar to figure 2.1.

Figure 2.1   A mockup of what you'll build in this chapter.

2.1.1 Designing the state shape

There's no single right way to approach problems with Redux, but we recommend taking time to think about how the application state should look before implementing a new feature. If React applications are a reflection of the current state, what should your state object look like to satisfy the requirements? What properties should it have? Are arrays or objects more appropriate? These are the kinds of questions you should ask when you approach new features. To recap, you know you need to do the following:

- Render a list of tasks.
- Allow users to add items to the list.
- Allow users to mark tasks as Unstarted, In Progress, or Completed.

What state do you need to track to make all this possible? It turns out that our requirements are straightforward: you need a list of task objects with a title, description, and status. Application state that lives in Redux is a simple JavaScript object. The following listing is an example of what that object might look like.

Listing 2.1 An outline of the Redux store

```
{
  tasks: [            ◁─── The tasks key represents one
    {                      "slice" of the data that could
      id: 1,               make up a store.             Each task is an object
      title: 'Learn Redux',                       ◁─── with several properties.
      description: 'The store, actions, and reducers, oh my!',
      status: 'In Progress',
    },
    {
      id: 2,
      title: 'Peace on Earth',
      description: 'No big deal.',
      status: 'Unstarted',
    }
  ]
}
```

The store is simple, a `tasks` field with an array of task objects. How you organize the data in your Redux store is completely up to you, and we'll explore popular patterns and best practices later in the book.

Deciding upfront how the data will look will be a big help down the road in determining what kinds of actions and reducers you might need. Remember, it may be helpful to think of client-side state like a database. Similarly to if you were dealing with a persistent data store such as a SQL database, declaring a data model will help you organize your thoughts and drive out the code you need. Throughout the book, you'll start each new feature by revisiting this process of defining a desired state shape.

2.2 *Using Create React App*

React has always enjoyed a reputation for being beginner-friendly. Compared with larger frameworks such as Angular and Ember, its API and feature set are small. The same can't be said for many of the surrounding tools you'll find in many production-ready applications. This includes Webpack, Babel, ESLint, and a dozen others with varying learning curves. We developers couldn't be bothered to do all this configuration for each new project or prototype from scratch, so an abundance of starter kits and boilerplate applications were created. Although popular, many of these starter kits became wildly complex and equally intimidating for beginners to use.

Fortunately, in mid-2016, Facebook released an officially supported tool that does this complex configuration work for you and abstracts most of it away. Create React App is a command line interface (CLI) tool that will generate a relatively simple, production-ready React application. Provided you agree with enough of the choices made within the project, Create React App can easily save days of setup and configuration time. We're sold on this tool as the preferred way to get new React projects off the ground, so we'll use it to kick-start this application.

2.2.1 *Installing Create React App*

Create React App is a module that can be installed using your favorite package manager. In this book, you'll use npm. In a terminal window, run the following command at the prompt:

```
npm install --global create-react-app
```

Once installed, you can create a new project with

```
create-react-app parsnip
```

Creating a new application can take a few minutes, depending on the time it takes to install the dependencies on your machine. When it completes, there will be a newly created `parsnip` directory waiting for you. Navigate to that directory now, and we'll get up and running.

To view the application, you'll start the development server, which takes care of serving your JavaScript code to the browser (among other things). Run the following command from within the `parsnip` directory:

```
npm start
```

If `create-react-app` didn't open a browser window automatically after starting the development server, open a browser and head to localhost:3000. You should see something similar to figure 2.2.

Go ahead and follow the instructions. Try changing the "To get started…" text by editing the src/App.js file. You should see the browser refresh automatically, without

To get started, edit `src/App.js` and save to reload.

Figure 2.2   The home page in a browser after bootstrapping a new React application with the create-react-app command

having to reload the page. We'll cover this feature and more development workflow enhancements in-depth in chapter 3.

2.3   Basic React components

Before you jump into configuring Redux, let's lay groundwork by building a few simple React components. We generally like to approach features "from the outside in," meaning you'll start by building the UI first, then hook up any necessary behavior. It helps you stay grounded in what the user will eventually experience, and the earlier you can interact with a working prototype, the better. It's much better to iron out issues with a design or feature spec early, before too much work gets underway.

You also want to make sure you're building flexible, reusable UI components. If you define your components with clear interfaces, reusing and rearranging them becomes easy. Start by creating a new directory under `src/` called `components/`, then create files for the new components, `Task.js`, `TaskList.js`, and `TasksPage.js`.

`Task` and `TaskList` will be stateless functional components, introduced in React v0.14. They don't have access to lifecycle methods such as `componentDidMount`, only accept props, don't use `this.state` or `this.setState`, and they're defined as plain functions instead of with `createReactClass` or ES2015 classes.

These kinds of components are wonderfully simple; you don't have to worry about `this`, they're easier to work with and test, and they cut down on the number of lines of code you might need with classes. They accept props as input and return some UI. What more could you ask for? Copy the code in the following listing to Task.js.

Listing 2.2   src/components/Task.js

```
import React from 'react';

const Task = props => {
  return (
    <div className="task">
      <div className="task-header">
        <div>{props.task.title}</div>
      </div>
```

Stateless functional components are exported anonymous functions.

These components receive and display props from parent components.

```
      <hr />
      <div className="task-body">{props.task.description}</div>
    </div>
  );
  }
```

```
export default Task;
```

> **NOTE** We aren't including the contents of CSS files in this book. They're verbose and don't aid in the understanding of Redux topics. Please see the supplementary code if you want to replicate the styles found in screenshots.

The implementation for the TaskList component is equally straightforward. The column name and a list of tasks will be passed in from a parent component. Copy the code in the following listing to TaskList.js.

Listing 2.3 src/components/TaskList.js

```
import React from 'react';
import Task from './Task';

const TaskList = props => {
  return (
    <div className="task-list">
      <div className="task-list-title">
        <strong>{props.status}</strong>
      </div>
      {props.tasks.map(task => (
        <Task key={task.id} task={task} />
      ))}
    </div>
  );
}

export default TaskList;
```

Redux allows you to implement a significant chunk of our React components as these stateless functional components. Because you get to offload most of the app's state and logic to Redux, you can avoid the component bloat that's typical of nearly all large React applications. The Redux community commonly refers to these types of components as *presentational components*, and we cover them in more detail later in the chapter.

Within TasksPage.js, import the newly created TaskList component and display one for each status (see the following listing). Although it doesn't yet, this component needs to manage local state when you introduce the new task form. For that reason, it's implemented as an ES6 class.

Listing 2.4 src/components/TasksPage.js

```
import React, { Component } from 'react';
import TaskList from './TaskList';
```

Tasks can have one of three states.

```
const TASK_STATUSES = ['Unstarted', 'In Progress', 'Completed'];

class TasksPage extends Component {           ES6 classes are used when
  renderTaskLists() {                          local state must be managed.
    const { tasks } = this.props;
    return TASK_STATUSES.map(status => {
      const statusTasks = tasks.filter(task => task.status === status);
      return <TaskList key={status} status={status} tasks={statusTasks} />;
    });                                        Display one column
  }                                            per status, with
                                               corresponding tasks.
  render() {
    return (
      <div className="tasks">
        <div className="task-lists">
          {this.renderTaskLists()}
        </div>
      </div>
    );
  }
}

export default TasksPage;
```

To start, TasksPage will receive mock tasks from the top-level component, App. App will also be created using an ES6 class, because it will eventually connect to the Redux store, as shown in the following listing.

Listing 2.5   src/App.js

```
import React, { Component } from 'react';
import TasksPage from './components/TasksPage';

const mockTasks = [                Until Redux is
  {                                introduced, mock tasks
    id: 1,                         will populate the UI.
    title: 'Learn Redux',
    description: 'The store, actions, and reducers, oh my!',
    status: 'In Progress',
  },
  {
    id: 2,
    title: 'Peace on Earth',
    description: 'No big deal.',
    status: 'In Progress',
  },
];

class App extends Component {
  render() {
    return (
      <div className="main-content">
        <TasksPage tasks={mockTasks} />
      </div>
```

```
    );
  }
}
```

```
export default App;
```

At this point, you can run your small React application with npm start and view it in the browser. Bear in mind that it'll look dreadfully boring until you circle back to apply styles. Again, you can borrow ours from the supplemental code if you like.

2.4 Revisiting the Redux architecture

Your small React application is now ready to be introduced to Redux. Before you dive straight in, let's consider the full arc of what will be required by revisiting the Redux architecture, introduced in chapter 1. See figure 2.3.

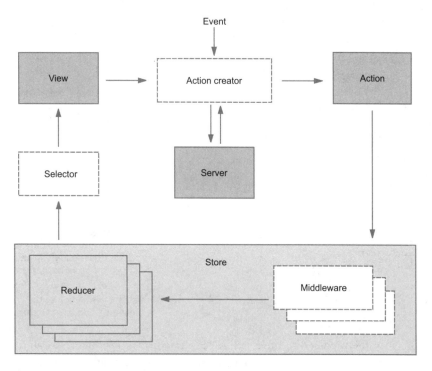

Figure 2.3   The Redux architecture

The store is a logical starting point for introducing Redux into an application. The Redux package exposes a few methods that facilitate the creation of a store. Once a store is created, you'll connect it to the React application using the react-redux package, enabling a view (component) to dispatch actions. Actions eventually return to the store, to be read by reducers, which determine the next state of the store.

2.5   *Configuring the Redux store*

The main hub of functionality in Redux is the store—the object responsible for managing application state. Let's look at the store and its API in an isolated context. As an example, we'll look at a tiny program to increment a number.

2.5.1   *The big picture and the store API*

In reading about Redux and talking with other community members, you'll see or hear references to the store, the Redux store, or the state tree often used interchangeably. Generally, what these terms refer to is a JavaScript object like any other. Let's look at the API that Redux provides to interact with the store.

The Redux package exports a `createStore` function that, you guessed it, is used to create a Redux store. Specifically, the Redux store is an object with a few core methods that can read and update state and respond to any changes: `getState`, `dispatch`, and `subscribe`. You'll capture all three in the quick example in the following listing.

Listing 2.6 The store API in action

```
import { createStore } from 'redux';

function counterReducer(state = 0, action) {        The store requires at least
  if (action.type === 'INCREMENT') {                one reducer function
    return state + 1;                               (counterReducer).
  }
  return state;
}

const store = createStore(counterReducer);          Creates a store
                                                    with the reducer

console.log(store.getState());                       Reads the current
                                                     state of the store

store.subscribe(() => {                              Does something after
  console.log('current state: ', store.getState()); the store has updated
});

store.dispatch({ type: 'INCREMENT' });              Sends a new action to the
                                                    reducers to update the store
```

The first argument passed to the `createStore` function is a reducer. Recall from chapter 1 that reducers are functions that inform the store how it should update state in response to actions. The store requires at least one reducer.

As promised, there are three methods on the store to show off. The first, `getState`, can read the contents of the store. You'll need to call this method yourself infrequently.

`subscribe` allows us to respond to changes in the store. For the sake of this example, you're logging out the newly updated state to the console. When you start connecting Redux to React, this method is used under the hood to allow React components to re-render when any state changes in the store.

Because you can't mutate the store yourself and only actions can result in a new state, you need a way to send new actions on to the reducers. That method is `dispatch`.

2.5.2 Creating a Redux store

Back to business! In this section, you'll begin to create your store and its dependencies. A store contains one or more reducers and, optionally, middleware. We'll save middleware for a subsequent chapter, but at least one reducer is required to create a store.

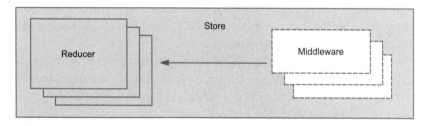

Figure 2.4   A store requires one or more reducers and may include middleware. The arrow between middleware and reducers indicates the order in which actions will eventually be handled.

Let's begin by adding Redux as a dependency of the project, then move your initial tasks data into Redux. Make sure you're in the `parsnip` directory and install the package by running the following command in a terminal window:

```
npm install -P redux
```

The `-P` flag is an alias for `--save-prod`, resulting in the package being added to your dependencies in the package.json file. Starting in npm5, this is the default install behavior. Now that Redux has been added, the next step is to integrate it into your existing React components. First create the store by adding the code shown in the following listing to index.js.

Listing 2.7   src/index.js

```
import React from 'react'
import ReactDOM from 'react-dom'
import App from './App';
import { createStore } from 'redux'
import tasks from './reducers'
import './index.css';

const store = createStore(tasks)
...
```

Imports the createStore function from the redux package

Because you need at least one reducer to create a Redux store, import the tasks reducer, which you'll define in listing 2.8.

Creates the store by passing the reducer to createStore

The next step is to make the store available to the React components in the app, but the code you added in listing 2.7 isn't functional yet. Before going any further in index.js, you need to provide a barebones implementation of the `tasks` reducer.

2.5.3   *The tasks reducer*

As you've learned, creating a new Redux store requires a reducer. The goal of this section is to get enough done to create a new store, and you'll fill out the rest of the functionality as you move through the chapter.

If you recall from chapter 1, a reducer is a function that takes the current state of the store and an action and returns the new state after applying any updates. The store is responsible for storing state, but it relies on reducers that you'll create to determine how to update that state in response to an action.

You won't handle any actions yet; you'll return the state without modifications. Within the `src` directory, create a new directory, `reducers`, with an index.js file. In this file, you'll create and export a single function, `tasks`, that returns the given state, as shown in the following listing.

> **Listing 2.8   src/reducers/index.js**

```
export default function tasks(state = [], action) {
  return state
}
```

Currently the action argument isn't being used, but you'll add more functionality to this reducer function once you start dispatching actions.

That's it! Do a little dance, because you've written your first reducer. You'll be back later to make this function more interesting.

2.5.4   *Default reducer state*

It's common to provide reducers with an initial state, which involves nothing more than providing a default value for the `state` argument in the `tasks` reducer. Before you get back to connecting the Redux store to your application, let's move the list of mock tasks out of App.js and into src/reducers/index.js, a more appropriate place for initial state to live. This is shown in the following listing.

> **Listing 2.9   src/reducers/index.js**

```
const mockTasks = [
  {
    id: 1,
    title: 'Learn Redux',
    description: 'The store, actions, and reducers, oh my!',
    status: 'In Progress',
  },
  {
    id: 2,
    title: 'Peace on Earth',
```

```
    description: 'No big deal.',
    status: 'In Progress',
  },
];

export default function tasks(state = { tasks: mockTasks }, action) {
  return state;
}
```

Sets the mock tasks
as the default state

Don't worry if your App component is breaking as a result of removing the mock data. You'll fix that shortly. At this point the store has the correct initial data, but you still need to somehow make this data available to the UI. Enter react-redux!

A note on immutability

Though it's not a strict requirement, it's highly encouraged to keep your data immutable; that is, not mutating values directly. Immutability has inherent benefits like being easy to work with and test, but in the case of Redux, the real benefit is that it enables extremely fast and simple equality checks.

For example, if you mutate an object in a reducer, React-Redux's connect may fail to correctly update its corresponding component. When connect compares old and new states to decide whether it needs to go ahead with a re-render, it checks only if two objects are equal, not that every individual property is equal. Immutability is also great for dealing with historical data, and it's required for advanced Redux debugging features such as time travel.

The long and short of it is to never mutate data in place with Redux. Your reducers should always accept the current state as input and calculate an entirely new state. JavaScript doesn't offer immutable data structures out of the box, but there are several great libraries. ImmutableJS (https://facebook.github.io/immutable-js/) and Updeep (https://github.com/substantial/updeep) are two popular examples, and in addition to enforcing immutability, they also provide more advanced APIs for updating deeply nested objects. If you want something more lightweight, Seamless-Immutable (https://github.com/rtfeldman/seamless-immutable) gives you immutable data structures, but allows you to continue using standard JavaScript APIs.

2.6 *Connecting Redux and React with react-redux*

As we discussed in chapter 1, Redux was built with React in mind, but they're two totally discrete packages. To connect Redux with React, you'll use the React bindings from the react-redux package. Redux provides only the means to configure a store. react-redux bridges the gap between React and Redux by providing the ability to enhance a component, allowing it to read state from the store or dispatch actions. react-redux gives you two primary tools for connecting your Redux store to React:

- Provider—A React component that you'll render at the top of the React app. Any components rendered as children of Provider can be granted access to the Redux store.

- connect—A function used as a bridge between React components and data from the Redux store.

Pause here to install the package: npm install -P react-redux.

2.6.1   *Adding the Provider component*

Provider is a component that takes the store as a prop and wraps the top-level component in your app—in this case, App. Any child component rendered within Provider can access the Redux store, no matter how deeply it's nested.

In index.js, import the Provider component and wrap the App component, using the code in the following listing.

Listing 2.10   src/index.js

```
import React from 'react';
import ReactDOM from 'react-dom';
import { createStore } from 'redux';
import { Provider } from 'react-redux';          Imports the Provider
import tasks from './reducers';                   component
import App from './App';
import './index.css';

const store = createStore(tasks);          Provider is now our most top-level React
                                           component. It works in conjunction with
ReactDOM.render(                           connect to make the store available to
  <Provider store={store}>                 any child component.
    <App />
  </Provider>,
  document.getElementById('root')
);
```

Think of the Provider component as an enabler. You won't interact with it directly often, typically only in a file such as index.js, which takes care of initially mounting the app to the DOM. Behind the scenes, Provider ensures you can use connect to pass data from the store to one or more React components.

2.6.2   *Passing data from Redux to React components*

You've laid the groundwork to pass data from the store into a React component. You have a Redux store with a tasks reducer, and you've used the Provider component from react-redux to make the store available to our React components. Now it's nearly time to enhance a React component with connect. See figure 2.5.

Generally, you can break visual interfaces into two major concerns: data and UI. In your case, the data is the JavaScript objects that represent tasks, and the UI is the few React components that take these objects and render them on the page. Without Redux, you'd deal with both concerns directly within React components.

As you can see in figure 2.6, the data used to render your UI is moved entirely out of React and into Redux. The App component will be considered an entry point for

The *connect* function will provide the link between a component and data in the store.

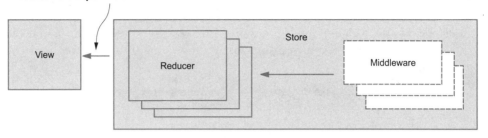

Figure 2.5 The connect method bridges the gap between the store and views (components).

data from Redux. As the application grows, you'll introduce more data, more UI, and as a result, more entry points. This kind of flexibility is one of Redux's greatest strengths. Your application state lives in one place, and you can pick and choose how you want that data to flow into the application.

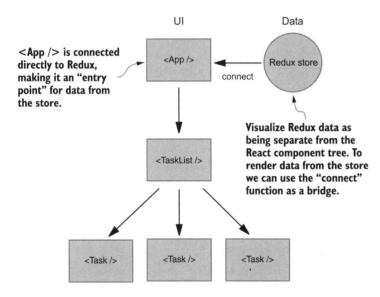

<App /> is connected directly to Redux, making it an "entry point" for data from the store.

Visualize Redux data as being separate from the React component tree. To render data from the store we can use the "connect" function as a bridge.

Figure 2.6 A visualization of how React and Redux work together

Listing 2.11 introduces a couple of new concepts: connect and mapStateToProps. By adding connect to the App component, you declare it as an entry point for data from the Redux store. You've only connected one component here, but as your application grows, you'll start to discover best practices for when to use connect with additional components.

Listing 2.11 passes `connect` a single argument, the `mapStateToProps` function. Note that the name `mapStateToProps` is a convention, not a requirement. The name stuck for a reason: because it's an effective descriptor of the role of this function. State refers to the data in the store, and props are what get passed to the connected component. Whatever you return from `mapStateToProps` will be passed to your component as props.

Listing 2.11   src/App.js: connecting components

```
import React, { Component } from 'react';
import { connect } from 'react-redux';          ◁─┐  Adds connect to
import TasksPage from './components/TasksPage';    │  the list of imports

class App extends Component {
  render() {
    return (                                          Tasks will be available via
      <div className="main-content">                  props after connected to
        <TasksPage tasks={this.props.tasks} />  ◁─┘   the store.
      </div>
    );
  }
}
                                                   The state argument is the entire
                                                   contents of the Redux store,
                                                   specifically the result of calling
function mapStateToProps(state) {     ◁─┘          getState on the store instance.
  return {
    tasks: state.tasks        ◁─┐  The return value of mapStateToProps is passed
  }                              │  into the App component as props, which is why
}                                │  render can reference this.props.tasks.

export default connect(mapStateToProps)(App);
```

Now the application successfully renders data from the Redux store! Notice how you didn't have to update the `TasksPage` component? That's by design. Because `Tasks-Page` accepts its data via props, it doesn't care what the source of those props is. They could come from Redux, from React's local state, or from another data library altogether.

2.6.3   *Container and presentational components*

Recall that `TaskList` is a presentational or UI component. It accepts data as props and returns output according to the markup you defined. By using `connect` in the App component, you secretly introduced their counterparts, known as container components.

Presentational components don't have dependencies on Redux. They don't know or care that you're using Redux to manage your application state. By using presentational components, you introduced determinism into your view renders. Given the same data, you'll always have the same rendered output. Presentational components are easily tested and provide your application with sweet, sweet predictability.

Presentational components are great, but something needs to know how to get data out of the Redux store and pass it to your presentational components. This is where container components, such as App, come in. In this simple example, they have a few responsibilities:

- Get data from the Redux store via connect.
- Use mapStateToProps to pass only relevant data to the component being connected.
- Render presentational components.

Again, separating things into container and presentational components is a convention, not a hard-and-fast rule that React or Redux enforces. But it's one of the most popular and pervasive patterns for a reason. It allows you to decouple how your app looks from what it does. Defining your UI as presentational components means you have simple, flexible building blocks that are easy to reconfigure and reuse. When you're working with data from Redux, you can deal with container components without having to worry about markup. The inverse applies for when you're working with a UI.

At this point, you can view the data being rendered in the browser; your app renders a simple list of tasks retrieved from the Redux store. Now it's time to wire up behavior! Let's see what it takes to add a new task to the list.

2.7 *Dispatching actions*

You'll follow the same workflow that you used to render the static list of tasks. You'll start with the UI, then implement functionality. Let's start with a "New task" button and a form. When a user clicks the button, the form renders with two fields, a title, and a description. Eventually, it'll look roughly like figure 2.7.

Figure 2.7   The New Task form

Modify the code in TasksPage.js to match the following listing. This code is still plain React, so much of it may be familiar to you.

Listing 2.12 Adding the New Task form

```
import React, { Component } from 'react';
import TaskList from './TaskList';

class TasksPage extends Component {
  constructor(props) {
    super(props);
    this.state = {
      showNewCardForm: false,
      title: '',
      description: '',
    };
  }

  onTitleChange = (e) => {
    this.setState({ title: e.target.value });
  }

  onDescriptionChange = (e) => {
    this.setState({ description: e.target.value });
  }

  resetForm() {
    this.setState({
      showNewCardForm: false,
      title: '',
      description: '',
    });
  }

  onCreateTask = (e) => {
    e.preventDefault();
    this.props.onCreateTask({
      title: this.state.title,
      description: this.state.description,
    });
    this.resetForm();
  }

  toggleForm = () => {
    this.setState({ showNewCardForm: !this.state.showNewCardForm });
  }

  renderTaskLists() {
    const { tasks } = this.props;
    return TASK_STATUSES.map(status => {
      const statusTasks = tasks.filter(task => task.status === status);
      return (
        <TaskList
          key={status}
          status={status}
          tasks={statusTasks}
        />
      );
```

It's often simpler to use React and setState for UI-related state, such as whether the form is open and for the current values of the form inputs.

A special syntax ensures the value of this will be correct.

Submitting the form is as simple as firing the onCreateTask prop.

Resets the form's state after submission

```
      });
    }

    render() {
      return (
        <div className="task-list">
          <div className="task-list-header">
            <button
              className="button button-default"
              onClick={this.toggleForm}
            >
              + New task
            </button>
          </div>
          {this.state.showNewCardForm && (
            <form className="task-list-form" onSubmit={this.onCreateTask}>
              <input
                className="full-width-input"
                onChange={this.onTitleChange}
                value={this.state.title}
                type="text"
                placeholder="title"
              />
              <input
                className="full-width-input"
                onChange={this.onDescriptionChange}
                value={this.state.description}
                type="text"
                placeholder="description"
              />
              <button
                className="button"
                type="submit"
              >
                Save
              </button>
            </form>
          )}

          <div className="task-lists">
            {this.renderTaskLists()}
          </div>
        </div>
      );
    }
  }

export default TasksPage;
```

Your `TaskList` component now tracks local state—whether the form is visible and the text values in the form. The form inputs are what's known in React as controlled components. All that means is the values of the input fields are set to the corresponding local state values, and for each character typed into the input field, local state is updated. When a user submits the form to create a new task, you call the `onCreate-Task` prop to indicate an event has taken place. Because you call `onCreateTask` from `this.props`, you know that this function needs to be passed down from the parent component, `App`.

> **POP QUIZ**   What's the only way to initiate a change in the Redux store? (No peeking at this section title.) Dispatching an action is exactly right. You have a good idea, then, of how to implement the `onCreateTask` function; we need to dispatch an action to add a new task.

In App.js, you know that `App` is a connected component and is enhanced with the ability to interact with the Redux store. Do you remember which of the store APIs can be used to send off a new action? Take a moment and log the value of `this.props` in the render method of App, as shown in the following listing. The resulting console output should match that of figure 2.8.

Listing 2.13   Logging this.props in src/App.js

```
...
render() {
   console.log('props from App: ', this.props)      ⟵   Logs the value of
   return (                                               this.props at the top
     ...                                                  of the render method
   )
 }
}
...
```

```
┆  Console                                                              ✕

⊘  ▽  top                          ▼  ☐ Preserve log

   props from App:                                              App.js:17
   ▶ Object {tasks: Array(2), dispatch: function}
>  |
```

Figure 2.8   Shows the console output from logging the props available to the App component

There it is: a `dispatch` prop in addition to your expected `tasks` array. What's `dispatch`? You know that the store is extremely protective of its data. It only provides one way to update state—dispatching an action. `dispatch` is part of the store's API, and `connect` conveniently provides this function to your component as a prop. Let's create a handler where you dispatch a `CREATE_TASK` action (see listing 2.14). The action will have two properties:

- `type`—A string that represents the category of action being performed. By convention, they're capitalized and use underscores as delimiters. This is the only required property for an action to be considered valid.

- payload—An object that provides the data necessary to perform the action. Having a payload field is optional and can be omitted if no additional data is required to perform the action. For example, an action to log a user out may contain a type of LOGOUT with no additional data requirements. If additional data is required, however, any keys may be passed in the action. The name payload isn't required by Redux, but it's a popular organizational convention that we'll stick with throughout the book. The pattern is commonly referred to as Flux Standard Actions (FSA); more details can be found in this GitHub repository at https://github.com/acdlite/flux-standard-action.

Listing 2.14 src/App.js: adding an action handler

```
import React, { Component } from 'react';
import { connect } from 'react-redux';
import TasksPage from './components/TasksPage';

class App extends Component {
  onCreateTask = ({ title, description }) => {
    this.props.dispatch({                          ◁── this.props.dispatch, injected
      type: 'CREATE_TASK',                              by connect, dispatches an
      payload: {                                        action to the store.
        title,
        description
      }
    });
  }

  render() {
    return (
      <div className="main-content">
        <TasksPage
          tasks={this.props.tasks}
          onCreateTask={this.onCreateTask}
        />                                         ◁── The onCreateTask handler is
      </div>                                           passed to TasksPage as a
    );                                                 simple callback prop.
  }
}
```

This listing also illustrates one of the other main roles of container components: action handling. You don't want TasksPage to worry about the details of creating a new task; it only needs to indicate that the user wishes to do so by firing the onCreate-Task prop.

2.8 Action creators

You dispatched the CREATE_TASK action object directly in the previous example, but it's not something you usually do outside of simple examples. Instead, you'll invoke action creators—functions that return actions. Figure 2.9 illustrates this relationship.

Figure 2.9   Although views can dispatch actions, they often invoke action creators instead—functions that return actions.

Actions and action creators are closely related and work together to dispatch actions to the store, but they fulfill different roles:

- *Actions*—Objects that describe an event
- *Action creators*—Functions that return actions

Why use action creators? Action creators have a friendlier interface; all you need to know is which arguments the action creator function expects. You won't have to worry about specifics, such as the shape of the action's payload or any logic that might need to be applied before the action can be dispatched. By the same token, an action creator's arguments are helpful because they clearly document an action's data requirements.

Later in the book, you'll implement a good chunk of your application's core logic directly within action creators. They'll do tasks such as make AJAX requests, perform redirects, and create in-app notifications.

2.8.1   *Using action creators*

From the last section, you know `dispatch` accepts an action object as an argument. Instead of dispatching the action directly, you'll use an action creator. Within the `src` directory, create a new directory called `actions` with an index.js file within it. This file is where your action creators and actions will live. Add the code in the following listing to that newly created file.

Listing 2.15   src/actions/index.js: the createTask action creator

```
let _id = 1;
export function uniqueId() {          uniqueId is a utility function to generate
  return _id++;                       numeric ids for tasks. When you hook up
}                                     the app to a real server in chapter 4, this
                                      will no longer be necessary.

export function createTask({ title, description }) {      The function signature
  return {                                                makes it clear that a title
    type: 'CREATE_TASK',                                  and a description are
    payload: {                      The payload property  required to dispatch the
      id: uniqueId(),               contains all the data CREATE_TASK action.
      title,                        necessary to perform
      description,                  the action.
      status: 'Unstarted',
    },
  };
}
```

There's one piece of cleanup you need to do after adding the `uniqueId` function. Update src/reducers/index.js to use `uniqueId` instead of hard-coded IDs, as shown in the following listing. This ensures your task IDs will increment correctly as you create them, and you'll use these IDs when you allow users to edit tasks later in the chapter.

Listing 2.16   src/reducers/index.js

```
import { uniqueId } from '../actions';        ◁─┐  Imports the uniqueId function you
                                                  created in src/actions/index.js
const mockTasks = [
  {
    id: uniqueId(),              ◁─┤  Uses uniqueId instead
    title: 'Learn Redux',              of hard-coded IDs
    description: 'The store, actions, and reducers, oh my!',
    status: 'In Progress',
  },
  {
    id: uniqueId(),
    title: 'Peace on Earth',
    description: 'No big deal.',
    status: 'In Progress',
  },
];
```

To finish the implementation, update the code in App.js to import and use your new action creator, as shown in the following listing.

Listing 2.17   src/App.js

```
...
import { createTask } from './actions';        ◁─┐  Imports the
                                                     action creator
class App extends Component {
  ...
 onCreateTask = ({ title, description }) => {
   this.props.dispatch(createTask({ title, description }));        ◁─┐
 }
 ...                                            Instead of passing an action
}                                               object to this.props.dispatch,
...                                             you'll pass the action creator.
```

To recap, the App container component has access to the dispatch method, thanks to connect. App imports an action creator, createTask, and passes it a title and a description. The action creator formats and returns an action. In the next section, you'll follow that action through to the reducer and beyond.

Remember that `uniqueId` function? How you generate the id field is particularly noteworthy, because it introduces a side effect.

DEFINITION   A side effect is any code that has a noticeable effect on the outside world, such as writing to disk or mutating data. Put another way, it's code that does anything but take inputs and return a result.

Functions with side effects do something other than return a value. `createTask` mutates some external state—the ID that you increment whenever you create a new task.

2.8.2   *Action creators and side effects*

Most of the code you've written so far has been deterministic, meaning it produces no side effects. This is all well and good, but you need to deal with side effects somewhere. Code that operates on data is easy to work with and think about, but side effects are necessary to do anything useful. Eventually you'll need to do things like write to the browser's local storage and communicate with a web server. Both are considered side effects and are ubiquitous in the world of web applications.

You know you can't do much without side effects. What you can do is isolate them by enforcing good practices around where they can be performed. Reducers must be pure functions, so they're out. You guessed it, that leaves action creators! The command `createTask` is non-deterministic, and that's perfectly okay. Chapters 4, 5, and 6 will explore various strategies for managing side effects.

2.9   *Handling actions with reducers*

You defined a simple tasks reducer when you used `createStore` to initialize your Redux store, but at this point it returns the current state, as shown in the following listing.

Listing 2.18   src/reducers/index.js

```
...
export default function tasks(state = { tasks: mockTasks }, action) {
  return state;
}
```

This reducer is completely valid and functional, but it doesn't do anything particularly useful. The real point of reducers is to handle actions. Reducers are functions that accept the store's current state and an action and return the next state after applying any relevant updates. You're still missing that last bit: you need to change our state.

The store's role is to manage application state; it's where the data lives, it controls access, and it allows components to listen for updates. What it doesn't, and can't, do is define how exactly its state should change in response to actions. That's up to you to define, and reducers are the mechanism Redux provides to accomplish this.

2.9.1   *Responding to actions in reducers*

You're correctly dispatching the `CREATE_TASK` action, indicating an event has occurred. But the action doesn't specify how to handle this event. How should state update in response to the action? You stored your task objects in an array, so all you need to do is push an element on to the list. Reducers check the action's type to determine if it should respond to it. This amounts to a simple conditional statement that describes how the state should update for a given action type. Figure 2.10 illustrates how the reducer responds to actions.

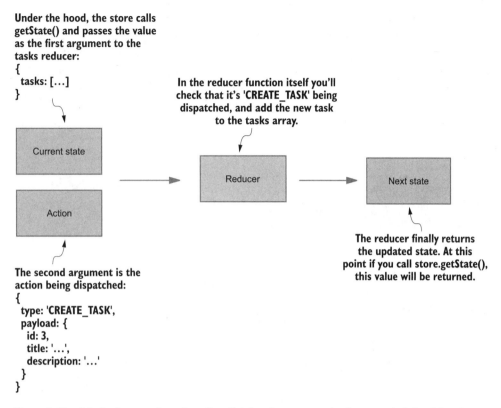

Under the hood, the store calls getState() and passes the value as the first argument to the tasks reducer:
```
{
  tasks: [...]
}
```

In the reducer function itself you'll check that it's 'CREATE_TASK' being dispatched, and add the new task to the tasks array.

Current state

Action

Reducer

Next state

The reducer finally returns the updated state. At this point if you call store.getState(), this value will be returned.

The second argument is the action being dispatched:
```
{
  type: 'CREATE_TASK',
  payload: {
    id: 3,
    title: '...',
    description: '...'
  }
}
```

Figure 2.10 A look at your reducer in action. It takes two arguments, the current state of the store and the CREATE_TASK action, and returns the next state.

In this case, if the reducer receives an action of type CREATE_TASK, you expect the next state tree to have one more task in the list but be otherwise identical to the previous state. An action of any other type will result in an unchanged Redux store, because CREATE_TASK is all you're listening for so far.

Update the tasks reducer to handle the CREATE_TASK action, as shown in the following listing.

Listing 2.19 src/reducers/index.js

Checks whether the action type is one that you care about

```
...
export default function tasks(state = { tasks: mockTasks }, action) {
  if (action.type === 'CREATE_TASK') {
    return { tasks: state.tasks.concat(action.payload) };
  }

  return state;
}
```

Always fall back to returning the given state in case a reducer receives an action it can't handle.

If the action is CREATE_TASK, add the task to the array and return the result.

Now the tasks reducer updates state in response to an action. As you continue to add functionality and dispatch new actions, you'll add more code like this that checks for a specific action type and conditionally applies any updates to application state.

At this point, you've completed an entire cycle within Redux's unidirectional data flow! Once the store updates, your connected component, App, becomes aware of the new state and performs a new render. Let's review the architecture diagram one last time to help it all sink in (figure 2.11).

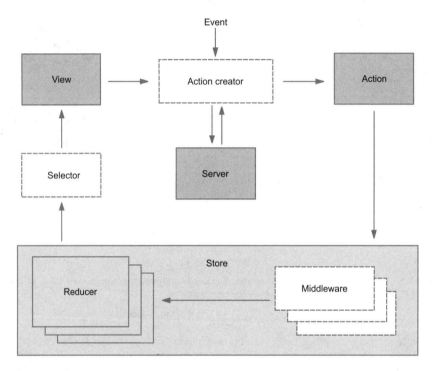

Figure 2.11   The Redux architecture

You started by creating a store, passing in the tasks reducer as an argument. After being connected to the store, the views rendered the default state specified by the tasks reducer. When a user wants to create a new task, the connected component dispatches an action creator. That action creator returns an action containing a CREATE _TASK type and additional data. Finally, the reducer listens for the CREATE_TASK action type and determines what the next application state should look like.

2.10   Exercise

More than anything, we want to help you develop the intuition that will help you solve unique problems on your own. You now know about the store, actions, reducers, and what roles they play. Using what you've learned from implementing task creation, try making Parsnip even more awesome by allowing users to update the status of each task.

Tasks have a status field, which can be one of three values: Unstarted, In Progress, and Completed. If you open the browser to localhost:3000, you'll see the UI already displays the status of each task, but users can now open a drop-down and choose a new status. See figure 2.12 for an example of the status selection UI.

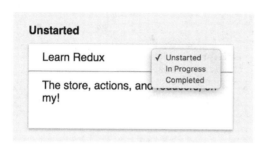

Figure 2.12 An example status drop-down

Try your hand first at an implementation; then we'll walk through how you can approach it. If the task seems daunting, try breaking the problem down until you have manageable, actionable steps. Before getting into any code, keep a few questions in mind:

- What am I allowing users to do? What UI do I need to build to allow them to access these features?
- Based on my requirements, what state might I need to track to fulfill them?
- When and how does that state change?

2.11 Solution

As always, let's start with a high-level description of what you want to accomplish, then work piece by piece toward an implementation. Your goal is to allow users to update a task's status by selecting either Unstarted, In Progress, or Completed from a select input. Let's break down the problem into manageable chunks:

- Add a select input with the three available statuses. Tasks already have a status field, and you can declare the possible states as a constant.
- When the user chooses a new status, dispatch an EDIT_TASK action with two pieces of data: the id of the task being updated and the desired status.
- The tasks reducer should handle EDIT_TASK, update the status of the correct task, and return the updated state tree.
- The view should re-render with the newly updated status.

Have you noticed how you tend to implement features in a particular order? It lines up nicely with the idea of a unidirectional data flow, one of the fundamental ideas in

React and Redux. A user interaction triggers an action, you handle the action, and close the loop by re-rendering the view with any updated state.

2.11.1 *The status drop-down*

Start by adding the status drop-down to the Task component, as shown in the following listing.

Listing 2.20   src/components/Task.js

```
import React from 'react'

const TASK_STATUSES = [          Defines the list of possible
  'Unstarted',                   statuses as a variable for
  'In Progress',                 clarity convenience
  'Completed'
]

const Task = props => {
  return (
    <div className="task">
      <div className="task-header">           Adds the status drop-
        <div>{props.task.title}</div>         down using the select
        <select value={props.task.status}>    and option elements
          {TASK_STATUSES.map(status => (
            <option key={status} value={status}>{status}</option>
          ))}
        </select>
      </div>
      <hr />
      <div className="task-body">{props.task.description}</div>
    </div>
  )
}

export default Task;
```

Now the user can interact with a drop-down that renders the correct values, but the task won't be updated when an option is selected.

> **TIP** For the sake of simplicity, you defined TASK_STATUSES directly in the Task component, but it's a common convention to define constants such as these in a separate file.

2.11.2 *Dispatching an edit action*

To indicate an event has occurred in your application—the user selecting a new status for a task—you'll dispatch an action. You'll create and export an action creator that builds the EDIT_TASK action. This is where you'll determine the arguments to the action creator (editTask), and the shape of the action payload, as shown in the following listing.

> **Listing 2.21 src/actions/index.js**

```
...
export function editTask(id, params = {}) {
  return {
    type: 'EDIT_TASK',
    payload: {
      id,
      params
    }
  };
}
```

By using an action creator, you can clearly communicate that the EDIT_TASK requires two arguments: the ID of which task to edit, and a params object with any fields being updated.

Next import editTask in App, your container component, add any necessary action handling, and pass down an onStatusChange prop to be fired eventually by the Task component, as shown in the following listing.

> **Listing 2.22 src/App.js**

```
...
import { createTask, editTask } from './actions';

class App extends Component {
  ...
  onStatusChange = (id, status) => {
    this.props.dispatch(editTask(id, { status }));
  }

  render() {
    return (
      <div className="main-content">
        <TasksPage
          tasks={this.props.tasks}
          onCreateTask={this.onCreateTask}
          onStatusChange={this.onStatusChange}
        />
      </div>
    );
  }
}
...
```

Imports the new action creator

Creates the onStatusChange handler, which dispatches the editTask action creator

Passes onStatusChange down to TaskList

Next move on to the TasksPage component and pass onStatusChange down to TaskList and finally on to Task, as shown in the following listing.

> **Listing 2.23 src/components/TasksPage.js**

```
  ...
return (
  <TaskList
    key={status}
    status={status}
    tasks={statusTasks}
```

```
      onStatusChange={this.props.onStatusChange}        ◁─────────────┐
    />                                                                 │
  );                          Task is ultimately what calls this.props.onStatusChange
  ...                          with the correct arguments, so TaskList only needs to
                                                    forward this prop along.
```

To reach the `Task` component, `onStatusChange` needs to travel through one more component: `TaskList`, as shown in the following listing.

Listing 2.24   src/components/TaskList.js

```
  ...
{props.tasks.map(task => {
  return (
    <Task
      key={task.id}                                    onStatusChange needs to
      task={task}                                      be passed once more as a
      onStatusChange={props.onStatusChange}      ◁─┘  prop to reach Task.
    />
  );
)}
  ...
```

Finally, in the `Task` component we can fire the `props.onStatusChange` callback when the value of the status drop-down changes, as shown in the following listing.

Listing 2.25   src/components/Task.js

```
...
const Task = props => {                                 Adds a callback to run
  return (                                              when the drop-down's
    <div className="task">                              change event fires
      <div className="task-header">
        <div>{props.task.title}</div>
        <select value={props.task.status} onChange={onStatusChange}>    ◁──┐
          {TASK_STATUSES.map(status => (
            <option key={status} value={status}>{status}</option>
          ))}
        </select>
      </div>
      <hr />
      <div className="task-body">{props.task.description}</div>
    </div>
  );                                          Calls onStatusChange with the
                                              ID of the updated task and the
  function onStatusChange(e) {        ◁──     value of the new status
    props.onStatusChange(props.task.id, e.target.value)
  }
}
...
```

The only thing missing at this point is update logic. An action is dispatched that describes an intent to edit a task, but the task itself still needs to be updated by a reducer.

2.11.3 *Handling the action in a reducer*

The last step is to specify how the task should be updated in response to the EDIT_TASK action being dispatched. Update the tasks reducer to check for the newly created EDIT_TASK action and update the correct task, as shown in the following listing.

Listing 2.26   src/reducers/index.js

Checks whether the action passed in has a type that you want to handle

Because the list of tasks is stored as an array, to update the right task iterate over the list of tasks with map, and if the current task matches the ID from the payload, update it with the new params.

```
...
export function tasks(state = initialState, action) {
  ...
  if (action.type === 'EDIT_TASK') {
    const { payload } = action;
    return {
      tasks: state.tasks.map(task => {
        if (task.id === payload.id) {
          return Object.assign({}, task, payload.params);
        }

        return task;
      })
    }
  }

  return state;
}
```

Uses Object.assign to update the task object by returning a new copy, not modifying the original object

First, you check whether the action being passed in is of type EDIT_TASK. If so, you iterate over the list of tasks, updating the relevant task and returning the remaining tasks without modification.

That completes the feature! Once the store updates, the connected components will perform another render and the cycle is ready to begin again.

You implemented a couple of relatively straightforward features, but in the process, you saw most of the core elements of Redux in action. It can be overwhelming, but it's not critical (or even feasible) that you leave chapter 2 with an ironclad understanding of every new concept we've introduced. We'll cover many of these individual ideas and techniques in greater depth later in the book.

Summary

- Container components receive data from Redux and dispatch action creators, and presentational components accept data as props and handle markup.
- Actions are objects describing an event. Action creators are functions that return actions.
- Reducers are pure functions that update state in response to actions.

- Side effects can be handled in action creators. Reducers, however, should be pure functions, meaning they don't perform any mutations and always return the same value given the same inputs.
- A configured Redux store can be made available to your app using react-redux and the `Provider` component.
- The commands `connect` and `mapStateToProps` pass data from Redux into a React component as props.

Debugging Redux applications

This chapter covers

- Working with the Redux developer tools
- Understanding the role of monitors
- Using hot module replacement

Debugging isn't only a thing you do when you're given a bug report. The same tools and developer experience are essential to developing new features, too. In chapter 1, you learned that Redux was born out of a desire for a better client-side development experience. In this chapter, we'll talk about a few areas where the Redux developer tools can provide better insight into an application, save valuable developer hours, and make for a more enjoyable day on the job.

Historically, time spent tracking down unexpected behavior could be one of the most egregious time sinks in a developer's day. Chasing state changes in a complex application using two-way databinding has sunk many developer days—we should know. However, the Flux architecture pattern successfully reduces part of the mental overhead required to keep up with state changes, thanks to its unidirectional dataflow. Standardizing on actions as the vehicles of state change introduced a certain clarity: regardless of what initiated it, a change in state can be traced back to an action.

As you've learned in the first two chapters, the list of actions dispatched in an application forms what can be thought of as a transaction log. When viewed sequentially, they can tell the story of a user's interaction with the application fairly comprehensively. Wouldn't it be nice to visualize those actions in real time? To see them as they're dispatched and the data they contain?

3.1   Introducing the Redux DevTools

The Redux developer tools, or DevTools for short, augment your development environment for real-time visualization of actions. Let's look at what the developer tools might look like in the context of Parsnip (figure 3.1), the task management application you started in chapter 2.

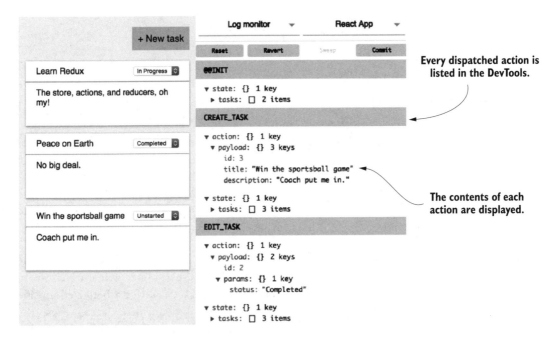

Figure 3.1   The Redux DevTools can be used to display actions in real time.

In the right panel (figure 3.1), you can see a highlighted list of items—the actions that have been dispatched to produce the state displayed. Given this list of actions, you can tell exactly what you've been up to within Parsnip without having to observe you do it: the app was initialized, a third task was created, and then the second task was edited. You can see why it might be handy to have immediate feedback on each new action as it's dispatched. For every action, you can be sure that the payload looks the way you intended. Still, there's much more that you can do with the DevTools.

You'll notice that beneath each action in the right page is a snapshot of the Redux store. Not only can you view the action produced, you can see the application state that resulted from that action. Better still, you can dig into the Redux store and see, highlighted, the exact values that changed as a result of the action. Figure 3.2 points out these details within the DevTools.

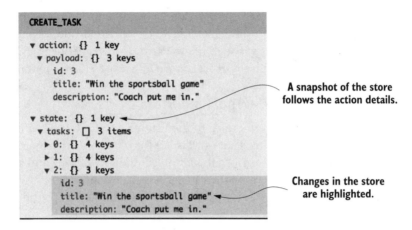

Figure 3.2 The DevTools highlight attributes of the Redux store that have changed as a result of the action.

3.2 Time-travel debugging

But wait, there's more! Clicking the title of an action in the DevTools toggles that action off. The application state is recalculated as if that action was never dispatched, even if the action is in the middle of a long list of actions. Click it again, and the application returns to its original state. See figure 3.3 for an example of this toggled state.

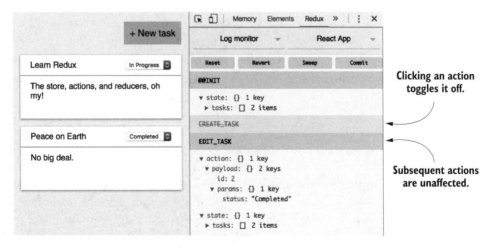

Figure 3.3 Toggling an action recalculates the application state as if the action was never dispatched.

The rewinding and replaying of actions like this is what inspired the name time-travel debugging. To determine what Parsnip would look like if you hadn't created a third task, there's no need to refresh and re-create the state—you can hop back in time by disabling that action.

One extension for the DevTools even provides a slider UI to scroll back and forward through actions, seeing their immediate effect on the application. Note that no extra configuration or dependency is required to use time-travel debugging; it's a feature of the DevTools. More specifically, it's a feature of many DevTools monitors.

3.3   *Visualizing changes with DevTools monitors*

The Redux DevTools provide an interface to the actions and Redux store, but don't provide a way to visualize that data. That work is left for monitors. This is a conscious decision to separate the two concerns, enabling the community to plug and play their own visualizations of the data to best fit their needs. Figure 3.4 illustrates this idea conceptually; one or more monitors can be configured to display the data provided by the DevTools.

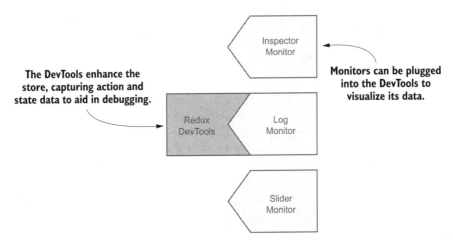

Figure 3.4   **Various monitors can be combined with the Redux DevTools to visualize actions and store data.**

Several of these monitors, including those listed in figure 3.4, are open source libraries and ready for use. In the screenshots from the previous sections, you viewed a simple monitor, the Log Monitor. Other monitors worth mentioning are the Slider Monitor, described in the previous section, and the Inspector Monitor, the default monitor of the Redux DevTools Chrome extension. Inspector provides a user interface similar to the Log Monitor but allows for easier filtering of actions and storing of data.

> **NOTE**   Several more monitors can be found in the README of the Redux DevTools repository on GitHub (https://github.com/gaearon/redux-devtools). Again, the DevTools will feed the data to any monitor, so if you can't find a monitor feature you're looking for, that may be your cue to build your own. The open source community will thank you for your contribution!

3.4   *Implementing the Redux DevTools*

Let's say that you're tasked with implementing the DevTools in your budding new application, Parsnip. The first choice you have to make is how you'd like to view the monitors. Here are a few popular options:

- In a component within the application
- In a separate popup window
- Inside your browser's developer tools

For a few reasons, our personal preference is the last option—to use the Redux DevTools using the Chrome browser developer tools. First, the installation is easier than any other option. Second, the integration with our existing development work-flow is seamless. Finally, the extension includes a robust set of monitors that continues to meet your needs out of the box.

As JavaScript developers, many of us already spend much time within the Chrome DevTools—inspecting elements, using breakpoints, flipping between panels to check the performance of requests, and so on. Installing the Redux DevTools Chrome plugin adds one more panel, and clicking it reveals the Inspector and other monitors. You don't miss a beat.

> **NOTE**   Redux and Chrome both refer to their developer tools by the abbreviation "DevTools." References to the Redux DevTools within the Chrome DevTools can get confusing, so pay extra attention to the difference. Going forward, we'll specify which we're referring to.

This process has two steps: installing the Chrome browser extension and hooking the Redux DevTools into the store. Installing the Chrome extension is the simpler of the two. Visit the Chrome Web Store, search for Redux DevTools, and install the first package by the author remotedev.io.

Now on to the second step, adding the Redux DevTools to the store. Although this configuration can be done without another dependency, the `redux-devtools-extension` package is a friendly abstraction that reads like English. You'll download and instrument the package now. Install and save the package to your development dependencies with the following command:

```
npm install -D redux-devtools-extension
```

Once installed, you'll import and pass a function called `devToolsEnhancer` to the store. As a refresher, Redux's `createStore` function takes up to three arguments: a reducer, an initial state, and an enhancer. In the case that only two arguments are passed, Redux presumes the second argument is an enhancer and there's no initial state. The following listing is an example of this case. Enhancers are a way to augment the Redux store and the `devToolsEnhancer` function is doing that: connecting the store with the Chrome extension to provide additional debugging features.

Listing 3.1   src/index.js

```
import { devToolsEnhancer } from 'redux-devtools-extension';
...
const store = createStore(tasks, devToolsEnhancer());
...
```

After you've completed adding the Redux DevTools enhancer to the `createStore` method, you can begin to use the tools. Flip back to the app in the browser and open the Chrome developer tools. If you're unfamiliar, from the Chrome navigation bar, select View, then Developer, and finally Developer Tools. The Chrome DevTools will open in a separate pane in your browser, typically with the Elements panel displayed by default. From the navigation bar within the Chrome developer tools, you can find the Redux DevTools by selecting the new Redux panel, made available by the Redux DevTools Chrome extension (figure 3.5).

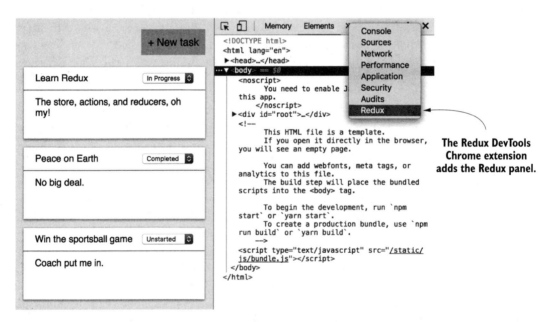

Figure 3.5   Navigate to the Redux DevTools via the Redux panel in the Chrome developer tools.

Once you've navigated to the Redux DevTools, you should see the Inspector Monitor by default, which you can confirm by verifying that the upper-left menu of the tools reads Inspector. If you've followed along and implemented the Redux DevTools in

Parsnip, test them by adding a couple of new tasks. You should see a new action listed in the Inspector Monitor for each task added. Click the Skip button for one of the actions in the monitor to toggle that action off, and notice the removal of that task in the user interface. Click the action's Skip button once more to toggle it back on.

When an action is selected, the other half of the Inspector Monitor will display data about the action or the Redux store, depending on the filter you've selected. The Diff filter is particularly helpful for visualizing the impact that an action had on the store. The menu in the upper left will change the display between the Inspector, Log, and Chart monitors. A button near the bottom on the panel with a stopwatch icon opens a fourth monitor: the Slider Monitor. Pause here to take time to explore these tools pointed out in figure 3.6, because they make for a delightful developer experience and will save your backside more times than you'll be able to count.

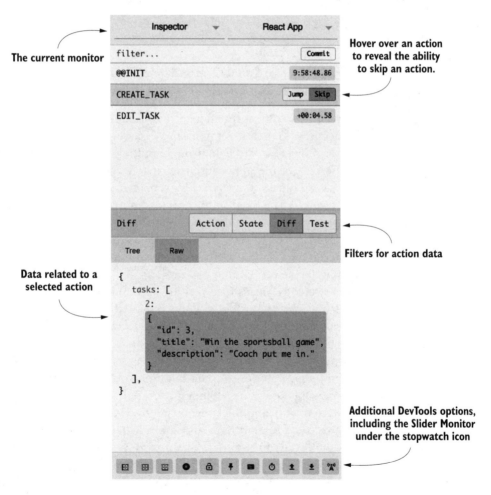

Figure 3.6 The skip, Diff filter, and monitor menu options offer unique ways to visualize and debug state effects.

If you think you'd prefer to use the Redux DevTools in a component within your app, the setup process is slightly more long-winded. You'll likely make use of the Dock Monitor—a component that can be shown or hidden in your application and that displays the Log Monitor, or another monitor, within it. Full instructions can be found in the README of the Redux DevTools repository on GitHub at https://github.com/gaearon/redux-devtools.

3.5   *The role of Webpack*

Are you already bored with your new debugging superpowers and looking for something else to optimize? As a JavaScript developer, you may be all too familiar with this workflow:

1 Place a `debugger` statement in an uncertain area of the code.
2 Click through the application until the `debugger` is triggered.
3 In the console, figure out what code should be written to make incremental progress.
4 Add the new code to your application and delete the `debugger`.
5 Return to step 1 and repeat until the bug fix or feature is complete.

Though `debugger` can be wildly more efficient than using console logs or alerts, this developer experience leaves much to be desired. We commonly burn a ton of time in the second step: after refreshing, we click through multiple extraneous screens before finally getting to the part of the application we're concerned about. We may make incremental progress each pass, but it may be repeated an inestimable number of times before we can call the bug fixed or the feature complete.

Let's start chipping away at these development-cycle times. Wouldn't it be nice if you no longer had to manually refresh the page after a change is made to your code? If you know you need to refresh the browser to view and test each code change, your build tools might as well take care of that for you.

Multiple tools are capable of this file-watching and updating on change, but we'll reference Webpack specifically throughout the rest of this chapter. Webpack isn't required to use Redux, but it's a favorite among React developers and it comes already configured within apps generated by Create React App.

Webpack is a type of build tool—a module bundler—capable of all kinds of tasks, thanks to rich plugin options. In this chapter, however, you're interested in only those features that improve your Redux development workflow. Don't panic, no Webpack expertise is required to understand the concepts in this chapter.

Webpack can save you a second here and there with automatic refreshing. Not bad, but we're not that excited yet either. The next opportunity for optimization is to more quickly bundle changes into the application and perform that refresh. Turns out that's a specialty of Webpack. By omitting the resources not required by a component, Webpack allows you to send less over the wire for each page load. These optimizations come enabled out of the box with Create React App and require no further configuration.

The combination of automatic refreshes and faster load times are nice wins that may add up over time, but they're still incremental improvements in a development workflow. You may be tempted to believe the Webpack bang isn't worth the buck, but you'll quickly discover that another feature, hot module replacement, is the foundation of an exceptional Redux development experience.

3.6 *Hot module replacement*

Hot module replacement enables an application to update without having to refresh. Let that sink in. If you've navigated deeply into an application to test a specific component, with hot module replacement, each code change updates in real time, leaving you to continue debugging uninterrupted. This feature all but eliminates that second, costly step in our example debugger workflow: "Click through the application until triggering the debugger." There's Webpack giving you your money's worth.

Note that hot module replacement doesn't outright replace debugger. The two debugging strategies can be used harmoniously together. Use debugger no differently than you already do, and let hot module replacement reduce the time you might spend navigating to reach the same breakpoint in the following development cycle.

It's worth clarifying at this point that hot module replacement is a feature of Webpack and isn't at all coupled or unique to React or Redux applications. Create React App enables the hot module replacement feature in Webpack by default, but it's still up to you to specify how to handle updates. You'll want to configure two specific updates for a React and Redux application. The first is how to handle updates to components.

3.6.1 *Hot-loading components*

Your next objective is to take Parsnip and augment it with hot module replacement. The first goal is to have Webpack update any components you touch without refreshing the page. Fortunately, the implementation logic is roughly that simple. See if you can make sense of the code in listing 3.2.

To summarize, Webpack will expose the `module.hot` object in development mode. One of the methods on that object is `accept`. The `accept` command takes two arguments: one or more dependencies and a callback. You'll want an update to any of your components to trigger the hot replacement, and fortunately, you don't have to list every React component in your application as a dependency. Whenever a child of the top-most component updates, the change will be picked up by the parent. You can pass the string location of `App` to the `accept` function.

The second argument passed to `accept` is a callback that gets executed after the modules have successfully been replaced. In your case, you want to render `App` and the rest of the updated components back to the DOM. In summary, each update to a component causes that module to be replaced, and then those changes are rendered to the DOM without reloading the page.

Listing 3.2 src/index.js

```
...
if (module.hot) {                              ◁————  The Create React App has hot module
  module.hot.accept('./App', () => {                  replacement enabled in development mode.
    const NextApp = require('./App').default;       ◁————
    ReactDOM.render(                                        Whenever the App
      <Provider store={store}><NextApp /></Provider>,       component (or one of
      document.getElementById('root')                       its children) changes,
    );                                                       re-render the component.
  });
}
```

Webpack won't expose `module.hot` in a production environment for good reason: you have no business making live changes to components in production. Remember that hot module replacement is a tool used only in development to accelerate development cycles.

3.6.2 *Hot-loading reducers*

It makes sense to add hot module replacement in one more location in the app: reducers. Manipulating data in reducers is another of those points in the development workflow that can really eat up the clock if you need to reload the page after each iteration. Consider instead the ability to make changes to a reducer and see data in its respective components update in real time.

In listing 3.3, you see a similar pattern to the implementation for components. In development mode, you listen for changes to your reducers and execute a callback after the modules have been replaced. The only difference now is that, instead of rendering new components to the DOM, you're replacing the old reducer with the updated one and recalculating what the state should be.

Listing 3.3 src/index.js

```
if (module.hot) {                                        Whenever the reducer
  ...                                                    updates, perform the hot
                                                         module replacement.
  module.hot.accept('./reducers', () => {        ◁————
    const nextRootReducer = require('./reducers').default;
    store.replaceReducer(nextRootReducer);       ◁————
  });                                                    The Redux store has a
}                                                        replaceReducer method
                                                         to facilitate this update.
```

Imagine that as you're developing the workflow for the CREATE_TASK action, you misspelled CREATE_TASK in the reducer. You might've created several tasks while testing the code you wrote, and even seen the actions logged in the Redux DevTools, but no new tasks appeared in the UI. With hot module replacement applied to the reducer, the correction of that typo results in the missing tasks appearing instantly—no refreshing required.

How is it that a change to a reducer can update the state of data already in the Redux store? The stage for this feature is set by the purity of the Redux architecture. You must rely on the reducer function to be deterministic; the same action will always produce the same change in state. If the Redux store is mutable, you can't be certain that a list of actions results in the same state each time.

Given a read-only store, this killer feature becomes possible with a clever combination of the Redux DevTools and hot module replacement. The short version of the answer is that the Redux DevTools augment the store with the ability to keep a running list of all the actions. When Webpack accepts an update to hot-load and calls `replaceReducer`, each of those actions is replayed through the new reducer. Presto! A recalculated state is born. This happens instantly and saves a ton of time having to re-create the same state manually.

Now you're cooking with fire! When developing, you can make changes to components or reducers and expect to see changes instantly while maintaining the state of the application. You can imagine this saves development time, but the real aha moments come with experience. Try implementing hot module replacement for yourself before moving on to the next section.

3.6.3 Limitations of hot module replacement

Note that hot module replacement currently has a few limitations. Updating non-component files may require a full-page refresh, for example, and a console warning may tell you as much. The other limitation to be aware of is the inability to maintain local state in React components.

Remember, it's perfectly reasonable to use local component state in combination with the Redux store. Hot module replacement has no trouble leaving the Redux store intact, but maintaining local state after an update is a tougher puzzle to solve. When App and its children components are updated and re-rendered to the DOM, React sees these as new and different components, and they lose any existing local state in the process.

One tool makes it possible to go that step further and maintain local component state after a hot module replacement: React Hot Loader.

3.7 Preserving local state with React Hot Loader

React Hot Loader is another of Dan Abramov's pet projects, and a version was demonstrated with Redux in his popular 2015 React Europe conference talk, "Hot Reloading with Time Travel." That early, experimental library has come a long way since then. Several iterations later, a stable package is available for use in your projects now.

As we've alluded, React Hot Loader takes the hot module replacement developer experience a step further. For every code update, not only will the Redux store be preserved, so too will each component's local state. React Hot Loader achieves this with the nuanced use of component proxies. Fortunately for us end users, those implementation details are hidden under the hood, and a simple configuration is all that's required to enjoy the fruits of that labor.

One downside to React Hot Loader is the unfortunate incompatibility with Create React App. It requires configuration of either Babel or Webpack, which necessitates ejecting (`npm run eject`) from Create React App. We won't eject from the application in this book, so implementing React Hot Loader is an exercise for you to do later. Please see the React Hot Loader GitHub repository at https://github.com/gaearon/react-hot-loader for instructions.

The value of adding React Hot Loader comes down to how large or how complex the local state in your application becomes. Many Redux applications rely on only simple local state to store the contents of a form, before the user submits it, for example. In these cases, vanilla hot module replacement is generally more than sufficient for an excellent developer experience.

3.8   *Exercise*

As a quick exercise to get more familiar with the Redux DevTools, try navigating to the Chart Monitor to view a graphic visualization of your application's state.

3.9   *Solution*

This is a quick one; the solution is only two clicks away. Recall that in the upper-left corner of the Redux DevTools, you can click the name of the current monitor to reveal a drop-down list of more available monitors (figure 3.7).

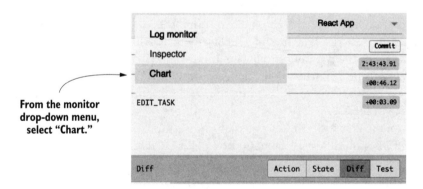

Figure 3.7   The location of the Chart Monitor

Clicking the Chart option reveals a graphical representation of the state in your application. It won't look so impressive now, because there's not much going on yet. You can imagine that a fully featured application would contain a much larger web of data, though. Using this perspective won't always be the best lens on your data, but it has its moments. See figure 3.8 for an example state payload displayed by the Chart Monitor.

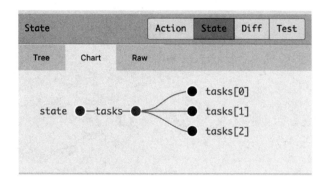

Figure 3.8 The Chart Monitor

Hovering over nodes in the Chart Monitor reveals their contents. This feature makes for a convenient way to quickly get to know an application. Navigation within the Chart Monitor can be controlled by zooming in and out or clicking and dragging to make lateral movements.

Your investment in learning the debugging tools and strategies covered in this chapter will start to pay immediate dividends, getting you unstuck in upcoming examples or on your own projects. The Redux developer experience is second to none and that's thanks in large part to the Redux DevTools.

The next chapter is a great place to put these new debugging skills to the test, where we'll introduce asynchronous actions and interact with an API.

Summary

- The Redux developer tools allow for the visualization and manipulation of actions in real time.
- Monitors determine how the data is visualized, and the DevTools can mix and match monitors.
- Hot module replacement takes the development experience to new heights by performing updates without refreshing the page.

Consuming an API 4

This chapter covers

- Using asynchronous actions
- Handling errors with Redux
- Rendering loading states

If you've kept up so far with the book, or completed a few of the more basic tutorials online, you know that we've reached a point where things traditionally start to get a little trickier. Here's where you are: a user interacts with the app and actions get dispatched to reflect certain events, such as creating a new task or editing an existing task. The data lives directly in the browser, which means you lose any progress if the user refreshes the page.

Perhaps without realizing, every action you've dispatched so far has been synchronous. When an action is dispatched, the store receives it immediately. These kinds of actions are straightforward, and synchronous code is generally easier to work with and think about. You know exactly the order things will execute based on where the code is defined. You execute line one and then line two, and so on. But you'd be hard-pressed to find any real-world JavaScript application that didn't involve any asynchronous code. It's fundamental to the language and required to do what this chapter is all about: talking with a server.

4.1 *Asynchronous actions*

To repeat a few fundamental Redux ideas

- Actions are objects that describe an event, such as CREATE_TASK.
- Actions must be dispatched to apply any updates.

Every action you dispatched in chapters 2 and 3 was synchronous, but, as it turns out, you often need a server to do anything useful. Specifically, you need to make AJAX requests perform actions such as fetch tasks when the app starts and save new tasks to a server, so they'll persist between page refreshes. Virtually every real-world application is backed by a server, so clear patterns for interacting with an API are crucial for an application's long-term health.

Figure 4.1 recaps how your dispatches have looked so far. You dispatch an action from the view, and the action is received immediately by the store. All this code is synchronous, meaning each operation will run only after the previous operation has completed.

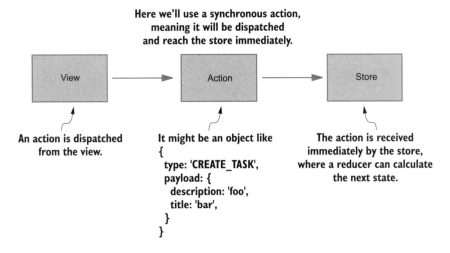

Figure 4.1   A synchronous action being dispatched

By contrast, asynchronous, or async, actions are where you can add asynchronous code such as AJAX requests. When dispatching synchronous actions, you don't have any room for extra functionality. Async actions provide a way to handle asynchronous operations and dispatch synchronous actions with the results when they become available. Async actions typically combine the following into one convenient package, which you can dispatch directly within your app:

- One or more side effects, such as an AJAX request
- One or more synchronous dispatches, such as dispatching an action after an AJAX request has resolved

Say you want to fetch a list of tasks from the server to render on the page when the app loads for the first time. You need to initiate the request, wait for the server to respond, and dispatch an action with any results. Figure 4.2 uses a `fetchTasks` async action, which you'll implement later in the chapter. Notice the delay between the initial async action being dispatched and when the store finally receives an action to process.

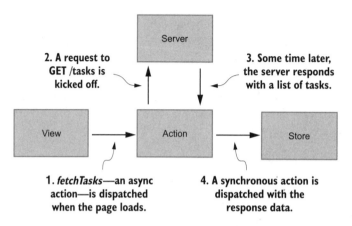

Figure 4.2   An example asynchronous action dispatch

Much of the confusion around async actions boils down to terminology. In this chapter (and throughout the book), we'll try to be specific about the terms we use, to avoid overloading certain language. Here are the fundamental concepts along with examples:

- *Action*—An object that describes an event. The phrase *synchronous action* always refers to these action objects. If a synchronous action is dispatched, it's received by the store immediately. Actions have a required `type` property and can optionally have additional fields that store data needed to handle the action:

```
{
  type: 'FETCH_TASKS_SUCCEEDED',
  payload: {
    tasks: [...]
  }
}
```

- *Action creator*—A function that returns an action.
- *Synchronous action creator*—All action creators that return an action are considered *synchronous* action creators:

```
function fetchTasksSucceeded(tasks) {
  return {
    type: 'FETCH_TASKS_SUCCEEDED',
```

```
    payload: {
      tasks: [...]
    }
  }
}
```

- *Async action creator*—An action creator that *does* contain async code (the most common example being network requests). As you'll see later in the chapter, they typically make one or more API calls and dispatch one or more actions at certain points in the request's lifecycle. Often, instead of returning an action directly, they may return synchronous action creators for readability:

```
export function fetchTasks() {
  return dispatch => {
    api.fetchTasks().then(resp => {
      dispatch(fetchTasksSucceeded(resp.data));
    });
  };
}
```

The syntax from the last example is a sneak peek at what's ahead. Soon we'll introduce the redux-thunk package, which allows you to dispatch functions in addition to standard action objects. Before you can dig into implementing async action creators, you need a simple server. Please go to the appendix and follow the instructions for setting up that server and installing two more dependencies: axios and redux-thunk. Don't miss the important tweak required in the Redux DevTools configuration either! When you've finished, go on to the next section to learn how to dispatch async actions.

4.2 *Invoking async actions with redux-thunk*

You know you can pass an action object to the dispatch function, which will pass the action to the store and apply any updates. What if you don't want the action to be processed immediately? What if you want to make a GET request for tasks and dispatch an action with the data from the response body? The first async action you'll dispatch is to fetch a list of tasks from the server when the app loads. At a high level, you'll do the following:

- From the view, dispatch an asynchronous action to fetch tasks.
- Perform the AJAX request to GET /tasks.
- When the request completes, dispatch a synchronous action with the response.

We've been going on about async actions, but we've yet to show you the mechanism to accomplish them. You can transition the fetchTasks action creator from synchronous to asynchronous by returning a function instead of an object. The function you return from fetchTasks can safely perform a network request and dispatch a synchronous action with response data.

It's possible to do this without another dependency, but you'll find that the code to facilitate it may quickly become unmanageable. For starters, each of your components will need to be aware if they're making a synchronous or asynchronous call, and if the latter, pass along the dispatch functionality.

The most popular option for handling async actions is redux-thunk, a Redux middleware. Understanding the ins and outs of middleware isn't necessary now; we'll cover middleware in depth in chapter 5. The most important takeaway is that adding the redux-thunk middleware allows us to dispatch functions as well as the standard action objects that you're already used to. Within these functions, you're safe to add any asynchronous code you might need.

4.2.1   *Fetching tasks from a server*

At this point, you have a functioning HTTP API, an AJAX library (axios), and the redux-thunk middleware, which will allow you to dispatch functions instead of action objects when you need to perform async operations such as network requests.

Currently, you're rendering the page with a static list of tasks defined in the tasks reducer. Start by removing the list of mock tasks in src/reducers/index.js and adjust the initial state for the reducer, as shown in the following listing.

Listing 4.1   src/reducers/index.js

```
import { uniqueId } from '../actions'          Remove the uniqueId
                                                import and mockTasks
const mockTasks = [                             array completely.
  {
    id: uniqueId(),
    title: 'Learn Redux',
    description: 'The store, actions, and reducers, oh my!',
    status: 'Unstarted',
  },
  {
    id: uniqueId(),
    title: 'Peace on Earth',
    description: 'No big deal.',
    status: 'In Progress',
  },
  {
    id: uniqueId(),
    title: 'Foo',
    description: 'Bar',
    status: 'Completed',
  },                                            Replaces mockTasks
];                                              with an empty array
                                                as the initial state for
export function tasks(state = { tasks: [] }, action) {  ◁──  the tasks property
  ...
```

At a high-level, here's what you need to add to fetch a list of tasks via AJAX:

- When the app loads, dispatch an async action, fetchTasks, to fetch the initial tasks.
- Make the AJAX call to /tasks.

- When the request completes, dispatch a synchronous action, `FETCH_TASKS` `_SUCCEEDED`, with the result.

Figure 4.3 shows the `fetchTasks` async action creator you're about to create in more detail.

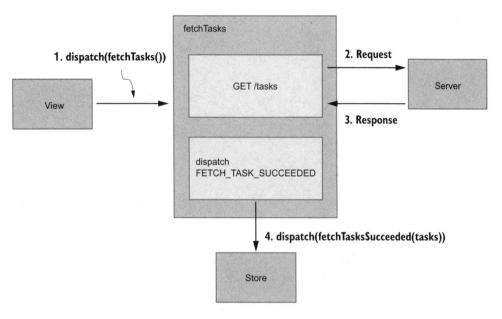

Figure 4.3 The chronological flow of fetchTasks as an async action

As with synchronous actions, the goal of dispatching `fetchTasks` as an async action is to load tasks into the store, so you can render them on the page. The only difference here is that you fetch them from a server instead of relying on mock tasks defined directly in the code.

Keeping figure 4.3 in mind, let's start from left to right by dispatching an action from the view. Import a soon-to-be-created `fetchTasks` action creator and dispatch it within the `componentDidMount` lifecycle method.

Listing 4.2   src/App.js

```
import React, { Component } from 'react';
import { connect } from 'react-redux';
import TasksPage from './components/TasksPage';
import { createTask, editTask, fetchTasks } from './actions';

class App extends Component {
  componentDidMount() {
    this.props.dispatch(fetchTasks());
  }
```

Imports the fetchTasks action creator from the actions module

Dispatches the fetchTasks action from componentDidMount

```
    . . .

    render() {
      return (
        <div className="main-content">
          <TasksPage
            tasks={this.props.tasks}
            onCreateTask={this.onCreateTask}
            onStatusChange={this.onStatusChange}
          />
        </div>
      );
    }
}

function mapStateToProps(state) {
  return {
    tasks: state.tasks
  };
}
```

It's useful to think about apps in terms of data dependencies. You should ask yourself, "What data does this page or page section need to render successfully?" When you're working in the browser, componentDidMount is the appropriate lifecycle callback to initiate AJAX requests. Because it's configured to run whenever a component is first mounted to the DOM, it's at this point that you can begin to fetch the data to populate that DOM. Furthermore, this is an established best practice in React.

Next, head to src/actions/index.js, where you'll need two things:

- An implementation of fetchTasks that performs the AJAX call
- A new synchronous action creator, fetchTasksSucceeded, to dispatch the tasks from the server response into the store

Use axios to perform the AJAX request. Upon a successful response, the body of that response will be passed to the synchronous action creator to be dispatched, as shown in the following listing.

Listing 4.3   src/actions/index.js

```
import axios from 'axios';

    . . .

export function fetchTasksSucceeded(tasks) {    ◁──┐  A new synchronous action will
  return {                                              be dispatched if the request
    type: 'FETCH_TASKS_SUCCEEDED',                      completes successfully.
    payload: {
      tasks
    }
  }
}
```

```
export function fetchTasks() {
  return dispatch => {
    axios.get('http://localhost:3001/tasks')
      .then(resp => {
        dispatch(fetchTasksSucceeded(resp.data));
      });
  }
}
```

fetchTasks returns a function instead of an action.

Makes the AJAX request

Dispatches a synchronous action creator

The biggest shift in listing 4.3 from any of the actions you've worked with so far is that `fetchTasks` returns a function, not an action object. The `redux-thunk` middleware is what makes this possible. If you attempted to dispatch a function without the middleware applied, Redux would throw an error because it expects an object to be passed to `dispatch`.

Within this dispatched function, you're free to do the following:

- Make an AJAX request to fetch all tasks.
- Access the store state.
- Perform additional asynchronous logic.
- Dispatch a synchronous action with a result.

Most async actions tend to share these basic responsibilities.

4.2.2 API clients

While you let async actions start to sink in, let's cover a common abstraction for interacting with servers. In listing 4.3, you used axios for the first time to make a GET request to the /tasks endpoint. This is fine for the time being, but as your application grows you'll start to run into a few issues. What if you change the base URL for the API from `localhost:3001` to `localhost:3002`? What if you want to use a different AJAX library? You have to update that code in only one place now, but imagine if you had 10 AJAX calls. What about 100?

To address these questions, you can abstract those details into an API client and give it a friendly interface. If you're working with a team, future developers won't have to worry about specifics around ports, headers, the AJAX library being used, and so on.

Create a new api/ directory with a single index.js file. If you're working in a large application with many difference resources, it can make sense to create multiple files per resource, but a single index.js file will be fine to get us started.

In src/api/index.js, create a `fetchTasks` function that will encapsulate your API call, and configure axios with basic headers and a base URL, as shown in the following listing.

Listing 4.4   src/api/index.js

```
import axios from 'axios';

const API_BASE_URL = 'http://localhost:3001';
```

Defines a constant for the API's base URL

```
const client = axios.create({
  baseURL: API_BASE_URL,
  headers: {
    'Content-Type': 'application/json',
  },
});
```

> The Content-Type header
> is required by json-server
> for PUT requests.

```
export function fetchTasks() {
  return client.get('/tasks');
}
```

> Exports a named
> fetchTasks function
> that will make the call

Here you're hardcoding the base URL for the API. In a real-world application, you'd likely get this from a server, so the value can be different based on the environment, like staging or production.

With `fetchTasks`, you're encapsulating the request method as well as the URL for the endpoint. If either change, you only have to update code in one place. Note that `axios.get` returns a promise, which you can call `.then` and `.catch` on from within an async action creator.

Now that you're exporting a `fetchTasks` function that wraps the API call, head back to src/actions/index.js and replace the existing API call with the new `fetch-Tasks` function, as shown in the following listing.

Listing 4.5   src/actions/index.js

```
import * as api from '../api';

...

export function fetchTasks() {
  return dispatch => {
    api.fetchTasks().then(resp => {
      dispatch(fetchTasksSucceeded(resp.data));
    });
  };
}

...
```

> Imports all available
> API methods

> Uses the friendlier
> interface for making
> an AJAX call

Not only are the details of the request safely hidden away, the `fetchTasks` action creator is also clearer and more concise. By extracting an API client, you've improved encapsulation, future maintainability, and readability at the cost of the overhead of another module to manage. Creating new abstractions isn't always the right answer, but in this case, it seems like a no-brainer.

4.2.3   *View and server actions*

You now know a few things about synchronous and asynchronous actions, but there's one more concept that can help you form a clearer picture around how updates are happening in our applications. Typically you have two entities that can modify application state: users and servers. Actions can be divided into two groups, one for each actor: *view actions* and *server actions.*

- View actions are initiated by users. Think `FETCH_TASKS`, `CREATE_TASK`, and `EDIT_TASK`. For example, a user clicks a button and an action is dispatched.
- Server actions are initiated by a server. For example, a request successfully completes, and an action is dispatched with the response. When you implemented fetching tasks via AJAX, you introduced your first server action: `FETCH_TASKS_SUCCEEDED`.

NOTE   Certain developers like to organize view and server actions in separate directories, with the argument being it can help to break up larger files. It's not a requirement, and we won't do it in this book.

Getting back to the code, you have a server action, `FETCH_TASKS_SUCCEEDED`, which you dispatch with the list of tasks sent back from the server. Server actions are initiated by a server event like a response, but they still behave like any other action. They get dispatched and then handled by a reducer.

Let's wrap up your initial fetching logic by updating the tasks reducer to handle receiving tasks from the server. It's also safe to remove the `mockTasks` array at this point. Because you can remove the `mockTasks` array, you can use an empty array as the initial state for the reducer, as shown in the following listing.

Listing 4.6   src/reducers/index.js

```
...
export default function tasks(state = { tasks: [] }, action) {    ⟵  Make sure to
                                                                      pass an empty
  ...                                                                 array as the
                                                                      initial state
  if (action.type === 'FETCH_TASKS_SUCCEEDED') {    ⟵              for tasks.
    return {
      tasks: action.payload.tasks,
    };                                              The reducer now listens
  }                                                 for the server action.

  return state;
}
```

Notice how you didn't have to make any updates to the view? That's by design! Your React components don't particularly care where the tasks come from, which allows you to totally change your strategy for acquiring tasks with relatively low effort. Keep this in mind as you continue to move through the book. When possible, you should be building each piece of your app with a clear interface—changing one piece (such as how you get a list of tasks to initially render) shouldn't affect another (the view).

At this point you've introduced most of the conceptual heavy lifting that chapter 4 has to offer, so let's do a quick recap before you move on to persisting new tasks to the server. We've covered the following:

- The use of asynchronous actions and `redux-thunk`. The `redux-thunk` package allows you to dispatch functions instead of objects, and inside those functions you can make network requests and dispatch additional actions when any requests complete.
- The role of synchronous actions. Dispatching an action object with a `type` and `payload` is considered a synchronous action, because the store receives and processes the action immediately after dispatch.
- Users and servers are the two actors that can modify state in your applications. As a result, you can group actions into view actions and server actions.

4.3 *Saving tasks to the server*

Now that you're fetching tasks from the server when the app loads, let's update creating tasks and editing tasks to be persisted on the server. The process will be similar to what you've seen with fetching tasks.

Let's start by saving new tasks. You already have a framework in place: when a user fills out the form and submits, you dispatch the `createTask` action creator, the store receives the `CREATE_TASK` action, the reducer handles updating state, and the changes are broadcast back to the UI.

The `createTask` command needs to return a function instead of an object. Within that function, you can make your API call and dispatch an action when a response is available. Here's a quick look at the high-level steps:

- Convert the synchronous `createTask` action creator into an async action creator.
- Add a new method to your API client, which will send a POST request to the server.
- Create a new server action, `CREATE_TASK_SUCCEEDED`, whose payload will be a single task object.
- In the `createTask` action creator, initiate the request, and dispatch `CREATE _TASK_SUCCEEDED` when the request finishes. For now, you can assume it will always be successful.

Remove the `uniqueId` function. It was originally meant as a stopgap until you could create tasks on a server, which would be responsible for adding an ID.

Now you're there! Create a new function for creating tasks in the API client, as shown in the following listing.

> **Listing 4.7   src/api/index.js**

```
...
export function createTask(params) {                    A POST request is required to add
  return client.post('/tasks', params);    ◁┘         or update data on the server.
}
```

Now you can modify the `createTask` action creator to return a function, as shown in the following listing.

Listing 4.8 src/actions/index.js

```
import * as api from '../api';

...

function createTaskSucceeded(task) {        Creates a new synchronous
  return {                                  action creator
    type: 'CREATE_TASK_SUCCEEDED',
    payload: {
      task,
    },
  };
}

export function createTask({ title, description, status = 'Unstarted' }) {
  return dispatch => {
    api.createTask({ title, description, status }).then(resp => {
      dispatch(createTaskSucceeded(resp.data));        Loads the newly created
    });                                                object into the store
  };
}
```

You know that reducers handle updates to state, so update the tasks reducer to handle the `CREATE_TASK_SUCCEEDED` action. After that, you'll be up to four action handlers, so now is as good a time as any to merge each `if` statement into a friendlier `switch` statement, as shown in the following listing. This is a common Redux pattern.

Listing 4.9 src/reducers/index.js

```
export default function tasks(state = { tasks: [] }, action) {
  switch (action.type) {
    case 'CREATE_TASK': {              Moves to a switch
      return {                         statement instead of
        tasks: state.tasks.concat(action.payload),   a long if-else chain
      };
    }
    case 'EDIT_TASK': {
      const { payload } = action;
      return {
        tasks: state.tasks.map(task => {
          if (task.id === payload.id) {
            return Object.assign({}, task, payload.params);
          }

          return task;
        }),
      };
    }
    case 'FETCH_TASKS_SUCCEEDED': {
```

```
      return {
        tasks: action.payload.tasks,
      };
    }
    case 'CREATE_TASK_SUCCEEDED': {                    ◁──┐ Shows the new
      return {                                              action handler
        tasks: state.tasks.concat(action.payload.task),
      };
    }
    default: {
      return state;
    }
  }
}
```

A switch statement is a slightly friendlier syntax when there are a significant number of cases to handle. This is the structure that you'll typically see most often in Redux reducers, but using a switch statement isn't a hard requirement.

Play around in the browser and create new tasks. When you refresh, they should appear again for the initial render. The big idea here is that the `createTask` action creator now returns a function instead of an object. The newly created task isn't received by the store immediately after being dispatched, but instead is dispatched to the store after the `POST` request to `/tasks` has completed.

4.4   *Exercise*

Task updates are the last feature you need to hook up to the server. The process for fetching, creating, and now editing tasks is nearly identical. This exercise is a good way to test whether you're ready to connect the dots on your own.

We'll outline the high-level steps needed to make everything work, but as a challenge, see if you can implement the code before glancing through the listings in the solution section. The requirements are the following:

- Add a new API function for updating tasks on the server.
- Convert the `editTask` action creator from synchronous to asynchronous.
- Within `editTask`, kick off an AJAX request.
- When the request is complete, dispatch an action with the updated object that comes back as part of the server response.

4.5   *Solution*

The first thing you'll do is add a new API function, `editTask`, as shown in the following listing.

Listing 4.10   src/api/index.js

```
export function editTask(id, params) {                              Uses an ES2015
  return axios.put(`${API_BASE_URL}/tasks/${id}`, params);   ◁──┤ template string to easily
}                                                                  construct the URL
```

Now that you have a function you can import to make the right AJAX request, create a new async action creator to make the request to the server, and a new synchronous action creator to indicate the request has completed, as shown in the following listing.

Listing 4.11   src/actions/index.js

```
...

function editTaskSucceeded(task) {          ◁──┐  Creates a new
  return {                                       synchronous action
    type: 'EDIT_TASK_SUCCEEDED',                 creator for edits
    payload: {
      task,
    },
  };
}

export function editTask(id, params = {}) {
  return (dispatch, getState) => {
    const task = getTaskById(getState().tasks.tasks, id);      ┐  Merges the new
    const updatedTask = Object.assign({}, task, params);       │  properties into the
                                                               ┘  existing task object
    api.editTask(id, updatedTask).then(resp => {
      dispatch(editTaskSucceeded(resp.data));
    });
  };
}

function getTaskById(tasks, id) {
  return tasks.find(task => task.id === id);
}
```

For each action that requires a network request (meaning you're dealing with an async action), you'll need at least one synchronous action creator to indicate where you are in the request/response lifecycle. Here, that's editTaskSucceeded, which indicates the request has completed successfully and passes data from the response body on to the reducer.

Because json-server requires a full object to be passed along for PUT requests, you must grab the task out of the store and merge in the new properties yourself, as shown in the following listing.

Listing 4.12   src/reducers/index.js

```
export default function tasks(state = { tasks: [] }, action) {
  switch (action.type) {

    ...

    case 'EDIT_TASK_SUCCEEDED': {          ◁──  Handles the new
      const { payload } = action;               server action
      return {
        tasks: state.tasks.map(task => {
```

```
          if (task.id === payload.task.id) {       ◁─┐  Replaces the old
            return payload.task;                      │  task with the
          }                                           │  updated one
          return task;
        }),
      };
    }
    default: {
      return state;
    }
  }
}
```

As you may have noticed, the process for saving updates to tasks is similar to the process for creating tasks. All interactions that trigger an async operation (usually a network request) tend to have these same high-level happenings:

- A user interacts with the UI in some way, triggering a dispatch.
- A request is started.
- When the request finishes, an action is dispatched with response data.

Go ahead and update a few tasks. The UI should be responsive, given that your server is running locally, and the work that the server is doing is inexpensive. But that won't always be the case. Requests in real-world applications inevitably will take longer due to latency or expensive operations, which means you need a kind of user feedback while a request is completing. Segue!

4.6   *Loading states*

As UI programmers, you always want to keep your users well-informed of what's happening in the application. Users have an expectation that certain things take time to complete, but they won't forgive being left in the dark. When creating user experiences, user confusion should be one of the primary things you try to eliminate completely.

Enter loading states! You'll use Redux to track the status of a request and update the UI to render the proper feedback when a request is in progress. One obvious place to start is during the initial fetch for tasks when the page loads.

4.6.1   *The request lifecycle*

With network requests, there are two moments in time that you care about: when the request starts, and when it completes. If you model these events as actions, you end up with three distinct action types that help describe the request-response lifecycle. Using fetching tasks as an example, note the following are the three action types:

- FETCH_TASKS_STARTED—Dispatched when a request is initiated. Typically used to render a loading indicator (which you'll do in this section).
- FETCH_TASKS_SUCCEEDED—Dispatched when a request is completed successfully. Takes data from the response body and loads it into the store.

- FETCH_TASKS_SUCCEEDED—Dispatched when a request fails for any reason, such as a network failure or a response with a non-200 status code. Payloads often include an error message from the server.

Right now, the fetchTasks action creator accounts for only one moment in time, when the request completes. Figure 4.4 is what fetchTasks might look like if you also want to track when the request was initiated.

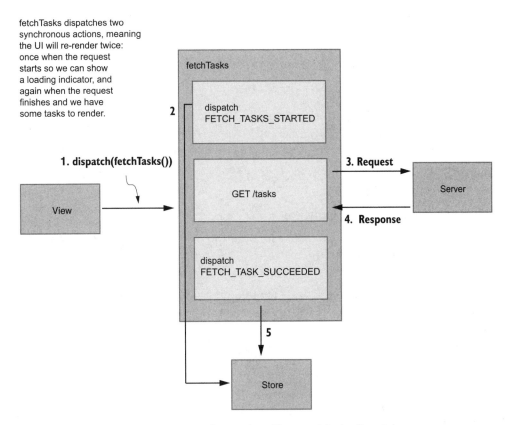

fetchTasks dispatches two synchronous actions, meaning the UI will re-render twice: once when the request starts so we can show a loading indicator, and again when the request finishes and we have some tasks to render.

Figure 4.4 The fetchTasks async action creator with support for loading states

Now your async action creator, fetchTasks, will be responsible for three things:

- Dispatching an action to signify a request has been started
- Performing the request
- Dispatching a second action with response data when the request completes

Think of async actions as orchestrations. They typically perform several individual tasks in pursuit of fulfilling a larger goal. Your goal is to fetch a list of tasks, but it takes several steps to get there. That's the role of the fetchTasks async action creator: to kick off everything that needs to get done to accomplish that goal.

Your store has only a single property, tasks:

```
{
  tasks: [...]
}
```

To render a loading indicator when a request for tasks is in progress, you need to keep track of more state. Here's how you want the store to track request status:

```
{
  tasks: {
    isLoading: false,
    tasks: [...]
  }
}
```

This structure is much more flexible, because it allows you to group the task objects, along with any kind of additional state or metadata. In any real-world application, you'd be much more likely to come across a structure like this. The specific naming convention of the keys is only one pattern you can choose to adopt, but you're not obligated to use it.

4.6.2   *Adding the loading indicator*

You have a few things to take care of in the code to move toward this new state structure. To start, update the `tasks` reducer to take a new initial state, and update the existing action handlers, as shown in the following listing.

> **Listing 4.13   src/reducers/index.js**

```
const initialState = {          Defines the new
  tasks: [],                    initial state for
  isLoading: false,             the reducer
};

export default function tasks(state = initialState, action) {
  switch (action.type) {
    case 'FETCH_TASKS_SUCCEEDED': {
      return {
        ...state,               Returns the next state
        isLoading: false,       with the list of tasks
        tasks: action.payload.tasks,   from the payload
      };
    }
    case 'CREATE_TASK_SUCCEEDED': {
      return {
        ...state,                                            Includes any existing
        tasks: state.tasks.concat(action.payload.task),      state when updating
      };                                                      the list of tasks
    }
    case 'EDIT_TASK_SUCCEEDED': {
      const { payload } = action;
```

```
      const nextTasks = state.tasks.map(task => {
        if (task.id === payload.task.id) {
          return payload.task;
        }

        return task;
      });                         Includes any existing
      return {                    state when updating
        ...state,            ◁──┘ the list of tasks
        tasks: nextTasks,
      };
    }
    default: {
      return state;
    }
  }
}
```

First, you made sure to set the isLoading flag to false by default when you defined the initial state for the reducer. This is always good practice, because it prevents any loading indicators from rendering when they're not supposed to. Let other actions that indicate a request has started set a flag like this to true.

When you handle the FETCH_TASKS_SUCCEEDED action, the obvious change is to update the array of tasks. You also have to remember to indicate the request is complete, so that any loading indicators are hidden, which you did by toggling the isLoading flag to false.

One important update you need to make is all the way up in the creation of the store, in index.js. Previously, you passed the tasks reducer directly to createStore. This was fine when all you had in your state object was a single array of tasks, but now you're moving toward a more complete structure with additional state that lives alongside the task objects themselves.

Create a small root reducer that takes the entire contents of the store (state) and the action being dispatched (action), and passes only the piece of the store that the tasks reducer cares about, state.tasks, as shown in the following listing.

Listing 4.14   index.js

```
...
import tasksReducer from './reducers';          A rootReducer function
                                                accepts the current state
const rootReducer = (state = {}, action) => {  ◁──┘ of the store and an action.
  return {
    tasks: tasksReducer(state.tasks, action),  ◁── Passes the tasks data and
  };                                               the action being dispatched
};                                                 to the tasks reducer

const store = createStore(
  rootReducer,
  composeWithDevTools(applyMiddleware(thunk)),
);
```

Adding a root reducer like this sets you up for the future as well. As you add more features to Parsnip, and, as a result, have more data to track in Redux, you can add new top-level properties to the store and create reducers that operate only on relevant data. Eventually you'll add the ability for users to have different projects, and each project will have its own tasks. The top level of the redux store might look like this:

```
{
  tasks: {...},
  projects: {...}
}
```

To configure the store, all you'd need to do is add a line of code to the root reducer:

```
const rootReducer = (state = {}, action) => {
  return {
    tasks: tasksReducer(state.tasks, action),
    projects: projectsReducer(state.projects, action),
  };
};
```

This allows each reducer to not care about the overall shape of the store, only the slice of data that it operates on.

> **NOTE** Using a root reducer like this is so common that redux exports a `combineReducers` function, which accomplishes the same thing as the `rootReducer` function you just wrote. Once you add a few more properties to your state object, you'll switch to the more standard `combineReducers`, but for now it's worth understanding how this process works under the hood.

Next, run through the following familiar process of adding a new action by updating the relevant action, reducer, and component:

- Add and dispatch a new synchronous action creator, `fetchTasksStarted`.
- Handle the `FETCH_TASKS_STARTED` action in the tasks reducer.
- Update the `TasksPage` component to render a loading indicator when the fetch is in progress.

First, dispatch the new action. For dramatic effect, you'll add a `setTimeout` of two seconds before you dispatch `fetchTasksSucceeded`, which indicates the request has completed, as shown in the following listing. Because the server responds almost instantly when running on your local machines, this delay gives you a chance to get a good feel for the loading state.

Listing 4.15   src/actions/index.js

```
function fetchTasksStarted() {
  return {
    type: 'FETCH_TASKS_STARTED',
  };
}
```

```
export function fetchTasks() {
  return dispatch => {
    dispatch(fetchTasksStarted());

    api.fetchTasks().then(resp => {
      setTimeout(() => {
        dispatch(fetchTasksSucceeded(resp.data));
      }, 2000);
    });
  };
}
```

Dispatches the fetchTasksStarted action creator to signify a request is in progress

setTimeout ensures the loading indicator will stay on the page for more than a fraction of a second.

Now as part of your async action, you have two synchronous dispatches to track the request lifecycle. One indicates when the request starts, the other when it completes. Next, handle the FETCH_TASKS_STARTED action by setting the isLoading property to true in the reducer, as shown in the following listing.

> **Listing 4.16 src/reducers/index.js**

```
...
export default function tasks(state = initialState, action) {
  switch (action.type) {
    case 'FETCH_TASKS_STARTED': {
      return {
        ...state,
        isLoading: true,
      };
    }
    ...
  }
}
```

Sets the isLoading flag to true, which we'll eventually use in a React component to conditionally render a loading indicator.

Finally, you'll update two components, App and TaskPage. In App, pass the value of isLoading to TasksPage via mapStateToProps, as shown in the following listing.

> **Listing 4.17 src/App.js**

```
...
class App extends Component {
  ...
  render() {
    return (
      <div className="main-content">
        <TasksPage
          tasks={this.props.tasks}
          onCreateTask={this.onCreateTask}
          onStatusChange={this.onStatusChange}
          isLoading={this.props.isLoading}
        />
      </div>
    );
  }
}
```

Passes the isLoading prop down to the TasksPage

```
function mapStateToProps(state) {
  const { tasks, isLoading } = state.tasks;
  return { tasks, isLoading };
}
...
```

> Updates mapStateToProps to pull isLoading out of the store and passes it to App as a prop

Finally, in `TasksPage`, you can check whether a request for tasks is in progress, then render a loading indicator if necessary, as shown in the following listing.

Listing 4.18   src/components/TasksPage.js

```
class TasksPage extends Component {
  ...
  render() {
    if (this.props.isLoading) {
      return (
        <div className="tasks-loading">
          Loading...
        </div>
      );
    }
    ...
  }
}
```

> Adds a fancy loading animation here

Tracking the status of a request to show a loading indicator isn't necessarily required, but it's become part of the expected experience in most modern web apps. This is one example of the increasingly dynamic requirements of modern web apps, but Redux was created in part to solve exactly these kinds of problems.

4.7   *Error handling*

With network requests, there are two moments in time you care about: the request starting and the request finishing. The invoking of the `fetchTasks` request will always be represented by the `FETCH_TASKS_STARTED` action, but request completion can trigger one of two dispatches. You've handled only the success case so far, but proper error handling is crucial for delivering the best experience possible.

Users are never thrilled when something goes wrong, but having an operation fail and being left in the dark is much worse than seeing an error with some feedback. Taking one last look at the async action diagram in figure 4.5, the second dispatch can now fork depending on the outcome of the request.

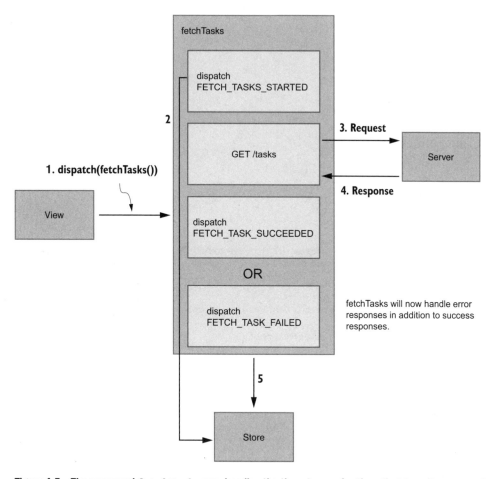

Figure 4.5 **The command `fetchTasks` now handles the three types of actions that describe a request.**

4.7.1 *Dispatching an error action*

You have plenty of ways to implement error handling in Redux. At a high level, these are the things you'll need:

- An action that dispatches an error message
- Somewhere to store the error message in the Redux store
- A React component to render the error

To keep things simple, you'll dispatch a single action, FETCH_TASKS_FAILED, with the error payload. When an error is present, you'll render the message at the top of the page, which will look something like figure 4.6.

Start from the outside-in by creating a new file for a FlashMessage component, as shown in listing 4.19. Its purpose is to accept an error message as a prop and display it in the DOM.

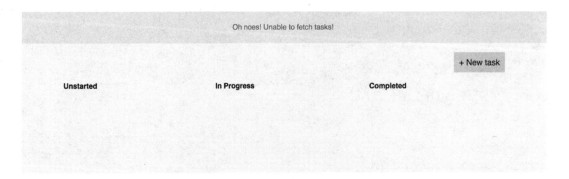

Figure 4.6   Rendering an error message

Listing 4.19   src/components/FlashMessage.js

```
import React from 'react';

export default function FlashMessage(props) {
  return (
    <div className="flash-error">
      {props.message}
    </div>
  );
}

Error.defaultProps = {
  message: 'An error occurred',
};
```

Even though you don't reference React directly in this file, the React object needs to be in scope to use JSX.

A default error message is set.

In the App component, pass along the yet-to-be-created error property from the redux store in mapStateToProps, as shown in the following listing.

Listing 4.20   src/App.js

```
...
import FlashMessage from './components/FlashMessage';

class App extends Component {
  ...
  render() {
    return (
      <div className="container">
        {this.props.error &&
          <FlashMessage message={this.props.error} />}
        <div className="main-content">
          <TasksPage
            tasks={this.props.tasks}
            onCreateTask={this.onCreateTask}
            onStatusChange={this.onStatusChange}
```

Conditionally renders the FlashMessage component

```
          isLoading={this.props.isLoading}
        />
      </div>
    </div>
  );
  }
}

function mapStateToProps(state) {
  const { tasks, isLoading, error } = state.tasks;
  return { tasks, isLoading, error };
}

export default connect(mapStateToProps)(App);
```

> Adds more map-
> StateToProps logic
> for passing data from
> the store into React

Because this.props.error is null for now, nothing will happen yet in the UI. You'll need to create a new synchronous action creator, fetchTasksFailed. You already have code to handle when the request promise resolves successfully, so go ahead and add a catch block to handle when the promise is rejected.

To make testing error handling easier, manually reject a promise in the then block, so that you're guaranteed to make it into the catch block, as shown in the following listing.

Listing 4.21 src/actions/index.js

```
function fetchTasksFailed(error) {
  return {
    type: 'FETCH_TASKS_FAILED',
    payload: {
      error,
    },
  };
}

export function fetchTasks() {
  return dispatch => {
    dispatch(fetchTasksStarted());

    api
      .fetchTasks()
      .then(resp => {
        // setTimeout(() => {
        //   dispatch(fetchTasksSucceeded(resp.data));
        // }, 2000);
        throw new Error('Oh noes! Unable to fetch tasks!'));
      })
      .catch(err => {
        dispatch(fetchTasksFailed(err.message));
      });
    };
  };
  ...
```

> Comments out the
> success handler
> for now

> Manually rejects
> the promise, to
> test the code in
> the catch block

> **Dispatches another
> synchronous action
> with an error message**

Finally, handle the update logic in the tasks reducer. This is a two-part change: add an error property to the initial state definition, then add a handler for the FETCH _TASKS_FAILED action. The case statement will mark the request as complete by setting isLoading to false and set the error message, as shown in the following listing.

Listing 4.22   src/reducers/index.js

```
const initialState = {
  tasks: [],
  isLoading: false,            Sets error to be
  error: null,             ←── null by default
};

export default function tasks(state = initialState, action) {
  switch (action.type) {
    ...
    case 'FETCH_TASKS_FAILED': {
      return {                    Indicates the request
        ...state,                 is complete by
        isLoading: false,         setting the isLoading
        error: action.payload.error,   flag and error value
      };
    }
    ...
    default: {
      return state;
    }
  }
}
```

All said and done, it's clear that fetching a list of tasks to render on the page is much more than making a GET request. These are the realities of modern web app development, but tools like Redux are here to help. You can handle tracking complex state to provide the best user experiences possible.

When first learning Redux, the stereotypical first tutorial is a todo app. It all seems so simple! Dispatch an action, update state in a reducer. But the question quickly turns to "How do you do anything useful?" Turns out you can't do much in a web application without being backed by a server.

Async actions are one of the real challenges for a budding Redux user. Compared to chapter 2, where only synchronous actions are found, the complexity level in this chapter was ramped up significantly. Hopefully you now have a sense for how to properly handle asynchronous code in Redux.

By using redux-thunk, you took advantage of middleware without needing to understand what that meant. The next chapter lifts the veil on middleware and shows you all there is to see.

Summary

- The difference between dispatching asynchronous and synchronous actions
- How `redux-thunk` enables the dispatching of functions, which can be used to perform side effects, like network requests
- How API clients can reduce duplication and improve reusability
- The two conceptual groups of actions: view actions and server actions
- The three important moments during the lifecycle of a remote API call: start, successful completion, and failure
- Rendering errors to improve overall user experience

Middleware 5

This chapter covers

- Defining what Redux middleware is
- Writing your own middleware
- Composing middleware
- Learning when to use middleware

We've covered most of the usual suspects you'd find in a React/Redux application: actions, reducers, and the store. To update a state in your application using Redux, you need all three. You have one more core actor that's key to this whole operation: middleware. If you've spent any time in chapter 4, you've already come face-to-face with middleware and lived to tell the tale. When you added redux-thunk to the Parsnip project, you learned how to apply middleware to Redux using the apply-Middleware function, but not necessarily how to create your own. In this chapter, we'll look more in depth at how middleware works, how to create it, and what use cases it can be a good fit for.

In the process, you'll improve Parsnip by creating custom middleware for a few classic use cases:

- Logging actions, which give us a quick look into what's happening in the app
- Analytics, which provide a convenient interface to track an event when an action is dispatched
- API calls, which will abstract away common tasks around making calls to the server

Let's get started!

5.1 *What's in middleware?*

What exactly is middleware? The concept isn't unique to Redux, and if you've worked with frameworks like Rails, Express.js, or Koa, you've likely used or been exposed to middleware in a shape or form. Generally, middleware is any code that runs between two other software components, typically as part of a framework. With a web server framework such as Express or Koa, you can add middleware that runs after an incoming request is received, and before the framework handles a request. This is useful for all kinds of things, such as logging data about each request and response, handling errors in a centralized way, authenticating users, and so on.

Frameworks such as Express and Koa are great for illustrating middleware, but you're here for Redux. If you know that middleware can be described as code that sits between two components, such as a framework receiving an HTTP request and generating a response, where does middleware in Redux live?

Redux middleware is code that sits between an action being dispatched and the store passing the action to the reducer and broadcasting the updated state. Similar to the way server middleware is useful for running code across many requests, Redux middleware lets you run code across many action dispatches.

Let's look again at our architecture diagram (figure 5.1). The middleware section is highlighted to give you an idea of where this kind of code fits in to the normal action dispatch cycle.

Notice that middleware in figure 5.1 exists within the store. Think of middleware as being "registered" with the store. When an action is dispatched, the store will know to pass that action through any middleware you've added. When the entire chain of middleware is complete, the action is finally passed to the reducers to calculate the updated state of the application.

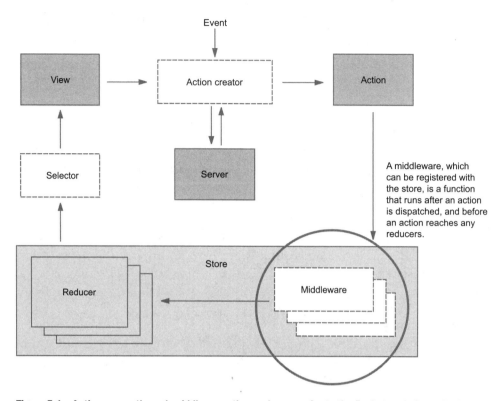

A middleware, which can be registered with the store, is a function that runs after an action is dispatched, and before an action reaches any reducers.

Figure 5.1   Actions move through middleware, then reducers, prior to the final state being calculated.

5.2   *Middleware basics*

Creating middleware involves a few basic steps:

- Define the middleware using the correct function signature
- Register the middleware with the store using Redux's `applyMiddleware` function

Let's start with the function definition. Here's the function signature for Redux middleware:

```
const middlewareExample = store => next => action => { ... }
```

Not confusing at all, right? In short, this amounts to writing three nested functions for each new middleware you write. Spelled out in a more verbose syntax, this looks like the following:

```
function storeWrapper(store) {
    return function middlewareWrapper(next) {
        return function handleAction(action) {
            ...
        }
    }
}
```

At this stage in the game, it's most important to know the nature of the arguments provided to your middleware:

- `store`—The redux store. You can use the store object directly in middleware when you need to make decisions based on an existing state. `store.getState` has you covered.
- `next`—A function that you'll call when you're ready to pass the action to the next middleware in the chain.
- `action`—The action being dispatched. Generally, your middleware will do something with every action (such as logging) or watch for a specific action by checking the value of `action.type`.

5.2.1 Composing middleware

One of the key aspects of middleware is its ability to be chained, meaning multiple middleware can be applied to the store. Each middleware, after completing any work it may decide to do, invokes the next middleware in the chain. As a result, any middleware you create should be focused and have a single purpose, making them easier to combine and reuse in different contexts. Maybe another app in your ecosystem can use a middleware you've created, or maybe you can open source it! Because all Redux middleware must be created the same way, it's perfectly fine (and expected) to combine your own middleware with third-party middleware.

Let's kick off your custom middleware creation with maybe the most classic middleware example around: logging.

> **NOTE** If you're coding along, pause here to start a new branch. Future chapters will require rolling back features created in this chapter.

5.3 Example: logging middleware

The goal: for every action dispatch, log the action being dispatched (including type and payload) and the new state of the store after the action is processed.

Because you need to run code for every action that's dispatched, logging fits the use case for middleware perfectly. It's also simple to implement, because it doesn't affect the normal flow of control within the app. You're not modifying the action or changing the outcome of a dispatch in any way. You want to hook into only the action lifecycle and log certain details about the action being dispatched and how it affects the state of the store.

It's also a bonus that logging fits Redux perfectly. Actions were invented in part to provide a trail of the events and data flying around your applications. Because events are modeled as objects with descriptive names and any data they might need, it's trivially easy for you to log an action's type and payload to get a quick sense of exactly what's happening at any given moment. Without a system such as Redux, where updates must pass through a central hub, it would be much more difficult to log state changes with the same kind of effort.

5.3.1   *Creating the logger middleware*

Given that this is the first custom middleware you'll add, let's take a high-level view at what it takes to go from zero to having a functioning logging middleware as part of your application:

- Create a new file for the logger in a src/middleware/ directory.
- Write the middleware.
- Import the middleware into index.js where you create the store.
- Add the middleware using Redux's `applyMiddleware` function.

Not so bad, right? For the middleware itself, you want to log two things: the type of the action being dispatched and the state of the store after it processes the action. Figure 5.2 shows the kind of output you'll see in the console after you've created the middleware and registered it with the store.

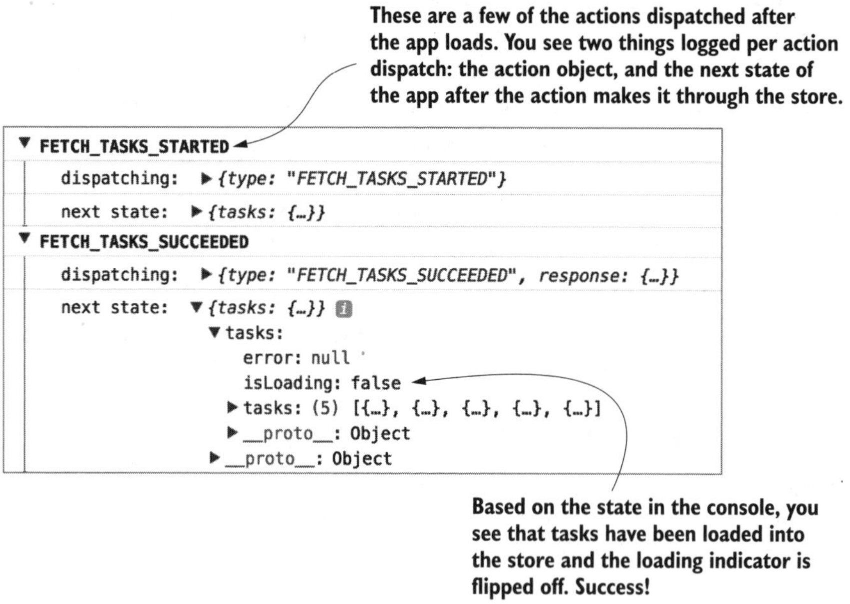

These are a few of the actions dispatched after
the app loads. You see two things logged per action
dispatch: the action object, and the next state of
the app after the action makes it through the store.

```
▼ FETCH_TASKS_STARTED ◄
      dispatching:   ▶ {type: "FETCH_TASKS_STARTED"}
      next state:    ▶ {tasks: {…}}
▼ FETCH_TASKS_SUCCEEDED
      dispatching:   ▶ {type: "FETCH_TASKS_SUCCEEDED", response: {…}}
      next state:    ▼ {tasks: {…}} ⓘ
                        ▼ tasks:
                            error: null
                            isLoading: false  ◄
                          ▶ tasks: (5) [{…}, {…}, {…}, {…}, {…}]
                          ▶ __proto__: Object
                      ▶ __proto__: Object
```

Based on the state in the console, you
see that tasks have been loaded into
the store and the loading indicator is
flipped off. Success!

Figure 5.2   Example console output after adding the logger middleware

Start by creating a new directory, src/middleware/, and a new file named logger.js. Inside the file, add the code from listing 5.1. Here you use all three of the arguments provided to your middleware, each to perform a different task:

- Use `action` to log the type of the action being dispatched.
- Use `store` to log the state of the store after applying the action with `store.get-State`.
- And finally, use `next` to pass the action to the next middleware in the chain.

Listing 5.1   Creating the logger middleware – src/middleware/logger.js

**Creates the middleware using
the correct function signature**

**Uses console.group to
style console output**

```
const logger = store => next => action => {
  console.group(action.type);
  console.log('dispatching: ', action);
  const result = next(action);
  console.log('next state: ', store.getState());
  console.groupEnd(action.type);
  return result;
};

export default logger;
```

**Uses next to ensure the
action gets passed to
the reducers and the
next state is calculated**

**Logs the state of the
store after the action
has been applied**

By now you know what action objects are and that they have a required `type` property, and you know how to retrieve the current state from the store with `store.getState`, so the `next` function is likely the most foreign concept in play here.

The `next` command, provided to us by Redux, is a way to signify when this middleware has completed its work and it's time to move on to the next middleware in the chain (if there is one). It's effectively a wrapped version of `dispatch`, so it has an identical API. Ensure you're always passing in the `action` argument whenever you call `next` within a middleware.

One curiosity here is that the middleware doesn't end after you use `next(action)`. You're free to carry on and reference the Redux state after the action passes through the logger middleware.

5.3.2   Using applyMiddleware to register the middleware

At this point you have a perfectly valid logger middleware, but it's not particularly useful on its own. To use it in Parsnip, you have to add the middleware to your store instance. If you've worked through chapter 4, then this should be familiar! It's the same process you went through to add the `redux-thunk` middleware when you introduced async actions.

Open index.js, import the logger, and add it to the argument list for `apply-Middleware` alongside `thunk`, as shown in listing 5.2. Whenever you want to add a new middleware to your applications, you'll follow this process. Note that you add the logger middleware last, and they run in the order that you pass them to `applyMiddleware`. It's not critical in this case, that the middleware be in any particular order, but you should be aware of the significance of their order.

Listing 5.2   Adding the logger middleware to the store – src/index.js

```
...
  import logger from './middleware/logger';
  ...
```

**Imports the newly
created middleware**

```
const store = createStore(
  rootReducer,
  composeWithDevTools(applyMiddleware(thunk, logger)),
);
```

Registers the logger middleware with the store

```
...
```

The middleware system is designed to be flexible and composable. As long as each middleware calls `next` to move to the next middleware in the chain, everything will work correctly.

After this last step of registering the middleware when the store is created, Parsnip has its first fully functioning custom middleware. Look at the app and open the browser console, where you can see the fruits of your labor. Try creating a new task or editing an existing task. You should see output similar to figure 5.3.

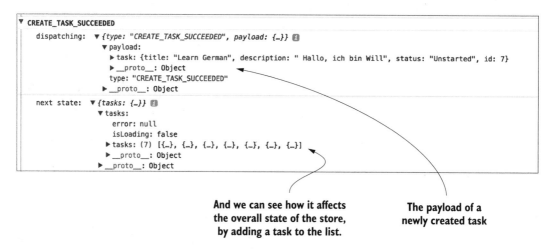

And we can see how it affects the overall state of the store, by adding a task to the list.

The payload of a newly created task

Figure 5.3   Another example of console output from the logger middleware

You might ask, "Isn't this a less powerful version of the Redux DevTools?", and you'd be correct! The dev tools are implemented using similar concepts as the middleware you created. We decided to start with middleware for logging because of how cleanly it demonstrates one of the core use cases for Redux middleware. In your own apps, you may choose to use a middleware like this if you want to keep things simple, but most likely you'll get the most bang for your buck with an established tool such as DevTools.

Parsnip now has its first custom middleware, but you've only scratched the surface. Let's explore another common use case for middleware: sending analytics events. The analytics middleware will be similar to the logger, but we'll introduce a new concept along the way: the `meta` property, which allows you to attach additional data to an action object. Then, in the middleware you can watch for the `meta` property on incoming actions and do work if the right conditions are satisfied.

5.4   Example: analytics middleware

Knowing what your users are doing is always preferable to not knowing, so in any real-world application, it's a good idea to have proper event tracking. In Parsnip, you can add tracking to most of the actions currently being dispatched. After all, actions are objects that describe an event, so you can hook into an action dispatch and record an analytics event whenever users view a page, create a task, or edit a task. You won't go as far as setting up a third-party analytics service such as Segment or Google Analytics, but you'll implement a Redux middleware that provides a convenient API for implementers of Parsnip to send new events. Analytics is a good use case for middleware for a few reasons:

- Like the other middleware you've worked with so far, you need to run analytics code across many different actions.
- It allows you to abstract the specifics of event tracking, such as which service is being used (for example, Segment, Keen) and any configuration.

For something like analytics, you're using middleware to encapsulate implementation details and provide a developer-friendly way to send analytics events. Other Parsnip developers won't need to know the specifics of how to send an event, they only need to know the high-level interface available to them.

5.4.1   The meta property

Up to now you've only dealt with two top-level properties as part of an action: `type`, a string which declares which action is being dispatched, and `payload`, any data that the action needs to be completed. A third action property has gained popularity within the community: the `meta` property. The `meta` property is designed to capture any data relevant to an action that doesn't fit within either `type` or `payload`. For your use case, you'll use it to send along analytics data, specifically an event name and metadata.

   In the yet-to-be-created analytics middleware, you'll watch for any action that has the relevant `meta` property. Every analytics event has two components: an event name and any metadata that the event might require. Let's name this event `create_task` and pass along the ID of the task being created.

   Fire an analytics event whenever the action is dispatched by heading to src/actions/index.js and updating the `createTaskSucceeded` action creator to match the following listing.

Listing 5.3   Adding the meta property – src/actions/index.js

```
function createTaskSucceeded(task) {
  return {
    type: 'CREATE_TASK_SUCCEEDED',
    payload: {
      task,
    },
    meta: {
      analytics: {
```

Adds the meta property at the same level as type and payload

Groups analytics-related data under a namespace key

```
        event: 'create_task',
        data: {
          id: task.id,
        },
      },
    },
  };
}
```

Indirection in the code is one of the potential downsides or costs of using middleware, but it isn't too much of an issue here. As you'll see in a moment, the action creator still gets to be explicit. Because you'll use the meta property directly on the action object, anyone reading the action creator will know that analytics will be captured whenever the action is dispatched. However, they won't need to know specifics about how to send events data. As users of the middleware, you can pass the right data with the right structure and let the middleware take care of the rest.

Now you have a sense of how we'll pass analytics data along with an action, but that's only one piece of the puzzle. You're using the meta property in the action creator, but you also need the middleware to take care of watching for actions with said meta property. In the next section you'll create the middleware, and you'll update a few of your actions to send analytics events by adding meta.

5.4.2   *Adding analytics middleware*

Now on to the middleware itself! Your goal is to create a middleware that, when an applicable action is being dispatched, will take care of everything related to recording an event. The action is responsible for passing any event data, and the middleware is responsible for encoding the details of how to send that event. For this example, you'll mock out an analytics API. In a production app, however, you'd likely use a third-party service, so the middleware is where you'd include any library code.

Here's how the flow of control in the middleware might look for dispatching an action with the meta and analytics properties:

- For each incoming action, check whether the meta and analytics properties exist.
- If not, call next(action) to move on to the next middleware.
- If so, get the event name and data and send it using a fictional analytics service.
- And finally, when that's complete, call next(action).

You already have the CREATE_TASK_SUCCEEDED action sending the meta/analytics properties; now you need to take a stab at implementing the middleware to satisfy the above criteria. Create a new file in src/middleware/ called analytics.js and add the code from listing 5.4.

Here, you introduce something that's a common practice you'll see with middleware. Instead of doing work for every action dispatch the way you did with the logger, you instead check for certain conditions before letting the middleware take over. In this case, if you see that the action has the `meta` and `analytics` properties, you know that the action has requested to track an event. In all other cases, you'll call `next(action)` right away without doing any further processing.

Checks whether the action wants to use the analytics middleware

```
const analytics = store => next => action => {
  if (!action || !action.meta || !action.meta.analytics) {
    return next(action);
  }

  const { event, data } = action.meta.analytics;

  fakeAnalyticsApi(event, data)
    .then(resp => {
      console.log('Recorded: ', event, data);
    })
    .catch(err => {
      console.error(
        'An error occurred while sending analytics: ',
        err.toString(),
      );
    });

  return next(action);
};

function fakeAnalyticsApi(eventName, data) {
  return new Promise((resolve, reject) => {
    resolve('Success!');
  });
}

export default analytics;
```

If the right action properties aren't found, move on to the next middleware.

Uses destructuring to get the event name and any associated metadata

Logs the event being recorded successfully

Logs an error if necessary

Moves on to the next middleware

As with the logger middleware, you'll also need to register the middleware with the store in src/index.js, as shown in the following listing.

Listing 5.5 Applying the analytics middleware – src/index.js

```
...
  import analytics from './middleware/analytics';
  ...

  const store = createStore(
    rootReducer,
    composeWithDevTools(applyMiddleware(thunk, logger, analytics)),
  );
  ...
```

Registers the analytics middleware by passing it to applyMiddleware

Head to the app, make sure your browser console is open, and try creating a new task. You should see output similar to figure 5.4, indicating that your analytics middleware is working properly. You're looking specifically for the event name, `create_task`, and the task object that we passed to the analytics middleware.

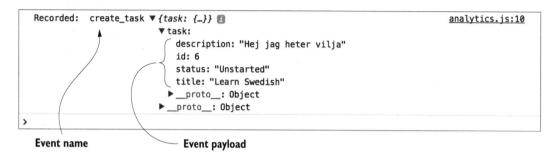

Event name   Event payload

Figure 5.4   Example output for the create_task analytics event

With logging, you did work in the middleware for every action, but not every middleware you write will want to respond in such a way. Here, you're doing something slightly different, but also extremely common: checking if the action being dispatched is one you care about. If it's not relevant to the middleware, you'll bail out and send the action on to the next middleware. If it's an action you care about, you'll take care of sending analytics before you move on.

This pattern of using a meta property to allow actions to indicate to a middleware that it should do work is great for a few reasons:

- It allows you to be explicit at the action level. Because the analytics data is baked directly in to the action object, it's clear that the action wants to do something analytics related.
- It lets the middleware stay generic. Instead of having the middleware watch for specific actions, letting actions specify they want additional work done using the `meta` property allows the middleware itself to remain relatively static.
- You now have an extremely friendly API for developers. Sending along an analytics object with an action is easier than having to import and use any analytics code directly.

Think of it as the best of both worlds. You get to abstract analytics functionality into the middleware, meaning you don't have to duplicate it around the app, but you also get to define actions in an explicit way.

> **INFO** Though you won't do it here, the middleware itself is also a great way to encapsulate any data that might apply to all analytics events. Because you have access to the state of the store, it's easy to get things like the ID of a logged-in user, or an identifier for the current build of your application.

If you want to add tracking to additional actions, follow a similar pattern to what you did with the CREATE_TASK_SUCCESS action. Using the meta property, specify an event name, any data the event might need, and let the middleware take care of the rest!

Now that you have experience creating two custom middleware, it's a good time for a brief conceptual interlude. Let's pause here to explore potential middleware pitfalls.

5.4.3 *Interlude: when and when not to use middleware*

The real benefit of middleware is the ability to centralize certain tasks that need to be applied across many actions. Again, let's use logging as an example. Say your goal is to log the type and payload of every action being dispatched. One way to accomplish this is to add logging statements at the point of every call to store.dispatch. Sure, you're logging action dispatches, which was your original goal, but this solution should make you cringe for at least one reason: it's not particularly scalable. Now you'll have to add logging for every action you create.

Middleware allows you to bypass this entirely by defining the logic for logging actions in a single place. All new actions will get logging for free, without any developer intervention.

When is it a good idea to use middleware? For us, there are two golden rules:

- Use middleware if you need to write code that applies across many, if not all, actions in the application. Logging is maybe the most classic example.
- But, use middleware only if the indirection caused by the middleware isn't overly damaging to the readability and understandability of the code.

In that last bit, there's a lot of nuance, and it's a good segue into an equally important question: When should you NOT use middleware?

Redux middleware in the right scenarios is incredibly useful and powerful, but like many things in life, it's possible to have too much of a good thing. The main tradeoff with middleware is indirection. This usually isn't an issue with big, cross-cutting concerns like logging, but you have to be wary when using middleware for tasks that affect the overall flow of control within your apps. For example, you'll build an API middleware later in the chapter that helps centralize tasks common to all async actions that require an AJAX request. It's a powerful abstraction, but because it directly impacts the flow of data, it's an added layer of complexity that's practically impossible for developers working in that area of the code to ignore.

Usage in cases like these will, as always, depend on the current situation and factors such as the size of your team and how much code you're dealing with. Redux is here to help you take back control of the flow of data through your applications, and responsible middleware usage is a big part of that.

5.4.4 *Case study: how not to use middleware*

Logging and analytics are great examples for when you *should* reach for middleware, but it's not always that light and breezy of a decision. It's worth covering the potential for misuse with middleware, and we'll use routing as a case study. The problem we're about to outline approximates something we dealt with in a real-world application, and highlights one of many hard lessons around best practices with middleware learned along the way.

Once upon a time, we had an application that needed a place for core routing code. Specifically, the goal was to redirect users to a dashboard after logging in. We decided to use middleware, but wrote it in a non-generic way. Instead of allowing actions to indicate they needed to perform a redirect, we watched for specific actions, such as LOGIN_SUCCESS, directly in the middleware.

From a readability perspective, we eventually lost the mental link between actions that triggered subsequent dispatches. The routing middleware became the de facto place for all routing, and the code blew up over time. In retrospect, it would have been better for us to use a more generic approach, something more along the lines of the meta property we used for analytics.

Again, the upside of the meta strategy is that it lets us keep actions explicit. Reading the action conveys everything you need to know that might affect the flow of control. The downside is that action creators become slightly larger and take on an additional responsibility. Ultimately, like everything in software, the best solution depends on your realities.

Let's look at several of the potential solutions to the original problem statement: a successful login should redirect the user to the /dashboard route. The following listing shows how you might do it using thunks and async action creators, which you learned about in chapter 4. Note that this code won't be part of Parsnip.

Listing 5.6 Redirecting after login

```
export function login(params) {
  return dispatch => {
    api.login(params).then(resp => {          Makes the call
      dispatch(loginSucceeded(resp.data));    to login

      dispatch(navigate('/dashboard'));       Dispatches an action
    });                                        indicating login was
  };                                           successful
}
                                              Performs the redirect
```

If you needed to interact with this login action creator, everything you need to know is contained within it. It's more imperative; the code reads like a list of step-by-step instructions, but login is transparent about its responsibilities.

On the other hand, you can add specific routing logic in a middleware like we did, shown in listing 5.7. Instead of dispatching the navigate action directly within the login action, you'll move that logic to a routing middleware. Middleware by default has a chance to inspect and respond to all actions, so in this case you'll wait until you see the LOGIN_SUCCEEDED action to redirect the user.

Listing 5.7　Routing logic in a middleware

```
function login(params) {
  return dispatch => {
    api.login(params).then(resp => {
      dispatch(loginSucceeded(resp.data));
    });
  };
}

// within a routing middleware file
const routing = store => next => action => {
  if (action.type === 'LOGIN_SUCCEEDED') {
    store.dispatch(navigate('/dashboard'));
  }
};
```

Watches for the LOGIN_SUCCEEDED action

When the action being dispatched is the one you care about, redirect to the dashboard.

This code seems harmless at first, and maybe it is, assuming the routing middleware doesn't grow too much. But it has one critical flaw: indirection. In our experience, it's usually a mistake to use middleware in this way.

You may be familiar with the decades-old concept of "the principle of least surprise." Liberally paraphrased, if users are consistently surprised by functionality, it might be time to re-think that experience. This user experience guideline may be extended to developers as well: if an implementation is surprising, consider an alternative. Future implementers of `login` need to somehow gain the unintuitive context of the middleware. If they're new to the project or Redux, there's a good chance they'll miss it at first, and be confused as to what exactly is triggering the redirection.

Let's look at this in a more visual way. Figure 5.5 illustrates the two different approaches for handling the redirect following a successful login.

The key takeaway here is the difference between explicit versus implicit approaches. With the action creator strategy on the left, you're explicit about the additional work taking place in the `login` example.

This is a small example, but picture middleware like this handling 5, 10, or 20 actions. Sure, much of the code around routing will be bundled in one place, but the flow of control for any individual action dispatch becomes more difficult to track down. Middleware can help you reduce duplication and centralize logic, but it comes at a cost, and it's up to you to use your best judgement. Middleware are abstractions and their primary purpose is to aid the development process. Like all abstractions, there's a point where they can go too far and negatively impact the overall design of your application.

Let's implement one more middleware, this time for API calls to the server, which will have the highest degree of difficulty.

Using a login async action creator, which dispatches at least two actions: one to indicate a user has logged in successfully, one to navigate to a new route

Using a generic routing middleware, which listens for the **LOGIN_SUCCEEDED** action

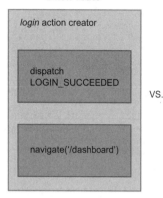
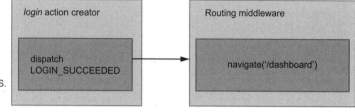

The link between these actions is implicit! The middleware will watch for the **LOGIN_SUCCEEDED** action to perform the redirect, instead of login dispatching it directly.

In some cases this may be convenient, but it comes at a complexity cost due to the route change not being declared explicity within the login action creator.

Figure 5.5   Modeling different strategies for routing as part of an async action

5.5   *API middleware*

You now know that middleware is meant to abstract logic that's common to many actions. Looking at Parsnip's existing functionality, is there any logic that we can abstract? Think about the actions in the app that make API calls to the server. Up to now, you have `fetchTasks`, `createTask`, and `editTask`. What do they all have in common? They all seem to

- Dispatch an action indicating that a request has started.
- Make an AJAX request.
- If the request succeeds, dispatch an action with the response body.
- If the request fails, dispatch an action with the error message.

If you recall from chapter 4, these steps relate to the three key moments in time for any server API call. You model each of these events with a standard set of action types. Using task creation as an example, you dispatch three actions:

- `CREATE_TASK_STARTED`
- `CREATE_TASK_SUCCEEDED`
- `CREATE_TASK_FAILED`

For any future action that you implement that requires an AJAX request, you'll have to create these three corresponding action types. Nothing is inherently wrong with this strategy. It has its own benefits, mainly that it's an explicit way to model the interactions in your application. But it's heavy on the boilerplate. You're doing the same type of work with different endpoints and different data. You can attempt to centralize much of the logic around sending requests by creating a new middleware to take care of the tasks common to all these async actions.

In our opinion, things like logging and analytics are no-brainers for middleware. They're generic, run across many actions, and don't interrupt the normal flow of control. The API middleware you're about to implement is slightly different. It directly affects how you interact with one of the core pieces of functionality in any application: AJAX requests. Whether you think adding this middleware is worth it in your own projects is up to you. Ultimately, the benefits are centralization of logic, at the cost of added complexity. Parsnip is all about exploring and experimenting with new technologies, so let's go for it and see how an API middleware like this might come together.

> **NOTE** This type of API middleware is popular both in production and as a teaching tool, because it's a great example of extracting repeated functionality. We took plenty of inspiration from two places: the "Real World" example that's part of the official Redux docs (https://github.com/reactjs/redux/blob/master/examples/real-world), as well as a popular open source variant (https://github.com/agraboso/redux-api-middleware/issues).

5.5.1 *The desired API*

What should the action creators look like? For this middleware, you'll require all actions with API calls to have three things:

- A CALL_API field defined and exported by the middleware
- A types property, an array of the three action types for the request starting, completing successfully, and failing
- An endpoint property, to specify the relative URL of the resource you want to request

You already have an existing implementation of the fetchTasks action, but for this middleware you'll replace it completely with a new implementation. The good news is that you'll have to make minimal updates elsewhere in the app. The App component, which dispatches the fetchTasks action, will notably require zero changes. Under the hood, the implementation of how the app fetches and stores tasks has changed, but the view layer (React components) is safely isolated from any of this work.

Using the code in listing 5.7, do the following:

- Import a CALL_API action from the yet-to-be-created middleware. This will be how fetchTasks will indicate that it wants to use the API middleware.

- Define and export constants for each action related to `fetchTasks`: FETCH_TASKS_STARTED, FETCH_TASKS_SUCCEEDED, and FETCH_TASKS_FAILED.
- From `fetchTasks`, return an object that uses the CALL_API action, passes the three action types, and finally passes the /tasks server endpoint.

Implementing the previous actions means you'll have the data you need when you get to the middleware itself in the next section. As you'll see in listing 5.8, the order in which you add the three action constants within the `types` array matters. The middleware will assume that the first action is request start, the second is request success, and the third is request failure.

TIP If the CALL_API syntax is new to you, the square brackets were introduced in ES6 and evaluate the variable within them to dynamically produce a key.

Listing 5.8 Updating fetchTasks – src/actions/index.js

```
...
import { CALL_API } from '../middleware/api';          ⟵⎯⎯ Imports the CALL_API
                                                            constant

export const FETCH_TASKS_STARTED = 'FETCH_TASKS_STARTED';       ⎫ Defines three
export const FETCH_TASKS_SUCCEEDED = 'FETCH_TASKS_SUCCEEDED';   ⎬ constants for
export const FETCH_TASKS_FAILED = 'FETCH_TASKS_FAILED';         ⎭ each action
                                                                 dispatched
                                                                 within fetchTasks
export function fetchTasks() {
  return {
    [CALL_API]: {
      types: [FETCH_TASKS_STARTED, FETCH_TASKS_SUCCEEDED,       ⎫ From fetchTasks,
      FETCH_TASKS_FAILED],                                      ⎬ returns the data
      endpoint: '/tasks',                                       ⎮ the middleware
    },                                                          ⎭ will need
  };
}

// function fetchTasksSucceeded(tasks) {      ⟵⎯⎯ Comments (or deletes) the
//   return {                                     existing implementation
//     type: 'FETCH_TASKS_SUCCEEDED',            of fetchTasks
//     payload: {
//       tasks,
//     },
//   };
// }
//
// function fetchTasksFailed(error) {
//   return {
//     type: 'FETCH_TASKS_FAILED',
//     payload: {
//       error,
//     },
//   };
// }
```

```
//
// function fetchTasksStarted() {
//   return {
//     type: 'FETCH_TASKS_STARTED',
//   };
// }
//
// export function fetchTasks() {
//   return dispatch => {
//     dispatch(fetchTasksStarted());
//
//     api
//       .fetchTasks()
//       .then(resp => {
//         dispatch(fetchTasksSucceeded(resp.data));
//       })
//       .catch(err => {
//         dispatch(fetchTasksFailed(err.message));
//       });
//   };
// }


...
```

You removed a whole lot of functionality from the fetchTasks action, and that's the whole point! The next step is to move request logic into a centralized place. In the next section, you'll create the API middleware that knows how to deal with an action like the one your new version of fetchTasks returns.

5.5.2 *Outlining the API middleware*

Because this middleware is more complex than the logger and analytics middleware, you'll create it in several smaller steps. Create a new file in the src/middleware/ directory named api.js. Using listing 5.9, start by creating the required middleware boilerplate: defining and exporting the main middleware function. Next, define the CALL_API action, and check if the current action includes the CALL_API type. If it doesn't, pass the action to next to move on to the next middleware.

Note the line in listing 5.9 where you check if callApi is undefined. You followed a similar process with the analytics middleware, where you checked for the existence of a meta property. In both cases, if the current action didn't satisfy the criteria for the middleware, you immediately called next(action) and moved on. This is a common pattern known as a guard clause. We're huge fans of guard clauses for readability purposes. They allow you to define exceptional cases for a function up front, freeing up the function body to be a clean, un-indented block. Once you get past a guard clause, you can assume any data that the middleware might need will be available.

**Defines the middleware-
specific action constant**

```
export const CALL_API = 'CALL_API';        ◁─┘

const apiMiddleware = store => next => action => {
  const callApi = action[CALL_API];
  if (typeof callApi === 'undefined') {
    return next(action);
  }
}
```

**Gets the object with
the types and endpoint
properties (if it exists)**

**If it's not an action meant
for this middleware,
continue without any
further work.**

```
export default apiMiddleware;
```

Because you now have a totally functional, albeit not useful, middleware, take this opportunity to register it with the store so you can use it within Parsnip. Head to src/index.js, import the middleware, and pass it to the applyMiddleware function, as shown in the following listing.

```
...
import apiMiddleware from './middleware/api';
...
const store = createStore(
  rootReducer,
  composeWithDevTools(applyMiddleware(thunk, apiMiddleware, logger,
    analytics)),
);
```

This time, the order in which you apply the middleware does matter. Because the API middleware requires a custom action shape, you want to include it first. If the logger or analytics middleware came before the API middleware, they wouldn't know how to handle an action without a type property and would throw an exception.

Now you can get to the meat of the middleware. You need to dispatch the first of your three actions, which will indicate that a request has started. Add the code from the following listing to src/middleware/api.js.

```
...
const apiMiddleware = store => next => action => {
  const callApi = action[CALL_API];
  if (typeof callApi === 'undefined') {
    return next(action);
  }

  const [requestStartedType, successType, failureType] = callApi.types;   ◁─┘
```

**Uses array destructing
to create variables with
each action type**

```
    next({ type: requestStartedType });          ⊲──┐  Dispatches the action
}                                                     │  which indicates the
                                                      │  request is in progress
...
```

Because `next` will ultimately dispatch an action to the store, you pass it an action object the same way you would if you were using `store.dispatch`. The result is identical to the old strategy of dispatching `FETCH_TASKS_STARTED` directly within the `fetchTasks` action. The reducer will update the correct state in response to the action, and the app will know to render a loading indicator.

The middleware uses array destructuring to create variables for each action type, which was why it was important to add the action types in the right order when you implemented the new `fetchTasks` action.

Next let's add a function for making the AJAX call. You already have an API client that lives at src/api/index.js, but for your purposes here you need a new, more generic function that accepts an endpoint as an argument. Update the code in src/middleware/api.js to match the following listing.

Listing 5.12   The makeCall function – src/middleware/api.js

```
import axios from 'axios';

const API_BASE_URL = 'http://localhost:3001';          ⊲──┐  Defines the base
                                                            │  URL for the API
export const CALL_API = 'CALL_API';

function makeCall(endpoint) {
  const url = `${API_BASE_URL}${endpoint}`;            ⊲──┐  Uses the given endpoint
                                                            │  to construct a final
  return axios                                              │  request URL
    .get(url)
    .then(resp => {
      return resp;                                     ⊲──┐  Returns the response
    })                                                      │  from the promise
    .catch(err => {                                         │  handler
      return err;                                      ⊲──┘
    });
}
```

...

The `makeCall` command is generic enough to work with our middleware. You'll pass it an endpoint defined by the action being dispatched, and then `makeCall` will return either a response or an error depending on the result of the request.

5.5.3   Making the AJAX call

Next let's go ahead and use the `makeCall` function you created. You've already dispatched the action to indicate the request has started. Now you'll make the API call and dispatch either the success action or the failure action depending on the result, as shown in the following listing.

Listing 5.13   Making the AJAX call – src/middleware/api.js

```
...
const apiMiddleware = store => next => action => {
  const callApi = action[CALL_API];
  if (typeof callApi === 'undefined') {
    return next(action);
  }

  const [requestStartedType, successType, failureType] = callApi.types;

  next({ type: requestStartedType });

  return makeCall(callApi.endpoint).then(          ⊲──┤ Passes the endpoint
    response =>                                          specified by the current
      next({                                   ⊲──┐     action to makeCall
        type: successType,                         │ If the request succeeds,
        payload: response.data,                    │ dispatches the success action
      }),                                          │ type with the response.
    error =>
      next({                                   ⊲──┐ If it fails, dispatches
        type: failureType,                         │ the failure type with
        error: error.message,                      │ an error message.
      }),
  );
};

export default apiMiddleware;
```

And now you've reached API nirvana. In this middleware, you managed to create a centralized place that implements a few of the tasks that are common across all AJAX requests you'll need to make in the app. The main benefit here is that you can drastically reduce any future boilerplate that might come along if you add additional async actions that require a server request. Instead of creating three new action types and dispatching them all manually, you can use the API middleware to do the heavy lifting.

5.5.4   *Updating the reducer*

You're finished with all the middleware-related work, but there's one last step you need to take. Ideally, you can update the implementation of fetchTasks without updating other components, such as the reducer, but to keep the middleware generic, you have to make a small concession and update the reducer to handle a slightly less friendly action payload. Update the handler for the FETCH_TASKS_SUCCEEDED action in src/reducers/index.js to use the payload defined by the API middleware, as shown in the following listing.

Listing 5.14 Updating the tasks reducer – src/reducers/index.js

```
const initialState = {
  tasks: [],
  isLoading: false,
  error: null,
};

export default function tasks(state = initialState, action) {
  switch (action.type) {
    ...
    case 'FETCH_TASKS_SUCCEEDED': {
      return {
        ...state,
        tasks: action.payload,          ◁──┐  Uses the new
        isLoading: false,                  │  action shape to
      };                                   │  update tasks state
    }

    ...
    default: {
      return state;
    }
  }
}
```

This is a change you'd rather not make, but it's not a disaster. New tasks being available in the reducer at `action.payload.tasks` was more descriptive, but it's a small price to pay in the larger picture. Libraries like normalizr can allow the API middleware to dispatch action payloads that are more specific, and we'll cover that process in a subsequent chapter.

5.5.5 *Wrapping up API middleware*

And there you have it: a powerful API middleware that helps centralize the common themes around sending an AJAX request with Redux. But remember, abstractions all have a cost, and the cost here is code complexity. Consider the tradeoffs and do whatever makes the most sense given your project realities.

5.6 *Exercise*

Because you've built this nice new API middleware, it makes sense to update other async actions to use it. See if you can migrate `createTask` similarly to how you migrated `fetchTasks` in the previous section. `createTask` currently dispatches the three typical request actions, request start, success, and failure.

It's not quite as simple as only implementing a new `createTask` that uses the API middleware. You'll also have to update the middleware itself to support a POST request in addition to a GET request.

5.7   *Solution*

Here's how you might break down this problem into manageable chunks:

- Update the API middleware to accept a request method and a request body, which it will use when it makes the AJAX request.
- Implement a new version of `createTask` that uses the `CALL_API` action constant and passes four arguments to the API middleware: an array of the three request-related actions, the endpoint, the request method, and any POST data.
- Update the reducer to handle the new action payload for `CREATE_TASK_SUCCEEDED` as supplied by the API middleware.

First, update the middleware to handle POST requests, as shown in the following listing.

Listing 5.15   Updating the API middleware – src/middleware/api.js

```
function makeCall({ endpoint, method = 'GET', body }) {        Updates makeCall
  const url = `${API_BASE_URL}${endpoint}`;                     to accept a method/
                                                                request body
  const params = {
    method: method,
    url,
    data: body,
    headers: {
      'Content-Type': 'application/json',
    },
  };

  return axios(params).then(resp => resp).catch(err => err);
}

...

const apiMiddleware = store => next => action => {
  ...

  return makeCall({
    method: callApi.method,          Passes the new arguments
    body: callApi.body,              provided by the action
    endpoint: callApi.endpoint,
  }).then(
    response =>
      next({
        type: successType,
        response,
      }),
    error =>
      next({
        type: failureType,
        error: error.message,
      }),
  );
};
```

It required a small effort, but this is a big win for us. You only had to add a few lines, but in the process, you made the middleware much more flexible for users of your code. Next, take care of updating `createTask` to use the `CALL_API` action, making sure to also provide a request method and body. Similar to `fetchTasks`, you can remove a ton of boilerplate here in favor of a much more declarative strategy, as shown in the following listing.

Listing 5.16 Implementing the new createTasks – src/actions/index.js

```
export const CREATE_TASK_STARTED = 'CREATE_TASK_STARTED';         Creates new action
export const CREATE_TASK_SUCCEEDED = 'CREATE_TASK_SUCCEEDED';     constants for the
export const CREATE_TASK_FAILED = 'CREATE_TASK_FAILED';          request actions

export function createTask({ title, description, status = 'Unstarted' }) {
  return {
    [CALL_API]: {
      types: [CREATE_TASK_STARTED, CREATE_TASK_SUCCEEDED,
      CREATE_TASK_FAILED],                           ◁─── Ensures that
      endpoint: '/tasks',                                 they're passed in
      method: 'POST',                                     the correct order
      body: {
        title,
        description,
        status,
      },
    },
  };
}
```

Passes the required arguments, including the new method/body properties

You're almost there, but you have one last small step. Similar to `fetchTasks`, you need to update the reducer to accept a new action shape for `CREATE_TASKS_SUCCEEDED`. Because you haven't added any logic to have the API middleware dispatch actions with custom payloads, the best you can do is pass the entire response object into the reducer. Head to src/reducers/index.js and make the final change, as shown in the following listing.

Listing 5.17 Updating the tasks reducer – src/reducers/index.js

```
...
  case 'CREATE_TASK_SUCCEEDED': {
    return {
      ...state,
      tasks: state.tasks.concat(action.payload),   ◁─┐ Adds the new
    };                                                │ task to the list
  }
...
```

Nice! If you're feeling industrious, update the `editTask` action to also use the API middleware. Overall, what style do you prefer? Would you rather have each action creator (`fetchTasks`, `createTasks`) explicitly dispatch multiple actions using `redux-thunk`? Or do you prefer the power of the API middleware? Redux isn't a large, opinionated framework, so there's always more than one way to peel the orange.

Middleware is fundamental to Redux and one of its most powerful features. But with great power, comes great responsibility. Middleware is a great way to centralize code and reduce duplication, and sometimes to create friendlier, more powerful APIs for yourself and for your collaborators.

In the next chapter, we'll explore another popular abstraction for async actions. Did you heed the warning in this chapter to commit your work before implementing all the middleware? Before beginning the next chapter, rollback your code to that commit or check out the appropriate branch. You'll need a clean slate before introducing Redux Sagas.

Summary

- Redux middleware is code that sits between an action being dispatched and the store processing the action.
- It's best used for generic tasks like logging, that need to be applied to many, if not all, actions.
- It can produce powerful abstractions like the API middleware, but it often comes at the cost of complexity and indirection.

Handling complex side effects

This chapter covers
- Looking again at redux-thunk
- Introducing generators
- Managing complex asynchronous operations with sagas

Eventually, you're going to want to handle more complex series of events in response to a user interaction. Using what you've learned so far, how would you handle logging in a user? The requirements will vary from app to app, of course, but let's consider what could be involved. Your application may need to verify login credentials, issue an authorization token, fetch user data, handle retries upon failure, and redirect upon success. What tools are at your disposal?

Up to now, we've explored thunks by way of the `redux-thunk` package as a way to handle side effects and asynchronous operations. Thunks have a friendly learning curve and are powerful enough to handle just about any use case you can throw at them. However, they aren't the only game in town. In this chapter, we'll revisit thunks, then introduce another paradigm for handling side effect complexity: Redux Sagas. By the end of the chapter, you'll have at least one more tool in your state-management toolbelt.

6.1 *What are side effects?*

Redux handles data with as much purity as possible, but for most applications you can't avoid side effects. Side effects are required to interact with the world outside of your client application. Side effects, in this context, are any interactions with the world beyond your Redux application. Most examples can be summarized as interactions with a server or local storage. For example, you might store an authorization token in a browser's `sessionStorage`, fetching data from a remote server, or recording an analytics event.

Where do you handle side effects? You know that reducers must be pure functions to get the full benefits of Redux, and components ought to dispatch action creators. That leaves action creators and middleware as options (figure 6.1).

Conveniently, you already have experience using both action creators and middleware to handle side effects. In the last chapter, you were exposed to an API middleware

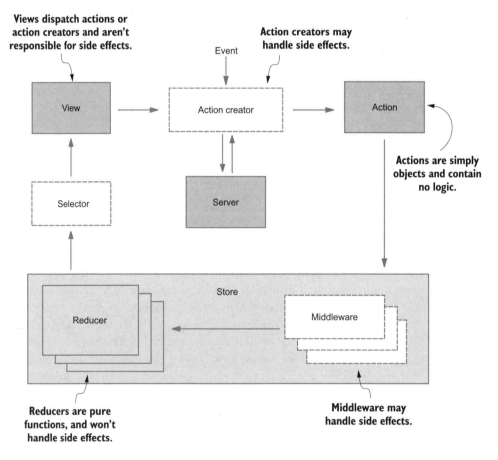

Figure 6.1   Within the Redux architecture, only action creators and middleware should handle side effects.

that handled AJAX requests. In chapter 4, you handled simple side effects within action creators by leveraging redux-thunk.

We should clarify: when asked where you want to handle side effects, the answer isn't restricted to either action creators or middleware. "Both" is an entirely reasonable answer! Remember, the redux-thunk package provides middleware to handle functions returned by action creators—an example of both action creators and middleware working together to manage side effects.

Over the next couple of sections, we'll compare and contrast thunks with Redux Sagas, another pattern that leverages middleware. We'll start with thunks.

6.2 Revisiting thunks

You've had great exposure to thunks already, having used them to interact with a remote server to fetch a list of tasks or create a new one. To review, the Redux store and its reducers know what to do with actions. Actions describe events—opening a modal, for example, can be the result of a clicked button dispatching an action of type OPEN_MODAL.

Things get more complicated when the contents of that modal need to be populated by an AJAX call. You could choose, for example, to dispatch an action only after the AJAX call returns, or dispatch several actions along the way to indicate loading progress. Again, the store deals in actions and is unequipped to handle functions or promises, so it's up to you to make sure that whatever reaches the store is an action.

When you need to perform asynchronous activities, redux-thunk makes it possible for an action creator to return a function in lieu of an action. Within the fetchTasks action creator, an anonymous function (thunk) is returned. The thunk middleware provides the dispatch and getState arguments, so the body of the function can view the contents of the current store and dispatch new actions to indicate loading, success, or failure states. View the following listing for a recap.

Listing 6.1 src/actions/index.js

```
export function fetchTasks() {                    The action creator returns a
  return (dispatch, getState) => {               function, also known as a thunk.
    dispatch(fetchTasksRequest());
    ...                                           Within the thunk, more
    dispatch(fetchTasksSuccess());                action creators can be
    ...                                           dispatched.
  }          Based on the results of a side effect,
}                  more dispatching may occur.
```

6.2.1 Strengths

Thunks have much going for them. They're dead simple, ubiquitous in documentation, and powerful enough to be the only side effect management tool you'll ever need.

SIMPLE

At the time of writing, the source code for `redux-thunk` is 14 lines—11 if you don't count line breaks. Installing and using the library is intuitive and newcomer-friendly. Additionally, you'll find excellent documentation in the GitHub repository and example usage in most Redux tutorials in the wild.

ROBUST

Although you'll learn about a few other side-effect management tools in this chapter, you can get the job done with thunks alone. They may be arbitrarily complex. Within a thunk, you're free to dispatch other action creators, make and respond to AJAX requests, interact with local storage, and so on.

GENTLE MIDDLEWARE INTRODUCTION

This is a tangential point, but worth mentioning. For most developers, `redux-thunk` is their first introduction to Redux middleware. Middleware tends to be one of the least accessible pieces of the Redux puzzle, and implementing `redux-thunk` is about as gentle a middleware introduction as you can get. That education is a net gain for the community and for you the developer, because it helps demystify part of the architecture.

6.2.2 Weaknesses

Any tool has tradeoffs, of course. The simplicity of thunks makes them something of a double-edged sword. Thunks are easy to write, but you're on your own to write advanced functionality.

VERBOSITY

Stuffing complex logic or multiple asynchronous events into a thunk can result in a function that's difficult to read or maintain. You won't find magic behind the scenes or accompanying utility functions to aid with that, so it's up to you to manage.

TESTING

Testing is one of the clearest weaknesses of thunks. The pain generally comes from needing to import, create, and populate a mock store before you can make assertions about actions being dispatched. On top of that, you'll likely need to mock any HTTP requests.

6.3 Introducing sagas

The name is telling. Sagas are built to handle the hairy and winding story of your data. Using an ES2015 feature, generators, the `redux-saga` package offers a powerful way to write and reason about complex asynchronous behavior. With a little new syntax, sagas can make asynchronous code as readable as synchronous code.

This chapter won't be an exhaustive look at `redux-saga` and all its use cases or features. The goal is to get you familiar enough with the basics to know whether your next feature could benefit from using a saga. The answer won't always be "yes."

A classic example of a good use case is a user login workflow. Logging in a user may require multiple calls to a remote server to validate credentials, issue or validate an authentication token, and return user data. It's certainly possible to handle all this with thunks, but this realm is where sagas really shine.

6.3.1 Strengths

As we've alluded, sagas aren't the answer to every problem. Let's explore what they're good for.

HANDLING COMPLEXITY AND LONG-RUNNING PROCESSES

Sagas helps you think about asynchronous code in a synchronous fashion. Instead of manually handling chains of promises and the spaghetti code that accompanies them, you can use an alternative control flow that results in cleaner code. Particularly challenging side effects to handle are long-running processes. A simple example where you'll run into these types of problems is a stopwatch application. Its implementation with redux-saga is trivial.

TESTING

Sagas don't perform or resolve side effects; they merely return descriptions of how to handle them. The execution is left to middleware under the hood. Because of this, it's straightforward to test a saga. Instead of requiring a mock store, you can test that a saga returns the correct side effect description. We won't walk through a saga test in this chapter, but there are examples in the official documentation at https://redux-saga.js.org/docs/advanced/Testing.html.

6.3.2 Weaknesses

With great power comes great responsibility. Let's look at the tradeoffs involved with using redux-saga.

LEARNING CURVE

When bringing a newly hired Redux developer onto your team, it's safe to assume they're proficient with thunks. The same cannot be said for sagas, however. A common cost for using redux-saga is the time it takes to bring an unfamiliar developer or team of developers up to speed with using it. The use of generators and an unfamiliar paradigm can make for a steep learning curve.

HEAVY-HANDED

Put simply, redux-saga may be overkill for simple applications. As a rule of thumb, we prefer to introduce a saga only when enough pain points are experienced while using a thunk. Keep in mind that there are costs associated with including another package—developer onboarding and the additional file size, in particular.

Generators are well-supported by most modern browsers, but that hasn't always been the case. If your application needs to support older browser versions, consider the impact of including a generator polyfill, if required.

6.4   *What are generators?*

This book assumes you're comfortable with the best-known ECMAScript 2015 syntax, but generators don't fall into that category. Generators enable powerful functionality, but the syntax is foreign, and their use cases are still being discovered. For many React developers, redux-saga is their first introduction to generator functions.

Put simply, generators are functions that can be paused and resumed. The Mozilla Developer Network describes generators as "functions which can be exited and later re-entered. Their context (variable bindings) will be saved across re-entrances." You may find it useful to think of them as background processes or subprograms.

6.4.1   *Generator syntax*

Generators look like any other function, except they're declared with an asterisk following the function keyword, as in the following example:

```
function* exampleGenerator() { … }
```

Note that when declaring a generator, the asterisk may come at any point between the function keyword and the function name. Each of the following are functionally the same:

```
function* exampleGenerator() { … }
function *exampleGenerator() { … }
function*exampleGenerator() { … }
function * exampleGenerator() { … }
```

This book standardizes on the first example, because it appears to be more popular in the wild and is the style preference chosen in the redux-saga documentation. Although you won't write any in this chapter, know that generators can also be anonymous:

```
function* () { … }
function *() { … }
function*() { … }
function * () { … }
```

Generators can yield results. The yield keyword can be used to return a value from the generator function. See the following listing for an example.

Listing 6.2   Basic generator example

```
function* exampleGenerator() {
    yield 42;
    return 'fin';
}
```

← The generator function is denoted with an asterisk.

← The yield keyword provides a return value from the generator function.

What do you suppose might happen if you execute the function, exampleGenerator()? Go ahead and try it out in your terminal. Assuming you have Node.js installed, start the Node.js REPL by entering node into your terminal window, then write the function in listing 6.2 and execute it. Not what you expected, was it? The terminal output appears to be an empty object.

6.4.2 *Iterators*

What the generator returns is called an iterator. Iterators are objects, but they're not empty. They keep track of where they are in a sequence and can return the next value in the sequence. Iterators have a next function that can be used to execute code within the generator up until the next yield, as shown in this example:

```
exampleGenerator();          //=> {}
exampleGenerator().next(); //=> { value: 42, done: false }
```

Notice the output of the next function. The result is an object with two keys, value and done. value contains the yielded content, 42. The done key has a value of false, indicating that the generator has more data to provide if called again. At this point, the generator function is effectively paused and waiting to be called on again to resume executing after the yield statement. Let's keep going:

```
exampleGenerator();          //=> {}
exampleGenerator().next(); //=> { value: 42, done: false }
exampleGenerator().next(); //=> { value: 42, done: false }
exampleGenerator().next(); //=> { value: 42, done: false }
```

Wait, what happened? Shouldn't value have been the string fin and done returned true? Don't let this one bite you. Each time exampleGenerator is executed, a new iterator is returned. You'll need to store the iterator in a variable, then call next on the stored iterator. See the following listing for an example.

Listing 6.3 Iteration with a generator example

```
const iterator = exampleGenerator();              ◁─┐  Stores the iterator
iterator.next(); // { value: 42, done: false }        created by the
iterator.next(); // { value: 'fin', done: true }    ◁─ generator function
iterator.next(); // { value: undefined, done: true } ◁─┐
                                                        Having reached the
        Continues to call next;                         return statement,
        returns an undefined value                      done flips to true.
```

Up to now, you've seen yield and return statements used in a generator. You've learned that yield will return a value with done set to false. return does the same, with done set to true. A third option exists: throw. You won't use it in this chapter, but throw can be used to break out of a generator function in the case of an error. You can find more details about the throw method at https://developer.mozilla.org/en-US/docs/Web/JavaScript/Reference/Global_Objects/Generator/throw.

6.4.3   *Looping with generators*

We're willing to bet that the last infinite loop you wrote was an accident. It happens to the best of us. In the case of generators however, infinite loops are a viable usage pattern. The next listing is an example of an intentional infinite loop.

Listing 6.4   Infinite loop example

```
function* optimisticMagicEightBall() {
    while (true) {                         ◁──┐  Creates an infinite
        yield 'Yup, definitely.';             │  loop with a while
    }                                          │  (true) block
}
```

Now, you can answer an unlimited number of questions with your generator function, `optimisticMagicEightBall`. Each call of the next function on the iterator will return the affirmative answer, then pause, waiting for the loop to begin again.

It's also possible to compose generators, or in other words, use generators within generators. In this case (listing 6.5), looping through the count function produces the numbers one through five in order as the count function becomes blocked until `middleNumbers` resolves. The `yield*` syntax is used to delegate out to another generator.

Listing 6.5   Composing generators example

```
function* count() {
    yield 1;
    yield 2;
    yield* middleNumbers();      ◁──┐  The middleNumbers
    yield 5;                         │  generator completes
}                                    │  before moving on to 5.

function* middleNumbers() {
    yield 3;
    yield 4;
}
```

Although these examples are contrived, be sure that they make sense before moving on. The `redux-saga` library makes heavy use of both.

6.4.4   *Why generators?*

Although capable, JavaScript has something of a reputation for its difficulty in managing series of asynchronous events. You may have heard the term "callback hell" used to describe a group of deeply nested, chained asynchronous functions regularly found in JavaScript codebases. Generators were created to offer an alternative control flow for asynchronous operations.

Generators are broadly applicable tools, and again, those applications are still being uncovered. Complex asynchronous operations and long-running processes are two of the most commonly cited opportunities to gain readability and maintainability by introducing a generator.

Generators are also a platform to build still more powerful or more developer-friendly tools. The popular ES7 feature, async/await, leverages generators to create another highly approachable way to handle complex asynchronous events. The doors are open for more intricate, domain-specific libraries to be built, such as `redux-saga`.

6.5 *Implementing sagas*

With an understanding of the fundamentals of generators, you're ready to step into sagas. As an exercise, try refactoring one of Parsnip's thunks into a saga: the `fetchTasks` action creator. Visually, the final result will look identical to existing functionality, but under the hood, you're using an entirely new paradigm. To be clear, the net gain from this refactor won't be much: easier testing in exchange for code complexity. The value is in the academic exercise.

The first step is to install the package. Within your Parsnip app, add `redux-saga`:

```
npm install redux-saga
```

In the following sections, we'll walk through configuring an application to use the `redux-saga` middleware, then you'll write your first saga. You'll discover that sagas and thunks are both a means to reach the same end, and for each feature you build, you may choose whichever tool fits the use case best.

6.5.1 *Connecting saga middleware to the store*

Sagas operate as middleware, and middleware gets registered in the store at the time of the store's creation. As a reminder, Redux's `createStore` function takes up to three arguments: reducers, initial state, and enhancers. In the last chapter, you learned that middleware gets applied in the last argument as a store enhancement. Here again, you'll register `redux-saga` as middleware. A final warning: this chapter uses the code from chapter 4 as a starting point. You'll need to roll back the changes or check out of the branch made in chapter 5 if you're coding along.

In listing 6.6, you import and use the `createSagaMiddleware` factory function. Redux's `applyMiddleware` function takes a list of arguments, so you can add the saga middleware right alongside the thunk middleware. Remember, the order you list middleware determines the order an action will pass through them.

Listing 6.6 src/index.js

```
import createSagaMiddleware from 'redux-saga';          ◁──┐   createSagaMiddleware
import rootSaga from './sagas';                         ◁──┤   is the default export of
                                                            │   redux-saga.
const sagaMiddleware = createSagaMiddleware();          ◁──┐
                                                            │
const store = createStore(            createSagaMiddleware is a    redux-saga needs to
    reducer,                          factory function, used to    know which saga (or
                                      create sagaMiddleware.       sagas) to run.
```

```
    composeWithDevTools(applyMiddleware(thunk, sagaMiddleware))
);

sagaMiddleware.run(rootSaga);
```

Finally, initiate the saga with the run method on the sagaMiddleware instance.

Adds the saga middleware to the list in applyMiddleware

Again, there's no reason you can't use both thunks and sagas in the same application, and indeed, many applications do.

It may be helpful to think of sagas as subprograms, and the run function on the last line of the listing is required for the subprogram to begin watching for actions. Once the saga middleware is configured, you can run the top-level, or root, saga. In the next section, you'll get a chance to put a generator into production by writing a root saga.

6.5.2   *Introducing the root saga*

The code in the previous listing won't do anything for you until you write the root saga you imported. Let's go only far enough to tell that we've configured redux-saga properly. Create a new file within the src directory and name it sagas.js. Within that file, write a rootSaga generator function and have it log a message to the console, as shown in the following listing.

Listing 6.7   src/sagas.js

```
export default function* rootSaga() {
    console.log('rootSaga reporting for duty');
}
```

Denotes generators with the asterisk following the function keyword.

If everything went smoothly, you should see your message logged to the console after restarting the server. (If you have trouble with the json-server, revisit the setup instructions in the appendix.) So far so good! Let's pause here to explore what you've got and where you're headed.

After configuring the store to use saga middleware, you instructed the middleware to run the root saga. Because it's simpler to keep track of a single entry point, the root saga's role will be to coordinate all other sagas used in the application. When that root saga is implemented, you'll expect it to kick off sagas to run in the background, watching for and reacting to actions of specific types. As mentioned, you can and will use thunks at the same time, so each saga will listen for and respond to only specific actions. See figure 6.2 for a visual representation.

You know that the order in which middleware is provided to the applyMiddleware function is the order that actions pass through them. Because you listed sagaMiddleware first, all dispatched values will pass through it before the thunk middleware. In general, a saga will react to an action, handling one or more side effects, and eventually return another action to be processed by the reducers.

Ready for the big reveal? The first saga you'll write will be a replacement for the thunk that handles tasks fetching. The first thing you'll need to do is let the root saga know about this new saga.

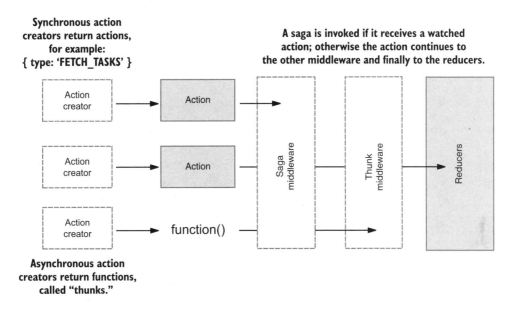

Synchronous action creators return actions, for example: { type: 'FETCH_TASKS' }

A saga is invoked if it receives a watched action; otherwise the action continues to the other middleware and finally to the reducers.

Asynchronous action creators return functions, called "thunks."

Figure 6.2 Sagas will respond to actions of a specific type. If another action type or thunk is received, it will pass through the saga middleware unchanged.

POP QUIZ What are the three generator-specific methods, and which is used to return a value from a generator without declaring it done? The three methods are `return`, `throw`, and `yield`. `yield` is the function that can return a value but provide a `done` value of `false`.

You're going to want to have our root saga yield each of the application's sagas. Could you use `return`? Sure, but only on the last line of the saga. The `redux-saga` documentation and examples choose to use only `yield`, so that's the pattern you'll stick with.

In the next listing, you'll see the root saga `yield` to another saga that will eventually watch for `FETCH_TASKS` actions. Sagas such as `watchFetchTasks` are sometimes called watchers, because they infinitely wait and watch for particular actions. A common convention for spinning up multiple watchers is to fork them. You'll learn what that means in a minute. You only have one watcher to write so far, but for the sake of example, you'll add a second in the following listing to demonstrate the conventions.

Listing 6.8   src/sagas.js

```
import { fork } from 'redux-saga/effects';        ◁─────┐  Imports fork from the
                                                         │  redux-saga/effects
export function* rootSaga() {                            │  package
    yield fork(watchFetchTasks);          ┐  Forking each
    yield fork(watchSomethingElse);       │  watcher allows
}                                         │  rootSaga to move
                                          │  on to the next one.
```

```
function* watchFetchTasks() {
    console.log('watching!');
}

function* watchSomethingElse() {
    console.log('watching something else!');
}
```

Each watcher is
also a generator.

What's `fork` doing here? When `rootSaga` executes, it's going to pause at every `yield` statement until the side effect is completed. The `fork` method, however, allows `root-Saga` to move onto the next `yield` without a resolution. Each of these forks are said to be non-blocking. This implementation makes sense, because you want to kick off all the watchers at initialization, not only the first in the list.

6.5.3   *Saga effects*

In listing 6.8, you'll notice that you imported `fork` not from `redux-saga`, but from `redux-saga/effects`. `fork` is one of many methods made available to help you manage what are referred to as effects. One common misconception for newcomers is that the logic you write within a saga needs to do the processing of your side effect, such as performing an AJAX request. That's not the case! Instead, the saga's role is to return a description of the logic needed in the form of an object. Figure 6.3 introduces the `call` method to illustrate this relationship.

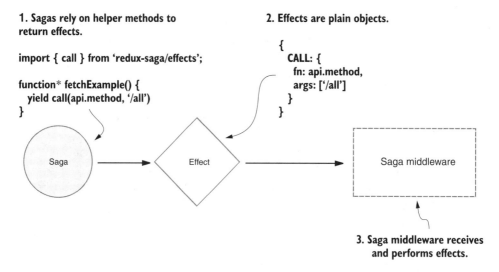

Figure 6.3 Sagas return effects, which are instructions for the saga middleware to perform.

The `call` method used here is analogous to JavaScript's `call` function. You'll use it again shortly to specify the AJAX request to fetch the tasks. Once you use the `redux-saga`-specific methods to generate an effect, the saga middleware will process and perform the required side effects out of view. You'll learn more about these methods in the implementation of the task fetching next.

6.5.4 *Responding to and dispatching actions*

Watchers reacting only when the right action comes along has generated a great deal of discussion. The method you're looking for is also among the group of helpers imported from `redux-saga/effects`: `take`. The `take` command is used to wake up and engage a saga when a particular action type arrives. Unlike `fork`, it is a blocking call, meaning that the infinite loop will halt while it waits for another action of type `FETCH_TASKS_STARTED` to come along. Listing 6.9 shows the basic usage.

Only after a `FETCH_TASKS_STARTED` action is dispatched and `take` is called will the `started!` log appear in your console. Notice that you've introduced an infinite loop into the saga to facilitate this feature. This technique shouldn't be alarming to you after reading the introduction to generators earlier in the chapter.

Listing 6.9   src/sagas.js

```
import { fork, take } from 'redux-saga/effects';     ⊲┐  Imports take from
...                                                    │  the effects package
function* watchFetchTasks() {
    while (true) {                                   ⊲┐  Watchers use infinite loops
        yield take('FETCH_TASKS_STARTED');       ⊲   │  to process actions as often
        console.log('started!');                     │  as they're needed.
    }
}
```
take waits for a given action type before allowing the saga to proceed.

If you're following along at home, you'll want to delete or comment out the related thunk feature. All you'll need to interact with this saga is to dispatch an action of type `FETCH_TASKS_STARTED`. You can accomplish this by exporting the `fetchTasks-Started` action and passing it to the dispatch in `componentDidMount` within the `App.js` component.

Now that you've got the basics of responding to actions covered, let's try out the other side of the coin, dispatching new ones. The method you're looking for this time is `put`. As an argument, `put` takes the action you'd like to pass through to the remainder of the middleware and to the reducers. Let's bring the `call` method back into the picture and connect the remaining dots to complete the feature.

Listing 6.10   src/sagas.js

```
import { call, fork, put, take } from 'redux-saga/effects';  ⊲┐  Imports each of the
...                                                            │  used helper methods
function* watchFetchTasks() {
    while (true) {
        yield take('FETCH_TASKS_STARTED');
        try {                                              ┐  call is a blocking
            const { data } = yield call(api.fetchTasks);  │  method used to specify
                                                       ⊲──┘  the AJAX request.
```

```
        yield put({
            type: 'FETCH_TASKS_SUCCEEDED',
            payload: { tasks: data }
        });
    } catch (e) {
        yield put({
            type: 'FETCH_TASKS_FAILED',
            payload: { error: e.message }
        });
    }
  }
}
```

> After a successful or unsuccessful request, put is used to dispatch an action.

The whole fetch tasks feature has been replaced by a saga! The saga wakes up when FETCH_TASKS_STARTED is dispatched. It next waits for the middleware to perform the AJAX request, then dispatches a success or failure action with the results.

To verify it works on your machine, be sure to delete or comment out the related thunk, within the action creator fetchTasks, so you don't have two systems competing to process actions. All you'll need is a synchronous action creator to dispatch a FETCH_TASKS_STARTED action. See listing 6.11 for an example. Remember though, you already have the know-how to debug that situation yourself. You know that whichever order you provide middleware to applyMiddleware is the order that actions will move through them.

Listing 6.11   src/actions/index.js

```
...
export function fetchTasks() {
    return { type: 'FETCH_TASKS_STARTED' };
}
...
```

> The saga middleware handles AJAX requests in response to this action type.

If you compare this complete saga implementation of the fetch tasks feature with the thunk implementation, you'll notice they're not all that different. They're roughly the same amount of code and the logic looks similar. Introducing sagas undeniably added complexity, though. Is it worth the learning curve?

We've mentioned, but not demonstrated, that sagas are easier to test than thunks. That's certainly worth something. It can also be valuable to learn a new programming paradigm. At this point, however, if your answer is still "no," we wouldn't blame you. It's a hard sell to convince your development team to introduce a complex new tool without clearer value.

Fortunately, we've barely scratched the surface of what sagas may be useful for. As a quick example, let's say you wanted to cancel an unfinished, old request whenever a new one came in. In a thunk, this requires extra labor, but redux-saga/effects provides a method, takeLatest, for this purpose. The command takeLatest replaces the use of fork in your root saga, as shown in the following listing.

Listing 6.12   src/sagas.js

```
import { call, put, takeLatest } from 'redux-saga/effects';
...
export default function* rootSaga() {
   yield takeLatest('FETCH_TASKS_STARTED', fetchTasks);      ◁—  takeLatest cancels
}                                                                 old processes when
                                                                  a new one begins.

function* fetchTasks() {
   try {                                              ◁—  No more infinite loop
      const { data } = yield call(api.fetchTasks);        is required, because
      yield put({                                         takeLatest continues to
         type: 'FETCH_TASKS_SUCCEEDED',                    listen for the action type.
         payload: { tasks: data },
      });
   } catch (e) {
      yield put({
         type: 'FETCH_TASKS_FAILED',
         payload: { error: e.message },
      });
   }
}
...
```

Behind the scenes, `takeLatest` is creating a fork with extra functionality. To provide its intended functionality, it will have to listen for every action of type `FETCH_TASKS _STARTED`. This keeps you from needing to do the same, so you can remove the infinite loop and `take` function from the `watchFetchTasks` saga. While you're at it, `watchFetchTasks` is no longer doing the watching, so you've tweaked the name to suggest that: `fetchTasks`.

That's the whole of it. Refresh your browser and you'll see identical results, but with more resource-conservative code underneath. To get that new feature, you deleted more code than you added. Sounds like a win-win to us.

6.6   *Handling long-running processes*

In the introduction of generators, we mentioned that handling long-running processes may be ideal use cases. Long-running processes may take many forms, and one of the textbook educational examples is a timer or a stopwatch. You're going to run with this idea to add an additional feature to Parsnip, but with a little twist. In this section, you'll add a unique timer to each task, which begins when the task is moved to "In Progress." By the time you're done with the feature, it will look something like figure 6.4.

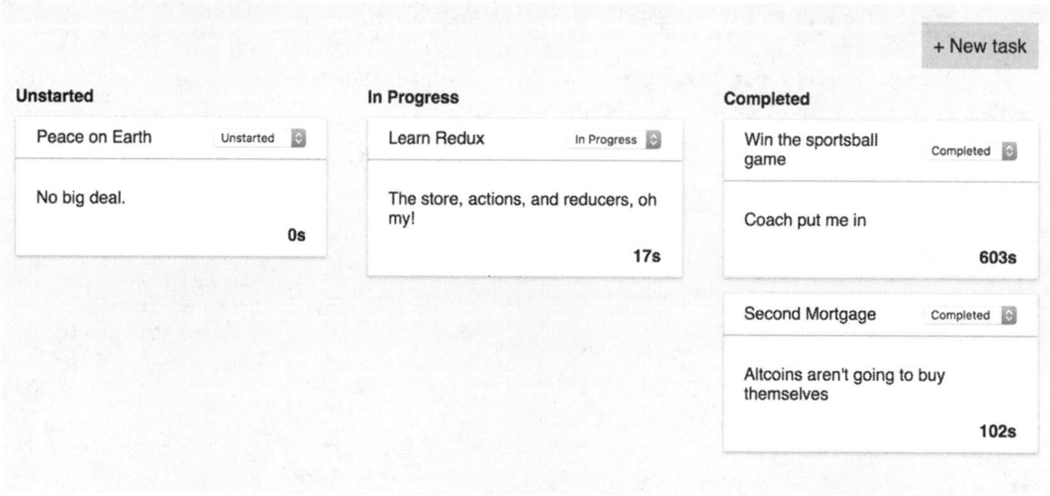

Figure 6.4   Tasks display a timer for how long they've been in progress.

6.6.1   *Preparing data*

You'll need the server to tell you at least what the timer starting value for each task is. To keep it simple, each task will have a timer key with an integer value, representing the number of seconds it has been in progress. See the following listing for an abbreviated example. The specific numbers you choose aren't important.

Listing 6.13   db.json

```
...
{
    "tasks": [
        ...
        {
            "id": 2,
            "title": "Peace on Earth",
            "description": "No big deal.",
            "status": "Unstarted",
            "timer": 0                      ⊲──┐ Gives each task
        }                                      │ a timer key and
        ...                                    │ number value
    ]
}
...
```

Be sure to add the `timer` key to every task record. Remember, this is JSON formatting, so don't forget your quotes around `timer`. Number values don't require them.

6.6.2 *Updating the user interface*

Next up is to display the new timer data in the tasks. This calls for a small addition to already straightforward React code, so you aren't going to publish the entire component here. Within the `Task` component, render the timer property somewhere within the body of the task. Use the following code as an example and style it as you please. The "s" is an abbreviation for seconds:

```
<div className="task-timer">{props.task.timer}s</div>
```

At this point, the timer values you entered in the db.json file should be visible in the UI. The parent components of the `Task` component already make the value available, so no additional configuration is required.

6.6.3 *Dispatching an action*

Before we get to the saga, you'll need to dispatch an action with which to get its attention. The goal is to turn the timer on whenever a task is moved into "In Progress." Mull it over: Where would you want to dispatch a `TIMER_STARTED` action?

You can piggyback onto existing logic to facilitate this. The action creator `editTask` already handles moving an action into each status column, so you can dispatch an additional action whenever the destination is the "In Progress" column. See the following listing for an example implementation.

Listing 6.14 src/actions/index.js

```
...
function progressTimerStart(taskId) {
    return { type: 'TIMER_STARTED', payload: { taskId } };      ⟵  The action that
}                                                                    the saga will
                                                                     be listening for
export function editTask(id, params = {}) {
    return (dispatch, getState) => {
        const task = getTaskById(getState().tasks.tasks, id);
        const updatedTask = {
            ...task,
            ...params,
        };                                                       Adds an additional
        api.editTask(id, updatedTask).then(resp => {            dispatch if the task
            dispatch(editTaskSucceeded(resp.data));             is moved into 'In
            if (resp.data.status === 'In Progress') {      ⟵    Progress'
                dispatch(progressTimerStart(resp.data.id));
            }
        });
    };
}
```

You need to pass the ID of the task to the action. When you have multiple timers incrementing at once, you need to know exactly which task to increment or pause.

6.6.4 Writing a long-running saga

If everything in this chapter is starting to click for you, you may already have an idea of where you'd like to go with this saga. One strategy is to listen for actions of type TIMER _STARTED, then increment the timer value once per second within an infinite loop. It's a good place to start!

You can begin by registering a handleProgressTimer saga with the root saga. This is an opportunity to introduce one more alternative to fork. The command take-Latest makes sense when you want to throttle API requests to a remote server. Sometimes you want to let everything through, though. The method you're looking for is takeEvery.

The implementation of handleProgressTimer will introduce one new method, but it's self-explanatory: delay. delay is a blocking method, meaning that the saga will pause at its location until the blocking method resolves. You can see a complete implementation in listing 6.15.

You'll notice that you're importing delay not from redux-saga/effects, but instead from redux-saga. The delay command doesn't help produce an effect object, so it doesn't reside alongside the other effect helpers. You'll lean on the call method in the following listing to produce the effect and pass in delay as an argument, the way you did when making an API request.

Listing 6.15 src/sagas.js

Adds the delay method from redux-saga

Adds the takeEvery method to the list of imports

```
import { delay } from 'redux-saga';        ◁──────┘
import { call, put, takeEvery, takeLatest } from 'redux-saga/effects';   ◁──────┘

export default function* rootSaga() {
    yield takeLatest('FETCH_TASKS_STARTED', fetchTasks);
    yield takeEvery('TIMER_STARTED', handleProgressTimer);   ◁──
}

function* handleProgressTimer({ payload }) {       ◁──────┐
    while (true) {                                  ◁──────
        yield call(delay, 1000);                    ◁──────
        yield put({
            type: 'TIMER_INCREMENT',
            payload: { taskId: payload.taskId },   ◁──────┐
        });
    }
}
...
```

Every time 'TIMER_STARTED' is dispatched, invoke the handleProgressTimer function.

Action properties are available as arguments.

The timer runs infinitely while in progress.

delay is used to wait one second (1000 ms) between increments.

The task ID is passed to the reducer to find the task to increment.

Without extra configuration, the take, takeEvery, and takeLatest methods will pass the action through to the function or saga you provide. handleProgressTimer can access the taskId from the action payload to eventually specify which task to update.

6.6.5   *Handling the action in the reducer*

Every second, the saga will dispatch a TIMER_INCREMENT action. By now, you know that it's the reducer's job to define how the store will update in response to that action. You'll want to create a case statement for handling the action within the tasks reducer. Much of this code is identical to the code for handling the EDIT_TASK_SUCCEEDED action in the same reducer. The goal is to find the desired task, update its timer value, then return the list of tasks, as shown in the following listing.

Listing 6.16   src/reducers/index.js

```
...
case 'TIMER_INCREMENT': {                          ◁─┐  Adds the new action type
    const nextTasks = state.tasks.map(task => {        to the tasks reducer
        if (task.id === action.payload.taskId) {   ◁─┐  Maps over the existing
            return { ...task, timer: task.timer + 1 };  tasks to create the
        }                                          ◁─┘  updated versions
        return task;
    });                                                 If the task ID matches,
                                                        increment the task's
    return { ...state, tasks: nextTasks };   ◁─┐        timer.
}
...
                                             Returns the
                                             updated tasks
```

That wraps up the implementation! If you try it out on your local machine, you should see the timer begin to tick up on any task that gets moved into the "In Progress" column. Multiple tasks increment uniquely, as you'd expect. Not bad, right?

Don't celebrate so quickly though; our solution is a short-sighted one. In the exercise for this chapter, you're asked to implement the ability to stop the timer when a task in progress is moved to "Completed" or back to "Unstarted." If you attempt to add this functionality to our existing saga, you'll eventually be left scratching your head as to why the tasks aren't responding to TIMER_STOPPED actions or breaking out of the increment loop.

6.6.6   *Using channels*

We'll save you the head-scratching trouble and reveal what's going on here. takeEvery is starting a new process for each TIMER_STARTED action it receives. Each time a task is moved into "In Progress," a separate process begins dispatching TIMER_INCREMENT actions. That's a good thing. You want each task to increment individually. However, if a TIMER_STOPPED action were to come through the handleProgressTimer saga, it too would start a new process, separate from the one busy incrementing the timer. You have no way to stop the incrementing process if you can't target it specifically. See figure 6.5 for an illustration.

In the figure, you can see that by the time you move the task into "In Progress" twice, you have two separate loops incrementing the timer every second. That's clearly not what you had in mind. If you use takeLatest instead of takeEvery, only

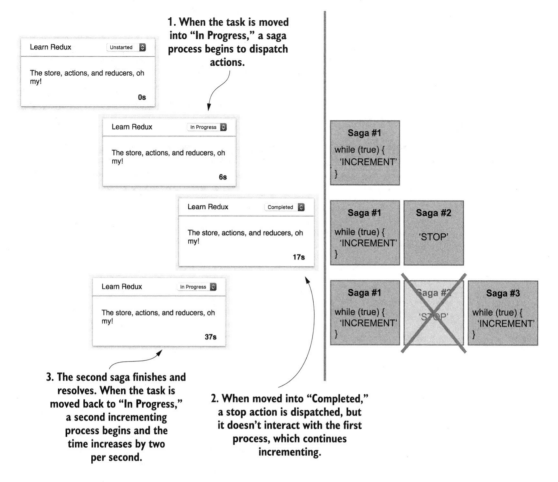

1. When the task is moved into "In Progress," a saga process begins to dispatch actions.

3. The second saga finishes and resolves. When the task is moved back to "In Progress," a second incrementing process begins and the time increases by two per second.

2. When moved into "Completed," a stop action is dispatched, but it doesn't interact with the first process, which continues incrementing.

Figure 6.5   The takeEvery method spawns a new saga process for each action.

one task could increment its timer at a time. Ultimately, what you want to achieve is the functionality of takeLatest, with a separate process per task. Simply stated, if you start a process, you need to stop the same process. That's exactly the functionality you'll build.

To build this feature, you're going to leverage another redux-saga utility called a channel. From the official documentation, channels are "objects used to send and receive messages between tasks." The tasks they reference are what we've referred to as processes, to avoid naming confusion with our Parsnip tasks. Essentially, you'll use channels as a way to give a name to a saga process, so that you can revisit the same channel again. If the language is confusing, the code should help to clarify it.

What you want to accomplish is to create a unique channel for each Parsnip task that starts a timer. If you keep a list of channels, you can then send a TIMER_STOPPED action to the correct channel when the task is moved to "Completed." You're going to go off the beaten path a little by creating a helper function to manage these channels.

You'll name the function `takeLatestById`, and it will send each action to the correct process. If a process doesn't already exist, a new one will be created. Listing 6.17 offers one implementation.

You'll see new code here, but there shouldn't be anything wildly surprising. `takeLatestById` is a generic helper function that is used to create rediscoverable processes. The function checks to see if a channel exists for a task, and if not, creates one and adds it to the mapping. After adding to the mapping, the new channel is immediately instantiated and the final line in the listing dispatches the action to the new channel. Conveniently, nothing about the `handleProgressTimer` function needs to change.

Listing 6.17 src/sagas.js

Adds channel to the list of imports

Adds take back to the list of effect helper imports

```
import { channel, delay } from 'redux-saga';
import { call, put, take, takeLatest } from 'redux-saga/effects';
...

export default function* rootSaga() {
    yield takeLatest('FETCH_TASKS_STARTED', fetchTasks);
    yield takeLatestById('TIMER_STARTED', handleProgressTimer);
}

function* takeLatestById(actionType, saga) {
    const channelsMap = {};

    while (true) {
        const action = yield take(actionType);
        const { taskId } = action.payload;

        if (!channelsMap[taskId]) {
            channelsMap[taskId] = channel();
            yield takeLatest(channelsMap[taskId], saga);
        }

        yield put(channelsMap[taskId], action);
    }
}
...
```

Have the root saga initiate the helper function.

Stores a mapping of created channels

If a task doesn't have a channel, create one.

Creates a new process for that task

Dispatches an action to the specific process

If you start the application on your machine, you should experience the same functionality with one important difference. Moving a task into "In Progress" twice should produce only one saga process, instead of two. The helper function has set up a `take-Latest` watcher for sagas being manipulated. The second time the task is moved to "In Progress," the `takeLatest` function cancels the first process and starts a new one, never producing more than one increment loop per task. That's more like it!

6.7   *Exercise*

Your turn! All the scaffolding is set up for you to write a few lines of code to add the stop timer functionality to Parsnip. Specifically, what you want is for a task's timer to stop any time it moves from "In Progress" to one of the other columns: "Unstarted" or "Completed."

Because there're only a few lines to write doesn't mean it's easy, though. Completing this exercise will be a good way to prove to yourself that everything you've done so far is beginning to make sense. We'll give you one hint to get started: functions such as take can be configured to accept and respond to more than one action type at a time. To do so, you can pass it an array of action type strings as the first argument.

6.8   *Solution*

Did you figure it out? The first step is to figure out when to dispatch the TIMER_STOPPED action. Right after the logic to determine whether to dispatch the TIMER_STARTED action is a reasonable opportunity. See the following listing for an example.

Listing 6.18   src/actions/index.js

```
...
export function editTask(id, params = {}) {
    ...
    api.editTask(id, updatedTask).then(resp => {
        dispatch(editTaskSucceeded(resp.data));          Don't forget the
                                                         return keyword
        if (resp.data.status === 'In Progress') {        on the start
            return dispatch(progressTimerStart(resp.data.id));   ◁─┘  dispatch.
        }

        if (task.status === 'In Progress') {          ◁──  Stops the timer if
            return dispatch(progressTimerStop(resp.data.id));    the task was "In
        }                                                        Progress" prior to
    });                                                          updating
}

function progressTimerStop(taskId) {              Return the new
    return { type: 'TIMER_STOPPED', payload: { taskId } };   ◁──  TIMER_STOPPED
}                                                        action with the
                                                         task ID.
```

The part that may be confusing here is that within the editTask function, task refers to the task before it was updated, and resp.data refers to the updated task returned from the AJAX request. To start the timer, check if the new task is in progress. If so, editTask dispatches another action and finishes there. You never move on to the check if the timer needs to be stopped. If the updated task isn't in progress, but the original task was, then stop the timer.

Next you need to handle the new TIMER_STOPPED action in the saga. This is going to be even less code than you expected.

Listing 6.19   src/sagas.js

```
...
export default function* rootSaga() {
    yield takeLatest('FETCH_TASKS_STARTED', fetchTasks);
    yield takeLatestById(['TIMER_STARTED', 'TIMER_STOPPED'],
        handleProgressTimer);
}

function* handleProgressTimer({ payload, type }) {
    if (type === 'TIMER_STARTED') {
        while (true) {
            ...
        }
    }
}
...
```

> Passes both action types in an array to the helper function

> Adds type to the list of destructured arguments

> Wraps all the function's logic in a conditional statement that executes if type is TIMER_STARTED

Seriously, that's it. Once you begin watching for both actions, the infrastructure you've already written will handle the rest. The helper function accepts the array of action types and passes the pattern into its `take` function. From that point on, start and stop actions will find themselves in the correct process, executing the code within the `handleProgressTimer` function.

Implementing the stop function doesn't require any other modifications to the function, because all you need it to do is not execute the increment logic. The TIMER _STOPPED function bypasses the infinite loop and moves on to the reducers, eventually becoming visible in the Redux DevTools.

6.9   *Additional side-effect management strategies*

Thunks and sagas are the most popular side-effect management tools around, but in the open source world, there's something for everyone. We'll discuss a few additional tools, but know that there are more options waiting for you to discover them.

6.9.1   *Asynchronous functions with async/await*

A feature introduced in ES7, async/await, has quickly found itself in many Redux codebases, often working in tandem with thunks. Using the feature is a natural step to take for those already comfortable with thunks. You'll notice the control flow feels similar to sagas, and that can be explained by the fact that async/await uses generators under the hood. See the following listing for an example within a thunk.

Listing 6.20   An async/await example

```
export function fetchTasks() {
    return async dispatch => {
        try {
```

> Adds the async keyword to the anonymous function

> One error handling strategy is to use a try/catch block.

```
      const { data } = await api.fetchTasks();
      dispatch(fetchTasksSucceeded(data));
    } catch (e) {
      dispatch(fetchTasksFailed(e));
    }
  }
}
```

> Uses the await keyword
> to block the function
> until the value returns

Why would you choose async/await? It's simple, powerful, and easy to learn. Why would you choose sagas? You need the functionality provided by the advanced features, the ease of testing is important to you, or maybe you prefer the paradigm.

6.9.2   *Handling promises with redux-promise*

The `redux-promise` library is another tool maintained by Redux co-creator, Andrew Clark. The premise is simple: whereas `redux-thunk` allows action creators to return functions, `redux-promise` allows action creators to return promises.

Also, like `redux-thunk`, `redux-promise` provides middleware that can be applied during the creation of the store. Several functional nuances exist for using promises over thunks, or both in tandem, but choosing is largely a matter of style preference. The package is available on GitHub at https://github.com/acdlite/redux-promise.

6.9.3   *redux-loop*

This library diverges from what you've learned so far about the Redux architecture. Ready for some rule-breaking? Using `redux-loop` permits side effects within reducers. Stressful, we know.

As you may recall, Redux draws inspiration from several sources, Elm among the most influential. Within the Elm architecture, reducers are powerful enough to handle synchronous and asynchronous state transitions. This is achieved by having the reducers describe not only the state that should update, but also the effects that cause it.

Redux, of course, didn't inherit this pattern from Elm. Redux can handle only synchronous transitions; all side effects must be resolved (by hand or by middleware) before they reach the reducers. However, the Elm effects pattern is available for use in Redux using `redux-loop`, a minimal port of the functionality. You can find the package on GitHub at https://github.com/redux-loop/redux-loop.

6.9.4   *redux-observable*

This package plays a similar role to `redux-saga` and even has kindred terminology. Instead of sagas, `redux-observable` has you create epics to handle side effects. Epics are implemented as middleware, like sagas, but instead of using generators to watch for new actions, you can leverage observables—functional reactive programming primitives. In English, epics can be used to transform a stream of actions into another stream of actions.

Using `redux-saga` and `redux-observable` are alternatives that accomplish roughly the same outcome. The latter is a popular choice for those already familiar with RxJS and functional reactive programming. One selling point for choosing epics over sagas is that the programming patterns learned can be carried over to other development environments. Rx ports exist in many other programming languages.

You have several options for handling complex side effects. The severity of the complexity will help you determine which tool is the right one for the job, but you'll probably develop favorites as you find strategies that make the most sense to you and your programming style.

The `redux-saga` tool is another option for your toolbelt. Certain folks will choose to replace all their thunks with sagas, while others will decide there's too much magic going on there. Again, you can still accomplish it all by using thunks. In practice, many applications succeed by finding a happy medium.

With `redux-saga` under your belt, you can confidently say you've got a handle on the messiest corners of Redux applications. You can move on to further optimizations elsewhere in the codebase by learning how to use selectors, such as `reselect`, in the next chapter.

Summary

- Thunks are sufficient for managing side effects of any size.
- Introducing sagas may help to tame especially complex side effects.
- Sagas are built using functions that can be paused and resumed, called generators.
- Sagas produce effects, descriptions of how to handle side effects.

Preparing data for components

This chapter covers

- Introducing selectors
- Organizing state in the store
- Using advanced selectors for deriving data
- Memoizing selectors with `reselect`

Our task management application, Parsnip, has everything it needs to be a successful production application, but there are still several optimizations that can be made to make the code more performant, better organized, and more maintainable. In this chapter, we'll explore selectors: functions used to compute derived data from the Redux store. Conveniently, the selector pattern manages to offer all three benefits.

Up to now, you've done a fine job of breaking down your code into manageable pieces by leveraging actions and reducers. Actions help model what is happening in the app; reducers allow you to apply updates to state in a centralized, testable way. Actions and reducers help in two more ways: they allow you to clean up your views (React components) by reducing the number of things the views are responsible for, and they help you decouple and modularize the different types of work happening in your application. Selectors may be slightly lesser known than actions and reducers, but as a software pattern, they offer similar benefits.

By the end of this chapter, you'll be ready to wield selectors in the battle against bloated and non-reusable React components.

7.1   *Decoupling Redux from React components*

We've covered the idea of decoupling concerns in previous chapters, particularly in relation to actions and reducers, but it's worth revisiting here as we prepare for a discussion about selectors. As a refresher, when you say things in a software system are coupled, you're talking about the relationships between them. If entity A relies on entity B to do its job, you can say that A and B are coupled. This, on its own, isn't necessarily a bad thing. After all, modern software systems are collections of different entities interacting to achieve a goal. In your application, those entities are actions, reducers, and components.

Where you can start to run into trouble is when different entities become too aware of, and reliant on, the implementation details of another entity. When this is the case, the entities are often referred to as being tightly coupled. You can figure out the degree to which components are coupled by thinking about what it will take to make a change to the system. If you update A, will you also have to make an update in B? If the answer is "yes," chances are you have entities that are tightly coupled, making maintenance more of a chore than it needs to be.

Decoupling has a few key benefits, namely, resilience to change and flexibility. When you have entities that have few responsibilities and don't know too much about the internals of other parts of the system, you can make changes with less fear of a ripple effect.

Flexibility is also a primary concern. Say you weren't using Redux for Parsnip, and the logic to create and update tasks was implemented directly within a React component. If you received new requirements to add that functionality elsewhere in the app (maybe in a modal or a new page), you'd likely have to shuffle around a good chunk of code to make sure the right props would be available to all components. By decoupling the tasks logic from React, you can reuse existing actions and reducers, with minimal to no impact on the components leveraging them.

If you agree that decoupling is something to shoot for, the good news is that you're already partway there. We've extracted a few major responsibilities out of the components with actions and reducers: the update logic and state management. If you're wondering if you can go further, making components even simpler and more flexible, you've come to the right place.

Another responsibility of your application architecture is to take application state from Redux and pass it to React via some plumbing code. React can then render the data received from the store to the page. On one hand, you could pass the entire Redux store to React and let the components figure out what they need. This could work for simpler cases, and might even be convenient and easy, but what if you need the same data in a different part of the app? Suddenly, you may need to duplicate logic that gets or transforms data from Redux. A better approach is to define more generic props for the components and extract out any logic to prepare data from Redux for React in one place.

What exactly are you decoupling in this case? You're decoupling the knowledge of the shape of the data in the Redux store from the React components that will eventually render that data. Nothing says that the React components you write need to know about Redux. You can, and most of the time should, write components in a way that's agnostic to the data source, allowing you to potentially use them in different configurations.

Maybe a day comes where you do a big store refactor. By keeping components generic, you need to update code in only one place—the plumbing code that connects Redux and React. Or maybe a day comes where you need to swap out Redux altogether. You can plug in existing components directly without requiring massive changes to the UI code.

We covered briefly in chapter 2 that at the highest level there are three things that make up a Redux application: Redux, React, and code that forms a bridge between them. In this chapter, we're mainly focused on the plumbing that connects React (the view) and Redux (the application state). Let's take another look at the high-level diagram (figure 7.1) that shows how Redux and React work together, focusing on the middle section, which provides the plumbing code.

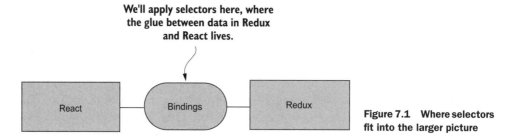

Figure 7.1 Where selectors fit into the larger picture

Certain components necessarily must interact with the Redux store and do so using the mapStateToProps function that gets passed into the connect function. Up until now, the mapStateToProps function hasn't needed to do much complex logic, so it acts mostly as a pass-through for data from Redux into React. We haven't drawn too much attention to it yet, but the goal of this chapter is to explore the ideas behind mapStateToProps, how to use it effectively, and how you can create reusable selector functions that ensure you need to do the same work only once.

The intention of the mapStateToProps function is to make it easy for even connected components to accept and render data passed to them. Instead of massaging or deriving data from the Redux store in the component, you typically reserve that role for the `mapStateToProps` function. In prior chapters, you saw how you could use `mapStateToProps` to effectively whitelist one or more slices of the Redux store that a connected component can read from.

Each slice of the Redux store is specified by what's sometimes called a transform. See the `mapStateToProps` function of the `App` component in listing 7.1 for an example of a transform. Thanks to the ES6 destructuring feature, the second line in the `map-StateToProps` function is effectively three transforms, one for each key: `tasks`, `isLoading`, and `error`. The implementation and outcome of these transforms are straightforward: for each key returned from the Redux store, make their data available to the component via props.

Listing 7.1 mapStateToProps - src/App.js

```
...
function mapStateToProps(state) {
  const { tasks, isLoading, error } = state.tasks;     ◁──── A transform of the Redux
  return { tasks, isLoading, error };                         store specifies which data
}                                                             to make available to the
...                                                           component.
```

That's roughly all that needs to be said about simple transforms. The remainder of this chapter will describe and discuss advanced transforms. These may be called transform functions, or more popularly, selectors.

7.2   *What are selectors?*

Selectors are functions that accept a state from the Redux store and compute data that will eventually be passed as props to React. Selectors are often thought of in terms of the `reselect` library, which you'll use later in the chapter, but any function that performs this role can be considered a selector. They're pure functions, meaning they don't produce any side effects. And like all pure functions, they're easy to write and maintain. This also makes them easy to memoize, an optimization you can apply which will store the result of each computation based on the arguments passed into a selector. More on that later when we get to `reselect`.

Let's look again at your overall architecture, seen in figure 7.2. Here you can see in greater detail where selectors fit into your architecture. Data comes out of the store, you run it through selectors, and the view (React, in your case) accepts selector output and takes care of any rendering.

Selectors, like all programming concepts, exist to solve a problem. The problem: without selectors, components would be coupled directly to the shape of the Redux store. If the structure of the store changes, you must update every component that may have relied on that structure.

Your end goal is to write your React components in a way that if the Redux structure changes, you won't need to update any of the components as a result. You lock in an interface at the component level and let code upstream take care of the changing

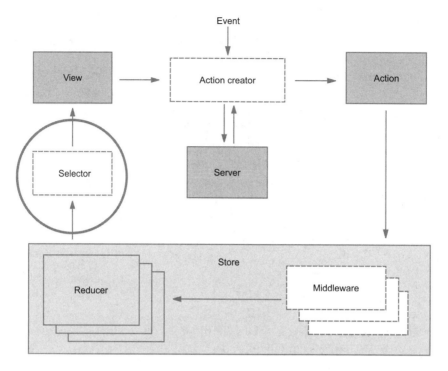

Figure 7.2   Selectors are optional entities that sit between the Redux store and components.

shape of the data. Not only do you not have to update components in response to changes in Redux, but it also means your components are generic enough to be used in different contexts. This might not be immediately relevant for you, but as applications grow, it can make a big difference.

To give you an idea of a real-world example, we once ran into this problem during a large Backbone refactor. Far too many components accepted Backbone models directly as props and operated on the models to get the data they needed to render something to the page. When you started to move away from Backbone, a huge effort to update each affected component was necessary. What was the lesson? If we'd written our components to accept simpler data types such as strings, numbers, and objects, we'd have saved a colossal effort because we'd have needed to update only the plumbing that connected the source of the data to the components.

7.3   *Implementing search*

The transforms used in Parsnip so far have been relatively straightforward. You have a single `mapStateToProps` function that takes care of bridging the gap between Redux and React. The value of introducing selectors becomes clearer when a more complicated feature necessitates doing so.

In this section, we'll introduce a new feature, search, to add complexity and better illustrate the point. Search is a classic example because it allows us to demonstrate how selectors are meant to compute derived data based on several inputs from the Redux store. As a reminder, when we discuss derived data, we're typically referring to any calculation or mutation of Redux state for displaying the data in a React component.

Coming up, you're going to add a text input where a user can type a search term and expect to have the tasks on the page filter to display only those with titles that match the search input. See figure 7.3 for a screenshot of the final result.

Figure 7.3 A screenshot of Parsnip with the completed search feature

One of the biggest advantages of selectors is they allow you to store the minimal possible state representation in Redux. For example, there's nothing stopping you from storing the list of filtered tasks directly in the store. Whenever the filter action is dispatched, you can apply the filter directly in the reducer and store the result in a key such as `filteredTasks`, and then pass that directly to React. You'd end up with a structure that looks something like the following listing.

Listing 7.2 filteredTasks persisted in Redux

```
{
  tasks: [
    {id: 1, title: 'foo'},
    {id: 2, title: 'bar'},
  ],
  filteredTasks: [
    {id: 1, title: 'foo'},
  ],
  searchText: 'foo',
}
```

Even an implementation like this hits two of your goals:

- Because the filter is applied directly in a reducer, the logic exists in only one place.
- Because the result is stored directly in the state tree, the value won't be recomputed after every render.

But something feels off about this implementation. The major issue is that you now have a task that's denormalized, meaning the same representation exists in multiple places. What happens if you want to edit a task? Now you have to make sure you find every reference in the state tree and update it accordingly, instead of updating one canonical representation.

> **TIP**   One rule of thumb for Redux is to try and always store a minimal representation of state. Selectors can be used to compute derived data like a filtered list of tasks.

Every new piece of data you add to the store is a piece of data you're now responsible for updating and keeping in sync. Or, it's one more place for bugs to creep in if that data ever becomes stale. More data in Redux, more problems.

Having written a few features, do you have a sense of how to implement this search functionality? As you've done in prior chapters, you'll start by fleshing out the UI, then move on to wiring up the Redux functionality. This is particularly relevant for you now, because one of your big goals is to have your components accept generic data as props and not have direct knowledge of Redux or the shape of the store. By starting from the outside in and defining the components first, you can decide up front what kind of interface you want. This will help clarify the kinds of selectors you eventually write to hook up real data to the components.

7.3.1   *Scaffolding out the UI*

Remember, starting with the UI helps you understand what you'll need from Redux and to decouple the views from the application logic. You can declare an interface (props) that makes sense from the component's perspective, without taking anything Redux-specific into consideration.

For this feature, little code is required to get a scaffold of the UI up. Ultimately, all that's required is a text input element. The ideal user experience is for visible tasks to update on each new character typed in the search field. No button is necessary to initiate the search.

Let's suppose that designs are ready and you've received marching orders from the product manager that the search field needs to be in the header, near the New Task button. You're tasked with this unit of work. Where do you jump in?

A reasonable starting point is to navigate to the TasksPage component and insert a text input above the New Task button. A good question to ask is, "Should this search form be its own component?" Maybe. This decision-making process is more of an art than a science. As a rule of thumb, we tend to prototype the UI for smaller features in an existing component before concluding whether it makes sense to refactor out into another component.

Many factors play into this decision. If a group of elements is a good candidate for reuse elsewhere in the app, for example, then you'll be much quicker to promote those elements to their own component. Don't panic if this decision-making process feels unnatural. Component composition is a fundamental React skill that takes time to hone.

Within the `TasksPage` component, add an input field alongside the New Task button. Because you'll want to perform the task filtering on every character added to or removed from the input, you're going to want to leverage the `onChange` callback. For now, that callback will log out the value of input.

In the `TasksPage` component, you added an input element with an `onChange` callback. This UI makes clear what the next required steps are. You want your search term to bubble up to the connected parent component, `App`, and ultimately affect which tasks are displayed, as shown in the following listing.

Listing 7.3 Adding the search input – src/components/TasksPage.js

```
...
onSearch = e => {                                          On every character
  console.log('search term', e.target.value);             typed, this callback
};                                                         will execute.

render() {
  if (this.props.isLoading) {
    return <div className="tasks-loading">Loading...</div>;
  }

  return (
    <div className="tasks">
      <div className="tasks-header">
        <input
          onChange={this.onSearch}                         A text input
          type="text"                                      captures search
          placeholder="Search..."                          terms.
        />

        <button className="button button-default"
  ➥ onClick={this.toggleForm}>
          + New task
        </button>
      </div>
...
```

We don't make a habit of including styles, but let's also add a few styles to ensure the text input appears in the top left of the page, as shown in the following listing.

Listing 7.4   Adding styles – src/index.css

```
...
.tasks-header {
  font-size: 18px;
  margin-bottom: 20px;
  text-align: right;
  display: flex;
  justify-content: space-between;
}
...
```

Adding flex and ensuring that the search input and the New Task button will appear at the top-left and top-right of the page, respectively

The next question you're confronted with is whether to handle the functionality within local state or Redux state. Can the filtering be handled within local state? If so, should it be? What do you think?

7.3.2   *Local state versus Redux state*

It's a good exercise to consider what functionality can and should be handled by local state versus Redux state. To answer the first question posed: it's absolutely possible to filter tasks using a search term that is stored in local state. The second question is a more philosophical one: Should you handle it with local state? For an example implementation, see the following listing. In this example, searchTerm is stored in local state and used with a regular expression to pare down all tasks to those that match the term.

Listing 7.5   Search with local component state – src/components/TasksPage.js

```
...
renderTaskLists() {
  const { onStatusChange, tasks } = this.props;

  const filteredTasks = tasks.filter(task => {
    return task.title.match(new RegExp(this.state.searchTerm, 'i'));
  });

  return TASK_STATUSES.map(status => {
    const statusTasks = filteredTasks.filter(task => task.status ===
  status);
    return (
      <TaskList
        key={status}
        status={status}
        tasks={statusTasks}
        onStatusChange={onStatusChange}
      />
    );
  });
}
```

Before displaying tasks, filter down to those that match the search term.

Keeps track of the searchTerm in the local state of the App component

That sure isn't much code. Is there any reason not to go this route? You can make the argument for using Redux state for this feature on a couple of grounds. First, using local state and requiring the component to calculate which tasks it should render couples the logic to the component. Remember, separating logic from the views is a major perk of using Redux. Second, there are performance gains to be had by using Redux and selector functions. You'll get into the details of this point later in the chapter.

The cost of implementing the feature using Redux state is the usual suspect: more boilerplate code. This is a tradeoff we've regularly examined throughout the book. Often, a little more code can result in an application that's easier to reason about and maintain.

7.3.3   Dispatching a filter action

As we've discussed, the first thing you'll wire up is the invoking of an action creator, which eventually will dispatch an action. Because `TasksPage` isn't a connected component, the dispatching will have to take place in its parent component, `App`. `App` will pass a callback to `TasksPage` to dispatch an action every time a character is added to or deleted from the search field. See the following listing for the additions to the `App` component.

> **Listing 7.6   Adding onSearch to App – src/App.js**

```
...
import { createTask, editTask, fetchTasks, filterTasks } from './actions';   ◁──┐
                                                          Imports the soon-to-be-created
class App extends Component {                                action creator, filterTasks
  ...
  onSearch = searchTerm => {
    this.props.dispatch(filterTasks(searchTerm));   ◁──┐  A callback invokes
  };                                                    │  the action creator.
  render() {
    return (
      <div className="container">
        {this.props.error && <FlashMessage message={this.props.error} />}
        <div className="main-content">
          <TasksPage
            tasks={this.props.tasks}
            onCreateTask={this.onCreateTask}
            onSearch={this.onSearch}              ◁──┐  Passes the callback
            onStatusChange={this.onStatusChange}     │  down to the component
            isLoading={this.props.isLoading}         │  with the search field
          />
        </div>
      </div>
    );
  }
}
...
```

Passing callbacks to a child component is something you've done a few times now, so nothing about this listing should be surprising. To finish out the views' portion of the

Redux workflow, you need a final tweak to the TasksPage component, as shown in the following listing. Instead of logging out the search term, execute the onSearch callback you wrote in the previous listing.

Listing 7.7 Using the onSearch prop – src/components/TasksPage.js

```
...
onSearch = e => {                              Trades out the console
 this.props.onSearch(e.target.value);    ◁—   log for the callback
};                                            execution
...
```

You're finished with the components for now. Refreshing the application in your browser will result in an error: `'./actions' does not contain an export named 'filterTasks'`. That's handy. It describes exactly where to direct your attention next: you need to implement the filterTasks action creator.

This is a good crossroads to pause at and plan ahead. What should happen inside this new filterTasks action creator? Will you need to use a thunk and handle any asynchronous activity? Your earlier local state exercise provides plenty of insight into these answers. No asynchronous activity was required to implement task filtering then, so you can expect the same here. All the Redux store needs to keep track of is the search term, so you're back in synchronous territory. See the following listing for the result in the actions file.

Listing 7.8 Adding a new action creator – src/actions/index.js

```
...                                                    Exports the new
export function filterTasks(searchTerm) {       ◁——    action creator
 return { type: 'FILTER_TASKS', payload: { searchTerm } };   ◁—┐
}                                                              Returns an
...                                                            action with the
                                                              search term
```

The application should compile now. Test the feature by typing a few characters into the search field. With your Redux DevTools open, you should see whether you've followed along correctly by the appearance of the FILTER_TASKS actions being logged out in the Inspector Monitor. See figure 7.4.

In this example, you typed "red" into the search field with the intention of displaying only tasks that include "Redux" in the title. An action is fired for each of the three characters you typed, as you can see in the figure. As you'd expect, the value of searchTerm is the complete contents of the search field after each change. The first action's searchTerm is r, the second's is re, and it's red in the final action.

With this success indicator, you can begin to consider the receiving end of actions. As it stands, no reducers are listening for FILTER_TASKS actions, so they float through without affecting the application. In the next section, we'll remedy that.

The "Action" tab
displays the content of
each action dispatched.

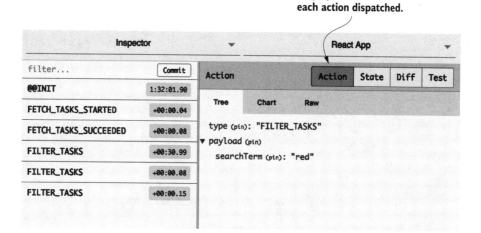

Figure 7.4   Each new character produces a new action logged by the Redux DevTools.

7.3.4   Handling filter actions in a reducer

Whenever handling a new action type, you should ask yourself if it makes sense to handle the action in an existing reducer or in a new reducer. Again, each reducer is meant to handle a logical domain or grouping of actions. There may be a case to make for introducing a new reducer that handles global UI concerns. Chapter 8 explores this topic more deeply.

In this case, the tasks reducer is still an appropriate place to handle an action that filters tasks. See the following listing for an example implementation. You'll augment the initialState and add one more case statement to the body of the reducer.

Listing 7.9   Adding update logic to the tasks reducer – src/reducers/index.js

```
const initialState = {
 tasks: [],
 isLoading: false,
 error: null,              Adds blank searchTerm
 searchTerm: ''           to the initialState
};

export default function tasks(state = initialState, action) {    Has the reducer
 switch (action.type) {                                          listen for the new
 ...                                                             action type
 case 'FILTER_TASKS': {
   return { ...state, searchTerm: action.payload.searchTerm };
 }
 ...                        Updates the searchTerm upon
}                           receiving the appropriate action
```

Now, whenever a character is added to that search field, a change in the Redux store will result. You can confirm this by observing the Redux DevTools when you type "red" in the input again. See figure 7.5.

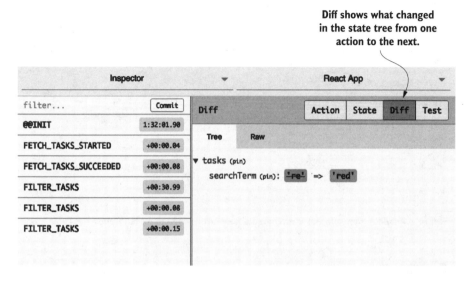

Diff shows what changed in the state tree from one action to the next.

Figure 7.5   The state Diff indicates that Redux state is updating as a result of the action.

Great! That's the whole Redux workflow playing nicely together. The Diff tab in the Inspector Monitor reveals that the `searchTerm` within the `tasks` key is updated after each `FILTER_TASKS` action. In the next section, we'll introduce a selector function and finish implementing the task filter.

7.3.5   *Writing your first selector*

Thinking back to the local state example implementation, the Redux store was unaware of the search term, so the filtering had to be done in the component. The advantage of using Redux is that you can complete the filtering before the component knows it's happened. All it has to do is accept and render whatever list of tasks you provide it.

The opportunity to derive data before making it available to a connected component is in the `mapStateToProps` function. Recall that `mapStateToProps` is where you add any plumbing code that bridges the gap between data in Redux and data that ultimately makes it into the component tree as props. It's where selectors in general should be applied (figure 7.6).

You don't want the components to have to accept a list of tasks and a search term. Instead, you want to treat this as the end of the line for certain details about the state of our application, and let the components receive more generic data.

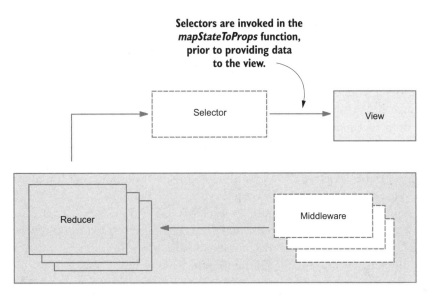

Selectors are invoked in the
mapStateToProps function,
prior to providing data
to the view.

Selector

View

Reducer

Middleware

Figure 7.6 Selectors calculate data required by the view.

In listing 7.10, you derive the list of tasks before making them available as props in the App component. The filtering and matching based on a regular expression is effectively the same implementation you used the first time around with local state. The match function takes a regular expression as the first argument and any modifiers as the second. In this case, i makes the matching case-insensitive. Nothing else in the App component needs to change.

Listing 7.10 Applying the filter in mapStateToProps – src/App.js

```
...
function mapStateToProps(state) {
 const { isLoading, error, searchTerm } = state.tasks;

 const tasks = state.tasks.tasks.filter(task => {
   return task.title.match(new RegExp(searchTerm, 'i'));
 });

 return { tasks, isLoading, error };
}
...
```

> **Removes tasks from the import and adds searchTerm**

> **Creates a new tasks variable that is a collection of filtered tasks**

This is decoupling in action. Because you declared a boundary between Redux and React, you can change how the data is transformed before it's passed into the component tree without requiring any changes to the components themselves. By implementing logic in a middleman function, mapStateToProps, you've allowed your components to be more generic and flexible. They know only what they need to do their job, and what they don't know can't hurt them. They render whichever tasks they're given and don't particularly care, or need to care, that a filter has been applied.

Technically, you've written a selector! The tasks made available using props are now derived from the search term and the list of all tasks. As we've discussed, there's much to like about this implementation. Components are decoupled from presentation logic and are easier to test.

Although it's an improvement, there are more optimizations to do. What if you needed half a dozen selector functions for one component? The mapStateToProps function could balloon to become as large as the component itself. What if you wanted to reuse selectors across multiple connected components? It makes no sense to write the same logic for each component.

A popular convention is to extract selectors out of the mapStateToProps function and into separate, reusable selector functions. Typically, you'll find these selectors collocated in the reducer file that best fits its domain. In the following listing, you're relocating the selector into the file containing the tasks reducer.

Listing 7.11 Moving filter logic into the tasks reducer – src/reducers/index.js

```
...
export function getFilteredTasks(tasks, searchTerm) {      Exports the generalized
  return tasks.filter(task => {                            selector function
    return task.title.match(new RegExp(searchTerm, 'i'));  Tweaks tasks to use
  });                                                       those passed in as
}                                                           an argument
```

Now, getFilteredTasks can be imported and used more than once, if the need arises. Conveniently, it can also be tested in isolation. Let's import it in the App component and finish the refactor in the following listing.

Listing 7.12 Importing and using the selector – src/App.js

```
...
import { getFilteredTasks } from './reducers/';           Imports the selector
...                                                        from the reducer
function mapStateToProps(state) {
  const { tasks, isLoading, error, searchTerm } = state.tasks;   Adds tasks back to
                                                                 the list of imports
  return { tasks: getFilteredTasks(tasks, searchTerm), isLoading, error };
}
```

Uses the selector to determine which
tasks to provide to the component

This refactor cleans up the mapStateToProps function by abstracting selectors into more appropriate places. You may be tempted to ask why selectors are placed in reducer files. It's a convention that you can choose to follow if you want. Selectors will generally be used in the domain of one reducer, but this may not always be the case. Remember, the default export of the reducer file is, of course, the reducer itself. Importing selectors from the same file requires the curly brackets to specify the specific export.

7.4   *Introducing reselect*

The `getFilteredTasks` is our first proper selector, and as far as functionality, it's perfectly fine as is. It does exactly what you want a selector to do: it takes one or more pieces of state from the Redux store and computes a value that you intend to pass directly to your React component tree. A popular library called `reselect` can be used for writing selectors; it also provides a few key benefits: memoization and composability. If you decide to use selectors in any kind of significant way in your apps, it's worth looking at `reselect` and getting to know its toolset.

7.4.1   *Reselect and memoization*

Memoization is another one of those terms in software that sounds more complicated than it is. In short, memoization is when a function stores the results of past computations and uses them for future calls. Let's use a simple `double` function as an example. The `double` takes a single number as an argument, and returns the value multiplied by two. Let's call the function a few times in the following listing. This code won't be part of Parsnip, so you can follow along in an interactive console by typing `node` in a terminal window or by using the JavaScript console in your browser's dev tools.

Listing 7.13   Exploring memoization

```
function double(x) {
   return x * 2;
}

double(2)

double(2)
```

The first call to add runs the computation and returns 4.

The second call to add reruns the computation and returns the same result.

The `double` is a pure function, meaning it accepts only a value and returns a value, producing no side effects. You also know that pure functions always return the same result given the same arguments. Can you use this to your advantage? You sure can. Look at listing 7.14.

Why don't you store the results of past computations and use them if `double` is called with the same arguments multiple times?

Listing 7.14   Adding memoization to double

```
const memoized = {};

function double(x) {
   if (memoized[x]) {
     console.log('Returning memoized value!');
     return memoized[x];
   }
```

Creates an object to store the result of each function call

When the function runs, first check whether the value has already been computed.

```
    console.log('No memoized value found, running computation and saving')   ◁─┐
    const result = x * 2;
    memoized[x] = result;                              If the value hasn't been computed,
                                                       run the computation and store the
    return result;                                                result for future use.
}

double(2);
double(2);
```

Figure 7.7 is what you should see as far as console output.

```
>  double(2)
   No memoized value found, running computation and saving
◁  4
>  double(2)
   Returning memoized value!
◁  4
```

Figure 7.7 Console output for the double function

Notice how you skipped running x * 2 the second time around? This is the heart of memoization. Memoization, as it's implemented in reselect, is slightly more complicated, but the core ideas are the same. In short

- When a function is called, check whether the function has been called with these arguments.
- If so, use the stored value.
- If not, run the computation and store the value for future use.

It might not make much of a difference with a function that takes a number and doubles it, but for more expensive operations, it can make a huge difference. Using reselect gives you this functionality out of the box for free.

7.4.2 Reselect and composition

Composition is the other major selling point of reselect. It means that selectors created with reselect can be chained together. The output of one selector can be used as an input to another. This is best demonstrated with a real example, so let's jump right into adding reselect to Parsnip and you can see selector composition in action.

7.5 Implementing reselect

Right now, you have a getFilteredTasks selector that takes two arguments: a list of tasks, and a search term. It filters the list of tasks using the search term and returns the result. The mapStateToProps is still doing a few more things that you can extract into selectors:

- Getting the list of tasks
- Getting the visibility filter

You want to extract as much as you can from mapStateToProps. If logic is implemented in mapStateToProps, it's "trapped" in a sense. If you need that logic elsewhere in your application, you have to go through the trouble of extracting as you add a new feature. It's always ideal to affect only the components directly relevant to whatever feature or change you're trying to implement, so you can do work upfront to make Parsnip slightly more modular. Here's a high-level look at what you'll do:

- Create two new selectors, getTasks and getSearchTerm.
- Update getFilteredTasks to be a reselect selector using the createSelector function.
- Use getTasks and getSearchTerm as inputs to getFilteredTasks.

First, let's start by defining your desired API by adjusting the code in mapStateToProps in App. All you're doing is modifying the arguments being passed to getFilteredTasks, as shown in the following listing. We'll leave it up to the selector to figure out where tasks and the search term live within the Redux store.

Listing 7.15 Updating mapStateToProps – src/App.js

```
...
function mapStateToProps(state) {
  const { isLoading, error } = state.tasks;

  return { tasks: getFilteredTasks(state), isLoading, error };   ⟵  Changes the arguments for getFilteredTasks
}
```

If you were to ever connect another component that needs a list of the filtered tasks, it wouldn't have to know tasks are available at state.tasks.tasks and the search term is available at state.tasks.searchTerm. You centralized that logic, making sure it doesn't leak out of getFilteredTasks.

Next, let's take a first look at how we'd use reselect. First, install the package:

```
npm install reselect
```

In the reducer, import the package, then create the getTasks and getSearchTerm selectors. Next, create a memoized getFilteredTasks selector via the createSelector function provided by reselect. This ensures that getFilteredTasks won't recompute the list of tasks when it receives the same arguments, as shown in the following listing.

Listing 7.16 Creating new selectors – src/reducers/index.js

```
import { createSelector } from 'reselect';   ⟵  Imports createSelector, which creates a memoized selector
...
const getTasks = state => state.tasks.tasks;   ⟵  Adds a selector for tasks
const getSearchTerm = state => state.tasks.searchTerm;   ⟵  Adds a selector for the search term
```

```
export const getFilteredTasks = createSelector(     ◁─┐  Changes getFilteredTasks
  [getTasks, getSearchTerm],                           │  to be a memoized selector
  (tasks, searchTerm) => {
    return tasks.filter(task => task.title.match(new RegExp(searchTerm,
➡ 'i')));
  },
);
```

Both getTasks and getSearchTerm are known as input selectors. They aren't memo-
rized; they're simple selectors intended to be used as inputs to other memoized
selectors. The getFilteredTasks is a memoized selector, created using the create-
Selector function. The createSelector takes two arguments: an array of input selectors, and a transform function. The transform function's arguments will be the result
of each input selector.

The goal is to run only the transform function when the result of the input selectors
changes. Remember that because the transform function is pure, you can safely store
the result of previous calls and use those results on subsequent calls. Input selectors
declare which slices of the Redux store a memoized selector cares about. If the full list of
tasks changes, or the search term changes, you want to compute a new result. Conversely, you want to avoid recalculating state unnecessarily, whenever possible.

Remember when we mentioned composition as a major benefit of reselect? This
is selector composition in action. Use getTasks and getSearchTerm as inputs to get-
FilteredTasks, and you're completely free to use them as input to other selectors as
well. You can even use getFilteredTasks as input to other selectors.

7.6   *Exercise*

Feeling good about selectors? One more task that components are currently responsible for seems like a good candidate for a selector. Currently, you group tasks by status
when you render them (unstarted, in-progress, or completed), with a column for each
status. If you recall, you're doing that work in the TasksPage component. To jog your
memory, look at the following listing.

Listing 7.17   Grouping tasks by status – src/components/TaskPage.js

```
renderTaskLists() {
  const { onStatusChange, tasks } = this.props;

  return TASK_STATUSES.map(status => {
    const statusTasks = tasks.filter(task => task.status === status);
    return (
      <TaskList
        key={status}
        status={status}
        tasks={statusTasks}
        onStatusChange={onStatusChange}
      />
    );
  });
}
```

The filtering of tasks seems like a good example of logic you can extract from a component into a selector. What if you decide to build out a new UI, where tasks are grouped in a list format instead of by columns? It's more convenient to have the component accept a pre-grouped list of tasks as a prop, where the keys are each status, mapped to a list of tasks. That data structure might look something like the following listing.

Listing 7.18 Grouped tasks

```
{
  'Unstarted': [...],
  'In Progress': [...],
  'Completed': [...]
}
```

Using what you've learned so far in the chapter, can you take a stab at a pre-filtered task implementation using one or more selectors?

7.7 Solution

Let's outline a few steps you can take to reach your goal:

- Update the component to expect a pre-grouped list of tasks instead of a flat list.
- Create a new selector in `src/reducers/index.js` that takes care of grouping the tasks by status.
- Import and use this selector in `mapStateToProps` in the `App` component.

Starting again from the outside in with the UI, let's update src/TasksPage.js to use the new expected structure. You'll remove a few key pieces of logic from the component:

- The `TASK_STATUSES` constant. The component doesn't need to know or care about the types of statuses, because it knows to render a column for each. This removes a dependency and makes the component easier to test.
- The logic for getting all tasks given a specific status. Again, you render whatever data you get.

Listing 7.19 Updating task rendering – src/components/TasksPage.js

```
...
renderTaskLists() {
    const { onStatusChange, tasks } = this.props;

    return Object.keys(tasks).map(status => {      ⟵─┐ Iterates over each
      const tasksByStatus = tasks[status];              │ status in the object
      return (
        <TaskList
          key={status}
          status={status}                          ┌─ For each status, render a
          tasks={tasksByStatus}               ⟵──┤  TaskList component with
          onStatusChange={onStatusChange}          └─ the appropriate tasks.
        />
```

```
    );
  });
}
...
```

Let's also create a new home for the TASK_STATUSES constant, as shown in the following listing. It's common to maintain a module or set of modules for application-wide constants, so create a new constants/ directory, and in it, create a file named index.js.

Listing 7.20   Create a new constants module – src/constants/index.js

```
export const TASK_STATUSES = ['Unstarted', 'In Progress', 'Completed'];
```

Next let's add a new getGroupedAndFilteredTasks selector, and use it within the mapStateToProps function in App (listings 7.21 and 7.22).

Listing 7.21   Creating the new selector – src/reducers/index.js

```
import { TASK_STATUSES } from '../constants';

...

export const getGroupedAndFilteredTasks = createSelector(  ⟵─┘ Creates the new selector
  [getFilteredTasks],                              ⟵─ Uses the result of another
  tasks => {                                           selector, getFilteredTasks,
    const grouped = {};                                 as an input

    TASK_STATUSES.forEach(status => {
      grouped[status] = tasks.filter(task => task.status === status);
    });

    return grouped;
  },
);
```

Builds up the object with each status as a key

Listing 7.22   Importing and using the new selector – src/App.js

```
...

import { getGroupedAndFilteredTasks } from './reducers/';  ⟵─┘ Imports the new selector

...
function mapStateToProps(state) {                          Uses the selector to
  const { isLoading, error } = state.tasks;                populate the tasks prop

  return { tasks: getGroupedAndFilteredTasks(state), isLoading, error };  ⟵─┘
}
```

The most noteworthy thing you did here was use the existing memoized selector getFilteredTasks as an input selector to the newly created getGroupedAndFilteredTasks. Selector composition in action!

Selectors play an important role in optimizing a Redux application. They prevent business logic from piling up inside components and boost performance by forgoing unnecessary renders via memoization.

The next chapter is heavily intertwined with the content of this chapter. Using selectors often has the biggest payoff when used with normalized data. Up next, we'll discuss and implement a normalized Redux store.

Summary

In this chapter you learned the following:

- The philosophy of decoupling logic from components
- Additional advantages of using Redux state over local state
- The role selectors play and how to implement them
- How to leverage `reselect` to gain clarity and performance when computing deriving data

Structuring a Redux store

8

This chapter covers

- Structuring relational data in Redux
- Learning the pros and cons of nested data versus normalized data
- Using the normalizr package
- Organizing different types of state within Redux

Parsnip is built using sound Redux fundamentals, but the app's data requirements up to this point are simple. You have a single tasks resource, meaning you haven't had any opportunities to deal with relational data. That's what this chapter is for! You'll double the number of resources in the app (from one to two!) by adding the concept of projects to Parsnip, meaning tasks will belong to a project. You'll explore the pros and cons of two popular strategies for structuring relational data: nesting and normalization.

This is one of the hottest topics for debate in the Redux community. For better or worse, the library offers no restrictions to how you organize data within the store. Redux provides the tools to store and update data and leaves it up to you to decide the shape of that data. The good news is that over time, and after no short period of trial and error, best practices started to emerge. One strategy emerged as a clear winner: normalization. It's not a concept that's unique to Redux, but you'll look at how to normalize data in Parsnip and the benefits normalization provides.

When you only had one resource, tasks, organizing the data wasn't a question you had to labor over. With the addition of projects, that changes. What's the most efficient way to store the data? Can you stick with one reducer or should you use multiple reducers? What strategy will make the data easier to update? What if you have duplicate data? Chapter 8 holds the answers to these questions and many more.

8.1 How should I store data in Redux?

The question of how and what to store in Redux surfaces regularly in the community. As usual, the answer varies, depending on whom you ask. Before you dig into the options, it's worth remembering that Redux doesn't necessarily care which strategy you decide on. If your data fits in an object, it can go in the Redux store. It's up to you to decide how to maintain order within that object.

> **NOTE** You may wonder if there's a limit to what you can keep in the Redux store. Official documentation strongly recommends storing only serializable primitives, objects, and arrays. Doing so guarantees the reliable use of surrounding tools, such as the Redux DevTools. If you'd like to handle a unique use case by storing non-serializable data in Redux, you're free to do so at your own peril. This discussion can be found in the documentation at http://redux .js.org/docs/faq/OrganizingState.html#can-i-put-functions-promises-or-other -non-serializable-items-in-my-store-state.

Up to now you've chosen a simple and common pattern for storing the task-related data currently in your system. You have one reducer which has a list of task objects, along with metadata: `isLoading` and `error`. These specific property names aren't significant; you may see many variations of them in the wild. You also introduced a `searchTerm` key in the last chapter to facilitate a filter feature.

With this pattern, the reducers (top-level state keys) tend to mimic a RESTful API philosophy. You can generally expect the `tasks` key to contain the data required to populate a tasks index page. Conversely, if you had a task show page, it would likely pull its data from a `task` (singular) reducer.

Having a single tasks reducer makes sense for Parsnip in its current state. Within connected components, you can easily read and display the tasks by referencing the attributes within the top-level `tasks` key. Parsnip is a small application, but this pattern scales efficiently, too. As each new domain is introduced to Parsnip, a new reducer is added to the store and contains its own resource data and metadata. If you decide you want to render a list of users, you can as easily introduce a `users` reducer that manages an array of users and metadata.

It's not so difficult to work with a Redux store like this, but things can start to get hairy once you introduce relationships between resources. Let's use Parsnip and projects as an example. The application may contain many projects, and each project may contain many tasks. How should you represent the relationship between projects and tasks in the Redux store?

As a starting point, let's consider the response from the server. If you make a GET request to /projects/1, at a minimum, you can probably expect to receive an ID, a project name, and a list of tasks associated with the project, as shown in the following listing.

Listing 8.1   Example API response

```
{
 id: 1,
 title: 'Short-Term Goals',
 tasks: [
   { id: 3, title: 'Learn Redux' },
   { id: 5, title: 'Defend shuffleboard world championship title' },
 ],
}
```

Having received this payload from a successful GET request, the next logical thing to do is stuff it into a project reducer, right? When viewing a project, you can iterate through and render each of its tasks. The entirety of the store may look something like this example.

Listing 8.2   An example Redux store with projects and tasks

```
{
  project: {
    id: 1,
    title: 'Short-Term Goals',
    tasks: [
      { id: 3, title: 'Learn Redux' },
      { id: 5, title: 'Defend shuffleboard world championship title' },
    ],
    isLoading: false,
    error: null,
    searchTerm: '',
  },
}
```

Not so fast. This pattern has a couple of shortcomings. First, your React components that render task data may require safeguards. Referencing nested data, such as task titles in this instance, requires that each of the parent keys exist. In similar scenarios, you may find yourself needing to guard against the nonexistence of parent keys.

What would it take to update a task? You now have to deal with tasks being nested one level deep, which requires you to navigate through a project object.

Managing one layer of nesting is generally manageable, but what happens when you want to list the user that each task is assigned to? The problem only worsens. See the following listing for the new Redux state.

Listing 8.3   Adding a user to each task

```
{
  project: {
    id: 1,
    title: 'Short-Term Goals',
    tasks: [
      {
        id: 5,
        title: 'Learn Redux',
        user: {
          id: 1,
          name: 'Richard Roe',
        }
      },
    ],
    isLoading: false,
    error: null,
    searchTerm: '',
  }
}
```

You haven't yet touched on the most egregious shortcoming of this pattern: duplicate data. If Richard is assigned to three different tasks, his user data appears in the state three times. If you want to update Richard's name to John, that user object needs to be updated in three locations. Not ideal. What if you could treat tasks and projects more like you would in a relational database? You could store tasks and projects separately but use foreign key IDs to maintain any relationships. Enter normalization, which prescribes exactly that.

8.2   *An introduction to normalized data*

Normalization can also be thought of as flattening a nested data structure. In a flat hierarchy, each domain receives its own top-level state property. Tasks and projects can be managed independently rather than as children of projects, and object IDs can be used to express relationships. The data would then be considered normalized, and this type of architecture is the recommendation found in the Redux documentation at http://redux.js.org/docs/faq/OrganizingState.html#how-do-i-organize-nested-or -duplicate-data-in-my-state.

What does this flat Redux store look like? It resembles a relational database architecture, with a table for each resource type. As discussed, projects and tasks each get a top-level key in the store, and relationships are linkable by foreign keys. You know which tasks belong to which projects, because each task contains a `projectId`. Here's an example of what a normalized store with projects and tasks looks like.

Listing 8.4   A normalized Redux store

```
{
  projects: {
```

```
    items: {                                  ⊳──┐ Resources are stored in
      '1': {                                       │ an object keyed by ID,
        id: 1,                                      │ instead of in an array.
        name: 'Short-Term Goals',
        tasks: [ 1, 3 ]          ⊲──┐
      },                             │ Each project has a list of task
      '2': {                         │ IDs, which can be used to
        id: 2,                       │ reference objects in another
        name: 'Long-Term Goals',    │ part of the store.
        tasks: [ 2 ]       ⊲──┘
      }
    },
    isLoading: false,
    error: null
  },
  tasks: {
    items: {
      '1': { id: 1, projectId: 1, … },
      '2': { id: 2, projectId: 2, … },
      '3': { id: 3, projectId: 1, … },
    },
    isLoading: false,
    error: null
  },
}
```

Projects and tasks are now stored in an object and keyed by ID, instead of an array. This makes any future lookups much less of a chore. Say you're updating a task: instead of looping over the entire array until you find the correct task, you can find the task immediately via its ID. Instead of nesting tasks within their respective projects, you now maintain relationships using a tasks array on each project, which stores an array of associated task IDs.

You'll find a few key benefits with normalized data that you'll explore over the course of the chapter:

- Reduced duplication. What if you allow tasks to belong to more than one project? With a nested structure, you'd wind up with multiple representations of a single object. To update a single task, you now must hunt down every individual representation of that task.
- Easier update logic. Instead of digging through nested objects, a normalized flat structure means you have to work only one level deep.
- Performance. With tasks in a totally separate section of the state tree, you can update them without triggering updates in unrelated parts of the store.

The decision to nest or normalize data depends on the situation. You'd typically opt to normalize your data in Redux. But it's not an open-and-shut case. You'll start implementing projects using nested data to get a sense of the benefits and costs.

8.3 Implementing projects with nested data

With all this talk around projects and actions, it's finally time to implement them and see what our store might look like beyond a single tasks reducer. Again, you chose to add projects because it means you now have relational data to manage. Instead of having a standalone tasks resource, tasks now belong to projects.

As far as user-facing changes, you'll add a new drop-down menu where users can choose between projects. Each task will belong to a project. When a user chooses a new project, you'll render the corresponding list of tasks. An example of what the UI might look like is shown in figure 8.1.

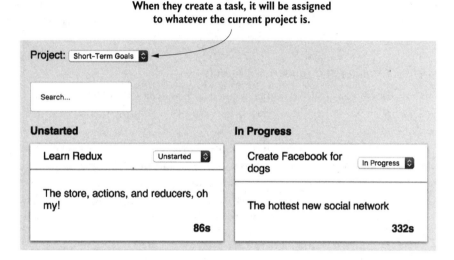

Figure 8.1   Allowing users to pick from a list of all projects

In the interest of time, you won't implement the ability to create new projects or update existing projects. To compensate for this, you'll use json-server and db.json to predefine a few projects, and assign them tasks.

We've talked about relational data and the two common methods for storing relational data in Redux: nested and normalized. We've already mentioned our preference for working with normalized data. It's becoming a standard community recommendation, particularly with apps of a certain size with a large amount of relational data.

This isn't to say that you should never store relational data in Redux in a nested fashion. For smaller apps, normalizing data can feel like overkill. Nested data structures are intuitive and can often make rendering friendlier. Take a blog application, for example. Instead of having to fetch an article, comments, and comment authors from three different sections of the store, you could pass into the view a single article object that contains all the necessary data. In this section, you'll implement a nested data structure without normalization to illustrate the pros and cons of the strategy.

When you have an API that needs to return relational data, such as with projects and tasks, it's a common strategy to nest any child data within its parent. You'll update your API to return nested data, and as a result, you'll end up storing roughly the same structure within the Redux store. Pretty intuitive, right? The API has defined a structure, so why not use that same structure in Redux? Any relationships between data are expressed using nesting, meaning you don't have to maintain any foreign key IDs manually. You don't need to do any translation between the API and Redux, and less code to maintain is often a good thing.

You'll see several of these benefits in the implementation, but in the process, the shortcomings will reveal themselves, too. You might see duplication, update logic could become more difficult, and you'll see decreased render performance due to re-rendering sections of the page unnecessarily.

8.3.1 *Overview: fetching and rendering projects*

Your new spec is to modify Parsnip to include projects. The main page should render the tasks for a given project, and users can choose which project to view using a drop-down menu.

These are the only user-facing changes. Turns out there's work you'll need to do under the hood to get things working, though. You need to update your data structure on the server as well as on the client. In addition to new features, you need to ensure existing functionality (creating or editing tasks, filtering) still works correctly. You'll break the work into three big chunks, based on the major events that take place in Parsnip:

- Fetch projects on initial load and render the main page (including the projects menu, and each column of tasks).
- Allow users to choose which project to display.
- Update task creation to use the new store structure and reducers.

Here's a high-level view of the changes you'll make, in order. You'll start with the initial page load and follow the flow of data through the entire stack, ultimately ending back at the view, where you'll render both projects and tasks. You'll loosely follow this path as you continue to make progress toward projects:

- As a prerequisite, update the server, which means modifying db.json. Add projects and update each task to belong to a project.
- Dispatch a yet-to-be-created `fetchProjects` action creator on initial page load.
- Create and implement `fetchProjects`, which is responsible for any actions related to fetching projects and loading them into the store.
- Replace the tasks reducer with a projects reducer.
- Update the reducer to handle projects coming from the server.

- Add the concept of a `currentProjectId`, so you know which project's tasks to render.
- Update any connected components and selectors to handle a new Redux store structure with both projects and tasks.
- Create the new projects drop-down menu and connect it to Redux.

To make these changes, you're truly hitting all parts of the stack. Take this as an opportunity to reinforce how you visualize data flowing through a Redux application. Figure 8.2 is a review of your architecture diagram, and where each change will fit in. It can be helpful to think about web applications such as Parsnip in terms of individual events. An event can be made up of multiple Redux actions, but typically it represents one thing that users can do (creating a task) or that can happen (initial page load) in your application. Here, you're visualizing what the initial page load looks like.

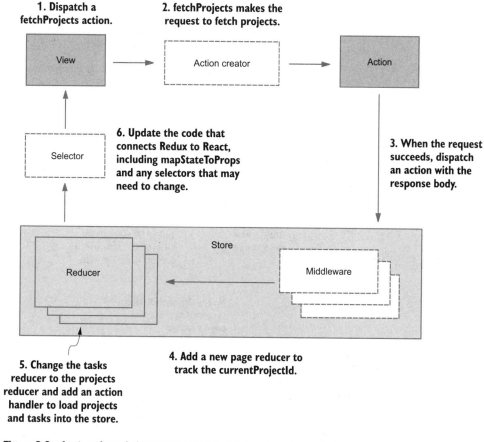

Figure 8.2 An overview of changes required to fetch and render projects

Listing 8.5 is a look at the desired store structure. You'll use this structure as a guide to create any actions you need (including payloads) and to create a particular reducer structure. Keep an eye on three things: adding a new top-level projects property, nesting tasks within each project, and the addition of a new top-level page property for storing currentProjectId. Note that you moved and renamed the search filter portion of your state. It's common to have UI state live in a different part of the tree as you add more typical application state such as projects and tasks. As a result, you renamed the property from searchTerm to tasksSearchTerm, because searchTerm is too generic, given that this piece of state isn't living directly under tasks.

Listing 8.5 The Redux store's structure using nested data

```
{
  projects: {
    isLoading: false,
    error: null,
    items: [                        Items hold each
                                    project object.
      {
        id: 1,                                  Each project's
        name: 'Short-term goals',               tasks are now
        tasks: [                                 nested.
          { id: 1, projectId: 1, ... },
          { id: 2, projectId: 1, ... }
        ]
      },
      {
        id: 2,
        name: 'Short-term goals',
        tasks: [
          { id: 3, projectId: 2, ... },
          { id: 4, projectId: 2, ... }
        ]
      }
    ]                        Adds a new              currentProjectId will
  },                         page property           be used to know which
  page: {                                            project is active.
    currentProjectId: null,
    tasksSearchTerm: null
  }                              Moves the search filter
}                                text for tags into the
                                 page reducer
```

Let's get the server updates out of the way so you can focus on the client.

8.3.2 *Updating the server with projects*

As a prerequisite before you get into the normal flow of the application, let's update the API to return both projects and tasks. As a refresher, you want your server to return a nested data structure when you make a GET request to /projects (as shown in the following listing).

Listing 8.6   An example API response

```
[
  {
    id: 1,
    name: 'Short-term goals',
    tasks: [
      { id: 1, title: 'Learn Redux', status: 'In Progress' },
      { id: 2, title: 'Defend shuffleboard championship title', status:
      'Unstarted' }
    ]
  },
  {
    id: 1,
    name: 'Short-term goals',
    tasks: [
      { id: 3, title: 'Achieve world peace', status: 'In Progress' },
      { id: 4, title: 'Invent Facebook for dogs', status: 'Unstarted' }
    ]
  }
]
```

json-server makes achieving this trivial for us. You don't have to bother writing any
code, you only need to update db.json with two things: `projects` and a `projectId` for
every task, as shown in the following listing.

Listing 8.7   Updating db.json

```
{
  "projects": [          ⟵──┐ Adds a new top-level
    {                        │ projects field, and a few
      "id": 1,               │ project objects
      "name": "Short-Term Goals"
    },
    {
      "id": 2,
      "name": "Long-Term Goals"
    }
  ],
  "tasks": [
    {
      "id": 1,
      "title": "Learn Redux",
      "description": "The store, actions, and reducers, oh my!",
      "status": "Unstarted",
      "timer": 86,
      "projectId": 1      ⟵──┐ Adds a projectId
    },                       │ to each task
    {
      "id": 2,
      "title": "Peace on Earth",
      "description": "No big deal.",
      "status": "Unstarted",
      "timer": 132,
```

```
    ⊢──▷   "projectId": 2
         },
         {
 Adds a         "id": 3,
projectId         "title": "Create Facebook for dogs",
 to each        "description": "The hottest new social network",
   task         "status": "Completed",
               "timer": 332,
    └───▷   "projectId": 1
         }
       ]
     }
```

Believe it or not, that's all you need on the server end. In an upcoming section, you'll use json-server's query syntax to get the nested response you're looking for.

8.3.3   Adding and dispatching fetchProjects

Because you're trying to model a single event—an initial page render—you'll start with the UI (see listing 8.8). Previously, you dispatched the `fetchTasks` action creator when the connected component App was initially mounted to the page (using the aptly named `componentDidMount` lifecycle hook). The only change you'll make here is to replace `fetchTasks` with `fetchProjects`, because you're moving to project-based API endpoints.

> **Listing 8.8   Importing and dispatching fetchProjects – src/App.js**

```
...
import {
  ...
  fetchProjects,
} from './actions';
...

class App extends Component {
  componentDidMount() {
    this.props.dispatch(fetchProjects());
  }
  ...
}
```

Before you get to the meat of the `fetchProjects` action creator, you'll make a quick quality-of-life update, shown in listing 8.9. Add a new function to your API client to deal with the specifics of the `/projects` endpoint. The actual request URL here may look foreign, but this is part of json-server's query language. This syntax will tell json-server to embed a project's tasks directly within each project object before it sends a response—exactly what you're looking for.

Listing 8.9   Updating the API client – src/api/index.js

```
...
export function fetchProjects() {
  return client.get('/projects?_embed=tasks');   <--
}
...
```
Uses json-server's query language to specify that tasks should be embedded within projects in the API response

Next, head to src/actions/index.js and implement `fetchProjects`. Like the old `fetchTasks`, `fetchProjects` will be an async action creator, responsible for orchestrating an API request and any related Redux actions. You won't use something like the API middleware you built in chapter 5. Instead, you'll use redux-thunk by returning a function from `fetchProjects`. Within that function, you'll make the API request and create/dispatch the three standard request actions: request start, success, and failure. See the following listing.

Listing 8.10   Creating fetchProjects – src/actions/index.js

```
function fetchProjectsStarted(boards) {
  return { type: 'FETCH_PROJECTS_STARTED', payload: { boards } };
}

function fetchProjectsSucceeded(projects) {
  return { type: 'FETCH_PROJECTS_SUCCEEDED', payload: { projects } };
}

function fetchProjectsFailed(err) {
  return { type: 'FETCH_PROJECTS_FAILED', payload: err };
}

export function fetchProjects() {
  return (dispatch, getState) => {
    dispatch(fetchProjectsStarted());   <--

    return api
      .fetchProjects()
      .then(resp => {
        const projects = resp.data;

        dispatch(fetchProjectsSucceeded(projects));   <--
      })
      .catch(err => {
        console.error(err);

        fetchProjectsFailed(err);
      });
  };
}
```
Dispatches an action to indicate the request has started

Dispatches an action with the projects from the response body

This pattern should start to look familiar. When using redux-thunk for async actions, most operations that involve an AJAX request consist of these same three request-based actions. Let's assume you're getting a successful response. Using `fetchProjects` dispatches two new actions, `FETCH_PROJECTS_STARTED` and `FETCH_PROJECTS_SUCCEEDED`. Like any other action, you need to add code to a reducer to handle any update logic.

8.3.4   *Updating the reducer*

You need to make a few major changes to the existing reducer code to fit projects and the new nested structure of the store. You'll take care of housekeeping first by renaming the `tasks` reducer to `projects` and updating the reducer's initial state to match the projects structure. Update the reducer code and update any imports and references in src/index.js, as shown in the following listing.

Listing 8.11   Updating the tasks reducer – src/reducers/index.js

```
...

const initialState = {
  items: [],
  isLoading: false,
  error: null,
};

export function projects(state = initialState, action) {     ◁──┐ Renames the
  switch (action.type) {                                          reducer
    ...
  }
}
...
```

Next let's handle two new actions (as shown in listing 8.12):

- `FETCH_PROJECTS_STARTED`—Handles loading state.
- `FETCH_PROJECTS_SUCCEEDED`—This payload is a list of projects from the server, which you'll have the reducer load into the store.

Listing 8.12   Handling new actions in the projects reducer – src/reducers/index.js

```
...
export function projects(state = initialState, action) {
  switch (action.type) {
    case 'FETCH_PROJECTS_STARTED': {          Sets the isLoading flag
      return {                                to true now that the
        ...state,                             request is in progress
        isLoading: true,               ◁──┘
      };
    }
    case 'FETCH_PROJECTS_SUCCEEDED': {
      return {                                     Loads the projects into
        ...state,                                  the store when the
        isLoading: false,                          request is complete
        items: action.payload.projects,    ◁──┘
      };
```

```
    }
      ...
    }
  }
}
...
```

This is standard Redux, so we won't spend too much time here. The reducers are calculating state correctly, so the next step is to update any code that connects Redux to React.

You added a new page property to the state tree to handle page-level state the same way as the current project and the current search term. Accordingly, you'll need a new reducer to handle updating this data in response to actions. Add the new page reducer as shown in the following listing.

Listing 8.13   Adding the page reducer – src/reducers/index.js

```
const initialPageState = {
  currentProjectId: null,          Declares the initial
  searchTerm: '',                  state for this part
};                                 of the state tree

export function page(state = initialPageState, action) {
  switch (action.type) {
    case 'SET_CURRENT_PROJECT_ID': {      ◁── Updates currentProjectId
      return {                                when users swap over to
        ...state,                            a new project
        currentProjectId: action.payload.id,
      };
    }                                              Updates searchTerm
    case 'FILTER_TASKS': {                   ◁──── when users filter tasks
      return { ...state, searchTerm: action.searchTerm };
    }
    default: {
      return state;
    }
  }
}
```

If you end up using Redux to handle UI-related state such as searchTerm, consider adding a ui reducer. You're only managing a few pieces of state here, so purely for convenience you can group them together within a single reducer/concept, page.

The page reducer won't be too useful on its own, so you also need to import and use it when you create the store in src/index.js, as shown in the following listing.

Listing 8.14   Update createStore – src/index.js

```
import React from 'react';
import ReactDOM from 'react-dom';
import { Provider } from 'react-redux';
import { createStore, applyMiddleware } from 'redux';
import { composeWithDevTools } from 'redux-devtools-extension';
```

```
import thunk from 'redux-thunk';
import createSagaMiddleware from 'redux-saga';
import { projects, tasks, page } from './reducers';      ⟵——  Adds page to
import App from './App';                                         the reducers
import rootSaga from './sagas';                                  import
import './index.css';

const rootReducer = (state = {}, action) => {
  return {
    projects: projects(state.projects, action),
    tasks: tasks(state.tasks, action),
    page: page(state.page, action),        ⟵——  Adds page to
  };                                              the rootReducer
};

const sagaMiddleware = createSagaMiddleware();

const store = createStore(
  rootReducer,
  composeWithDevTools(applyMiddleware(thunk, sagaMiddleware)),
);
...
```

8.3.5   *Updating mapStateToProps and selectors*

The role of selectors is to translate data between the Redux store and React components. Because you updated the structure of the store, you need to update your selectors to handle this new structure, as shown in the following listing. Your point of connection is mapStateToProps in the App component, Parsnip's only connected component to date.

> **Listing 8.15   Connecting projects to React – src/App.js**

```
function mapStateToProps(state) {                         Grabs relevant data
  const { isLoading, error, items } = state.projects;  ⟵  from projects state

  return {
    tasks: getGroupedAndFilteredTasks(state),   ⟵——  Uses the same selector to
    projects: items,   ⟵                              retrieve tasks, which you'll
    isLoading,                                         update in a moment
    error,              Passes in the list of projects
  };                    to eventually render in a
}                       drop-down menu
```

You needed only minimal changes within mapStateToProps, the point of connection between Redux and React, but the getGroupedAndFilteredTasks isn't functioning correctly in its current state. It still expects the old Redux store with a single tasks property. You need to modify a few of the existing selectors to handle a new store structure. Because you no longer have a single list of actions, you also need to add a new selector to find the right tasks to pass into the UI to render given the currentProjectId. Most noteworthy here is the addition of getTasksByProjectId, which replaces getTasks. The getFilteredTasks requires two input selectors: one to retrieve tasks and one to retrieve the current search term, as shown in the following listing.

**Adds a new selector to get
tasks based on a project ID**

**Updates
getSearchTerm
to use the new
page reducer**

```
const getSearchTerm = state => state.page.tasksSearchTerm;

const getTasksByProjectId = state => {
  if (!state.page.currentProjectId) {
    return [];
  }

  const currentProject = state.projects.items.find(
    project => project.id === state.page.currentProjectId,
  );

  return currentProject.tasks;
};

export const getFilteredTasks = createSelector(
  [getTasksByProjectId, getSearchTerm],
  (tasks, searchTerm) => {
    return tasks.filter(task => task.title.match(new RegExp(searchTerm,
      'i')));
  },
);
```

**If no project is currently
selected, it returns early
with an empty array.**

**Finds the
correct project
from the list**

**Updates getFilteredTasks
input selectors**

Now that you're rendering tasks for a specific project, you need additional logic to find the tasks for a given project.

Parsnip was in a broken state while you made these updates, but now things should be up and running again.

8.3.6   Adding the projects drop-down menu

Before you get into creating and editing tasks, let's do one last thing to make the app feel more complete, by allowing users to choose which project to display from a drop-down. Up to now, you've had only a single connected component, App, and one major page section that displayed a list of tasks. Now you have projects, and along with them comes another major page section to maintain.

You'll add the drop-down in a new Header component (see figure 8.17). Create a new file in the src/components directory named Header.js. Based on Header's requirements, you'll need at least two props:

- projects—A list of projects to render
- onCurrentProjectChange—A callback to fire when a new project is selected

```
import React, { Component } from 'react';

class Header extends Component {                        Renders an option
  render() {                                             for each project
    const projectOptions = this.props.projects.map(project =>
      <option key={project.id} value={project.id}>
        {project.name}
      </option>,
    );

    return (
      <div className="project-item">
        Project:
        <select onChange={this.props.onCurrentProjectChange}
          className="project-menu">
          {projectOptions}
        </select>
      </div>
    );
  }
}

export default Header;
```

Hooks up the
onCurrentProjectChange
callback

Now that you have a Header component, you need to render it. This includes not only including it somewhere in the component tree but also passing Header its required data. Because App is the only connected component, it needs to pass in projects and define an onCurrentProjectChange handler that dispatches the correct action, as shown in the following listing.

```
import React, { Component } from 'react';
import { connect } from 'react-redux';
import Header from './components/Header';
import TasksPage from './components/TasksPage';
import {
  ...
  setCurrentProjectId,
} from './actions';

class App extends Component {
  ...
  onCurrentProjectChange = e => {
    this.props.dispatch(setCurrentProjectId(Number(e.target.value)));
  };

  render() {
    return (
      <div className="container">
        {this.props.error && <FlashMessage message={this.props.error} />}
```

Adds an
event handler
for changing
the current
project

```
                    <div className="main-content">
   Renders the          <Header
header with the            projects={this.props.projects}
necessary data             onCurrentProjectChange={this.onCurrentProjectChange}
                        />
                        <TasksPage
                          tasks={this.props.tasks}
                          onCreateTask={this.onCreateTask}
                          onSearch={this.onSearch}
                          onStatusChange={this.onStatusChange}
                          isLoading={this.props.isLoading}
                        />
                    </div>
                  </div>
                );
              }
            }
            ...
```

The app won't run in its current state because you need to do one last thing: define
the setCurrentProjectId action creator. It's a simple, synchronous action creator
that accepts a project ID as an argument and returns an action object with the correct
type and payload. Head to src/actions/index.js, where you defined all your action-
related things so far, and add the code from the following listing.

> **Listing 8.19   Adding setCurrentProjectId – src/actions/index.js**

```
...
export function setCurrentProjectId(id) {        ⟵── Exports a synchronous
  return {                                            action creator that accepts
    type: 'SET_CURRENT_PROJECT_ID',       ⟵┐        a project ID as an argument
    payload: {                              │
      id,         Sets the correct payload,  │   Sets the correct
    },            a single ID property       │   action type
  };
}
...
```

You can now switch between projects by choosing from the drop-down menu. The
role of the App component is varied at this point. It needs to get the right data from
Redux, render any children, and implement small wrappers around action dispatches.
Its purpose could be described as orchestrator. This is fine for the time being, but it's
something to keep an eye on. If this component becomes too bloated, Parsnip could
become more difficult to maintain.

   At this point, you have two major pieces of functionality left to update: creating
and updating tasks. Loading initial projects data was relatively straightforward. Projects as returned from the API are already in a shape that's friendly to render. All you
needed to do was load the data into the store, adjust part of the code that connects
Redux and React, and everyone's happy.

With creating tasks, you'll get your first taste of making updates to nested data. To fetch projects, you threw an entire API response directly in the store. Now you need to pluck out individual tasks and operate on them, which won't be as easy.

Recall one of the major downsides of having a store with nested data—updating nested data comes with a high-complexity cost. At the risk of spoilers, the next few sections are meant to demonstrate these issues first-hand.

You won't need to make any UI changes to get task creation working again, you need to change only how things work under the hood. You'll make two changes:

- Ensure the current project ID is passed to the `createTask` action creator.
- Update the `projects` reducer to add the task to the correct project.

That last bullet is the most significant change. As a refresher, let's look at the existing implementation for handling `CREATE_TASK_SUCCEEDED`, which is responsible for taking the newly created task and adding it to the store. This is about as straightforward as it gets. You take the new task from the action's payload and add it to the existing list of tasks, as shown in the following listing.

> **Listing 8.20   Existing code for CREATE_TASK_SUCCEEDED – src/reducers/index.js**

```
export function projects(state = initialState, action) {
  switch (action.type) {
    ...
    case 'CREATE_TASK_SUCCEEDED': {
      return {
        ...state,
        tasks: state.tasks.concat(action.payload.task),
      };
    }
    ...
  }
}
```

With projects, you need one additional step: finding the project that the task belongs to. You first use the `projectId` from the task as part of the action payload to find the project that you need to update. In the following listing, you start to see real shortcomings with storing lists of objects in an array.

> **Listing 8.21   Updating the projects reducer – src/reducers/index.js**

```
export function projects(state = initialState, action) {
  switch (action.type) {
    ...
    case 'CREATE_TASK_SUCCEEDED': {
      const { task } = action.payload;
      const projectIndex = state.items.findIndex(
        project => project.id === task.projectId,          Finds the right
      );                                                   project to
      const project = state.items[projectIndex];           update
```

```
      const nextProject = {                        Merges the new
        ...project,                                tasks array into
        tasks: project.tasks.concat(task),         the project
      };

      return {
        ...state,
        items: [                                   Inserts the
          ...state.items.slice(0, projectIndex),   updated project at
          nextProject,                             the correct place
          ...state.items.slice(projectIndex + 1),  in the array
        ],
      };
    }
    ...
  }
}
```

The immutability restriction of reducers enables great features within Redux, such as time travel, but it can make updating nested data structures harder. Instead of modifying a project's task array in place, you must take care to always create new copies of objects. Using arrays to store lists of objects makes this extra problematic, because you have to loop through the entire list to find the project you'd like to work with.

8.3.7 Editing tasks

With creating tasks, you started to see how updating nested data in a way that preserves immutability can become tricky. Editing tasks will be even more complex, because you can't take a new task and add it to a list. Now you need to find the right project and find the right task to update—all while avoiding mutating any existing data in place. Again, let's look at the following listing to see the existing implementation before you introduced projects. In this instance, you chose to map over the list of tasks and return the updated task when you found the task being updated.

> **Listing 8.22 Existing EDIT_TASKS_SUCCEEDED code – src/reducers/index.js**

```
export function projects(state = initialState, action) {
  switch (action.type) {
    ...
    case 'EDIT_TASK_SUCCEEDED': {
      const { payload } = action;
      const nextTasks = state.tasks.map(task => {
        if (task.id === payload.task.id) {       Finds and replaces
          return payload.task;                   the desired task
        }

        return task;
      });
      return {
        ...state,                       Returns the
        tasks: nextTasks,               updated tasks
      };
```

```
      }
      ...
    }
  }
}
```

As with task creation, you also have to find the project for the task being updated, as shown in the following listing.

Listing 8.23   Finding the project – src/reducers/index.js

```
export function projects(state = initialState, action) {
  switch (action.type) {
    ...
    case 'EDIT_TASK_SUCCEEDED': {
      const { task } = action.payload;
      const projectIndex = state.items.findIndex(
        project => project.id === task.projectId,       Determines the
      );                                                project to update
      const project = state.items[projectIndex];
      const taskIndex = project.tasks.findIndex(t => t.id === task.id);

      const nextProject = {              Updates the project
        ...project,
        tasks: [
          ...project.tasks.slice(0, taskIndex),
          task,
          ...project.tasks.slice(taskIndex + 1),
        ],
      };
                                         Returns the updated
      return {                           projects list
        ...state,
        items: [
          ...state.items.slice(0, projectIndex),
          nextProject,
          ...state.items.slice(projectIndex + 1),
        ],
      };
    }
  }
}
```

If you think this code is dense, it's not you. You had to

- Find the associated project for the task being updated.
- Replace the updated task at the correct index.
- Replace the updated project at the correct index.

All this to update a single task! Granted, tools such as Immutable.js are designed to make updating nested data structures easier. If you find that nested data works for you, it can be worth considering such a tool to help save you the boilerplate you wrote.

As you'll see later in the chapter, using a normalized state shape can remove the need for this kind of logic entirely.

8.3.8 Unnecessary rendering

It's obvious that updating nested data is more complex than updating flat structures. Another downside exists to nested data that we covered earlier in the chapter but haven't had a chance to look at in detail yet: updates to nested data causing parent data to change. It's not something that's going to make or break an app such as Parsnip, but it's something to be aware of.

Most design-related problems that require nuance are hot topics of debate within the React community. As you've see in this chapter, how to structure data within a store is a big point of debate. Related but distinct are strategies around how to best connect Redux and React. How you decide what the entry points are for your app has a big effect on overall architecture and data flow.

You know nested data makes updates harder. Recall that one of the other big downsides of nested data is performance. Here's what we mean by that.

Figure 8.3 is a diagram of your current component structure and how it connects to Redux. You have two major page sections to manage, `Header` and `TasksPage`, and `App` is still the lone connected component.

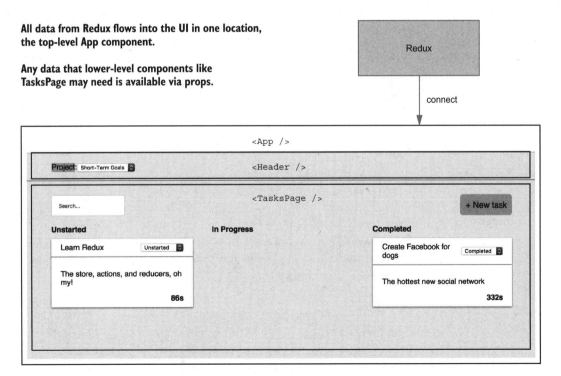

Figure 8.3   An overview of Parsnip's components and how they connect to Redux

Let's look at the `Header` and `TasksPage` components in terms of their data dependencies. `Header` requires projects, `TasksPage` requires tasks. You have two resources in Redux, projects and tasks. `App` will re-render if any contained within `state.projects` changes, including tasks.

Let's say you're updating a task, where ideally only that particular `Task` component should re-render. Whenever `App` receives new data from the store, it will automatically re-render all of its children, including `Header` and `TasksPage`. See figure 8.4.

App is connected to projects' state, meaning whenever any data nested underneath the projects property changes, App, Header, and TasksPage will re-render. Updates to a single task will cause every component to re-render, even though TasksPage is the only component that directly relies on tasks.

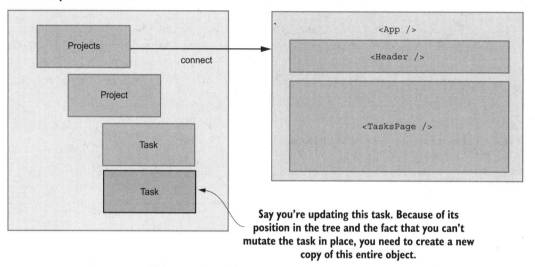

Say you're updating this task. Because of its position in the tree and the fact that you can't mutate the task in place, you need to create a new copy of this entire object.

Figure 8.4   Updates to any part of projects' state will cause App to re-render.

Because you only have one connected component, you can't be any more granular about which components should be notified when certain data changes. And because you have nested data, any updates to tasks will automatically update the entire projects portion of the state tree.

8.3.9   Summary—nested data

Now you have a good sense of what it's like to fetch, create, and update nested data. In certain ways, it's an intuitive way to structure data. It's tricky to express relationships between data, so leaving tasks nested within their respective projects saves you from having to manage any relationships in a more manual way.

We also reinforced a few of the shortcomings of nested data:

- Update logic became more complex. Instead of adding or updating, you had to find the relevant project for each operation.
- Because your data was nested, you were forced to re-render the entire app whenever any projects-related state changed. For example, updating a task also required the header to update, even though the header didn't rely on tasks.

Now we'll look at normalization, one of the most effective ways for managing relational data in Redux.

8.4 Normalizing projects and tasks

The alternative to nesting relational data in Redux is normalization. Instead of using nesting to express relationships between projects and tasks, you'll treat the Redux store more like a relational database. Instead of having one projects reducer, you'll split things up into two reducers, one per resource. You'll use selectors to fetch and transform the necessary data for the React components.

This allows you to keep a flat structure, which means you won't need to bother with updating nested resources. It also means you can adjust how you connect your React components for improved performance.

To accomplish this, you'll use the popular normalizr package. You'll pass into normalizr a nested API response and a user-defined schema, and it will return a normalized object. You could do the normalization yourself, but normalizr is a great tool and you don't need to reinvent the wheel. Note that you'll be using the finished code from section 8.3 as a base.

Figure 8.5 shows the current structure of the store, side-by-side with the structure you'll end up with after you finish this section.

Note that tasks is back to being a top-level property in your normalized state tree. This means when you're creating or editing tasks, you no longer have to dig through a list of projects to find the task you want to update; you can look at each task using its ID.

You're also no longer storing lists of tasks or projects in arrays. Now you're using objects with the ID of the resource as a key. Regardless of whether you choose to nest or normalize your data, we usually recommend storing your lists in this way. The reason is simple: it makes lookups roughly a thousand times easier. The following listing shows the difference.

Listing 8.24 Why objects with IDs make lookups easier

```
const currentProject = state.projects.items.find(project =>
  project.id === action.payload.id
);
```

versus

```
const currentProject = state.projects.items[action.payload.id];
```

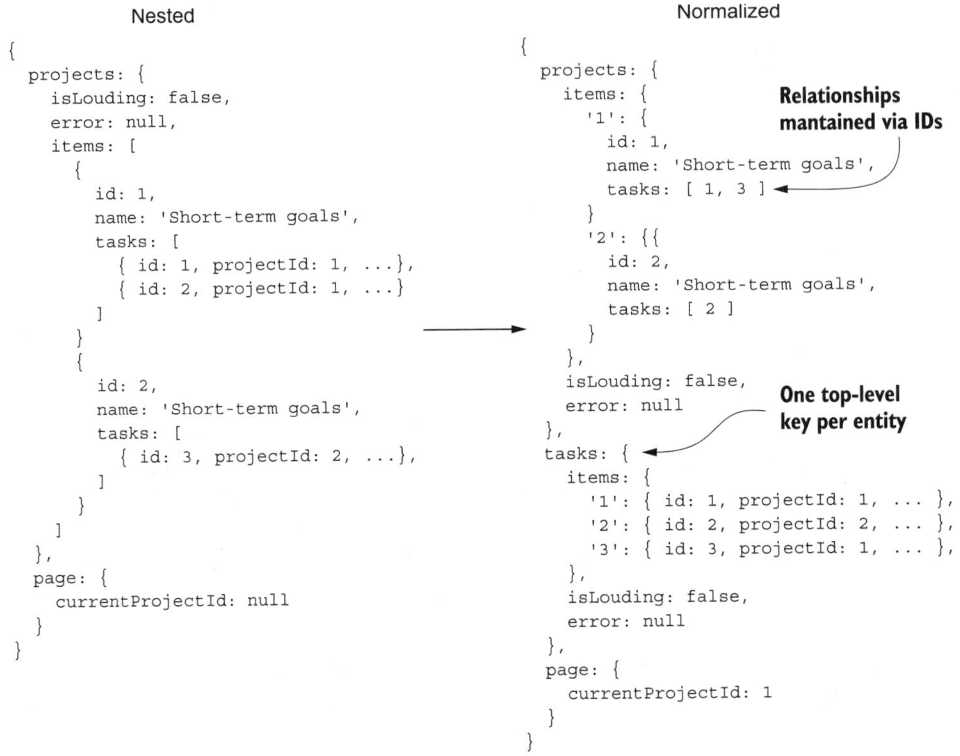

Nested

```
{
  projects: {
    isLouding: false,
    error: null,
    items: [
      {
        id: 1,
        name: 'Short-term goals',
        tasks: [
          { id: 1, projectId: 1, ...},
          { id: 2, projectId: 1, ...}
        ]
      }
      {
        id: 2,
        name: 'Short-term goals',
        tasks: [
          { id: 3, projectId: 2, ...},
        ]
      }
    ]
  },
  page: {
    currentProjectId: null
  }
}
```

Normalized

```
{
  projects: {
    items: {                        Relationships
      '1': {                        mantained via IDs
        id: 1,
        name: 'Short-term goals',
        tasks: [ 1, 3 ]
      }
      '2': {{
        id: 2,
        name: 'Short-term goals',
        tasks: [ 2 ]
      }
    },
    isLouding: false,               One top-level
    error: null                     key per entity
  },
  tasks: {
    items: {
      '1': { id: 1, projectId: 1, ... },
      '2': { id: 2, projectId: 2, ... },
      '3': { id: 3, projectId: 1, ... },
    },
    isLouding: false,
    error: null
  },
  page: {
    currentProjectId: 1
  }
}
```

Figure 8.5   The transition from nested to normalized

This not only simplifies lookups, it improves performance by removing unnecessary loops.

8.4.1   Defining a schema

The first step on the road to normalization is to define a normalizr schema. Schemas are how you tell normalizr what shape to give back when you run the API response through the normalize function. You'll put your schemas along with the actions in src/actions/index.js for now, but it's also common to use a separate file for schemas. The following listing tells normalizr that you have two top-level entities, tasks and projects, and that tasks belong to projects.

Listing 8.25   Adding normalizr schemas – src/actions/index.js

```
import { normalize, schema } from 'normalizr';

...

const taskSchema = new schema.Entity('tasks');
const projectSchema = new schema.Entity('projects', {
  tasks: [taskSchema],
});
```

Next you run the API response from the /projects endpoint through normalizr's normalize function, which takes an object and a schema and returns a normalized object. This is the piece that transforms the nested API response into the normalized structure you'll use in Redux. Also, create a new receiveEntities action creator, which will return a RECEIVE_ENTITIES action. You'll then handle this action in both reducers, tasks and projects, as shown in the following listing. This helps you reduce boilerplate by not having to dispatch multiple actions, such as FETCH_PROJECTS_SUCCEEDED and FETCH_TASKS_SUCCEEDED.

Listing 8.26   Normalizing the response – src/actions/index.js

```
function receiveEntities(entities) {          ◁──┐ Creates a generic
  return {                                         receiveEntities action
    type: 'RECEIVE_ENTITIES',
    payload: entities,
  };
}

...

export function fetchProjects() {
  return (dispatch, getState) => {
    dispatch(fetchProjectsStarted());

    return api
      .fetchProjects()                              Passes the response
      .then(resp => {                              and the schema into
        const projects = resp.data;                        normalizr

        const normalizedData = normalize(projects, [projectSchema]);   ◁──

        dispatch(receiveEntities(normalizedData));   ◁──┤ Dispatches the
                                                          normalized result
        if (!getState().page.currentProjectId) {
          const defaultProjectId = projects[0].id;          Sets a
          dispatch(setCurrentProjectId(defaultProjectId));  default
        }                                                   project ID
      })
      .catch(err => {
        fetchProjectsFailed(err);
      });
  };
}
```

You added only one new step to your existing code within the fetchProjects action creator, but because it fundamentally changes the structure of the data within the store, it will require profound changes to your reducers.

8.4.2   *Updating reducers for entities*

You currently have a single `projects` reducer that handles everything related to both projects and tasks. Now that you're normalizing your data and tasks are back to being a top-level property in your store, you need to bring back the `tasks` reducer. Rumors of its demise have been greatly exaggerated.

You'll split up the existing actions you have per resource. Task-related actions will go in the `tasks` reducer, while project-related actions go in the `projects` reducer. Note that you'll change the implementation for many of these actions to support this new normalized structure. In the process, you'll see a big improvement in terms of complexity, especially for any code that handles modification of nested tasks. Both the tasks and projects reducers need to handle `RECEIVE_ENTITIES`. To be extra safe, in each reducer you'll check if the action payload includes relevant entities and load them in if so, as shown in the following listing.

> **Listing 8.27   Creating the tasks reducer and RECEIVE_ENTITIES – src/reducers/index.js**

```
const initialTasksState = {
  items: [],
  isLoading: false,
  error: null,
};                                                              Creates new tasks
                                                                reducers, including
                                                                any initial state
export function tasks(state = initialTasksState, action) {   ◁
  switch (action.type) {
    case 'RECEIVE_ENTITIES': {
      const { entities } = action.payload;
      if (entities && entities.tasks) {        ◁        If tasks are part of this
        return {                                         RECEIVE_ENTITIES
          ...state,                                      action, it loads them
          isLoading: false,                              into the store.
          items: entities.tasks,
        };
      }

      return state;
    }
    case 'TIMER_INCREMENT': {
      const nextTasks = Object.keys(state.items).map(taskId => {
        const task = state.items[taskId];

        if (task.id === action.payload.taskId) {
          return { ...task, timer: task.timer + 1 };
        }

        return task;
      });
      return {
        ...state,
        tasks: nextTasks,
      };
    }
```

```
      default: {
        return state;
      }
    }
  }
}

const initialProjectsState = {
  items: {},
  isLoading: false,
  error: null,
};

export function projects(state = initialProjectsState, action) {
  switch (action.type) {
    case 'RECEIVE_ENTITIES': {
      const { entities } = action.payload;
      if (entities && entities.projects) {                    ◁─┐ Repeats the
        return {                                                 │ same process
          ...state,                                              │ for projects
          isLoading: false,
          items: entities.projects,
        };
      }

      return state;
    }

    ...

    default: {
      return state;
    }
  }
}
```

You also need to include the new `tasks` reducer when you create the store. Head to
src/index.js and set up the `tasks` reducer. You need to import the reducer and take
care of passing the relevant state slice, as shown in the following listing.

Listing 8.28   Using the tasks reducer – src/index.js

```
...

import { projects, tasks, page } from './reducers';          ◁─┐ Imports the
                                                                │ reducer
...

const rootReducer = (state = {}, action) => {
  return {
    projects: projects(state.projects, action),
    tasks: tasks(state.tasks, action),                       ◁─┐ Passes the
    page: page(state.page, action),                             │ relevant state
  };                                                            │ slice and action
};
```

You're not quite to the point of rendering tasks: you still need to get the data out of the store. That's where selectors and `mapStateToProps` come in.

8.4.3   *Updating selectors*

You changed the structure of the store yet again, and that means you need to update any selectors that may reference outdated data structures. First, you'll make one quick change to `mapStateToProps` in the connected `App` component, as described by the following listing. You'll import a new `getProjects` selector (that you'll define in a moment) that will return an array of projects.

Listing 8.29   Updating App – src/App.js

```
import { getGroupedAndFilteredTasks, getProjects } from './reducers/';   ◁─┐

...                                                            Imports a new
                                                          getProjects reducer

function mapStateToProps(state) {
  const { isLoading, error } = state.projects;

  return {
    tasks: getGroupedAndFilteredTasks(state),
    projects: getProjects(state),        ◁─┐ Uses getProjects to
    isLoading,                               pass an array of
    error,                                   projects into the UI
  };
}


...
```

Minus the new `getProjects`, you've left everything else as is. You won't need to change how the React portion of the app works. It will still accept the same props. This is decoupling between Redux and React in action. You can radically change how you manage state under the hood, and it won't affect any UI code. Pretty cool.

Next, update the existing `getGroupedAndFilteredTasks` selector to handle normalized data and implement `getProjects`. Arrays are much easier to work with in React, so a simple `getProjects` selector handles the simple transform of an object of projects keyed by ID to an array of project objects.

The high-level logic behind `getTasksByProjectId` is the same—it uses `projects`, `tasks`, and a `currentProjectId` and returns an array of tasks for the current project. The difference here is that you're operating on normalized data. Instead of having to loop over all projects to find the correct object, you can look up the current project by ID. Then you use its array of task IDs to subsequently look up each task object, as shown in the following listing.

Listing 8.30 Updating selectors – src/reducers/index.js

```
...

export const getProjects = state => {
  return Object.keys(state.projects.items).map(id => {
    return state.projects.items[id];
  });
};
```
Creates a selector to convert the object containing all projects back into an array

```
const getTasksByProjectId = state => {
  const { currentProjectId } = state.page;

  if (!currentProjectId || !state.projects.items[currentProjectId]) {
    return [];
  }

  const taskIds = state.projects.items[currentProjectId].tasks;

  return taskIds.map(id => state.tasks.items[id]);
};

...
```
If there's no current project, or no project matching the currentProjectId, it returns early.

Gets the list of task IDs from the project

For each task ID, it gets its corresponding object.

8.4.4   Creating tasks

The only things you haven't ported over to this new normalized structure are creates and updates. You'll leave updates as an exercise toward the end of the chapter. Creating tasks is an interesting case, because it's the first example where you have to handle a single action in multiple reducers. When you dispatch CREATE_TASK_SUCCESS, you need to do a few things:

- In the tasks reducer, add the new task to the store.
- In the projects reducer, add the ID of the new task to the corresponding reducer.

Recall that because you're tracking related entities in different sections of the store, you need to use IDs to maintain these relationships. Each project has a tasks property that's an array of tasks belonging to that project. When you create a new task, you have to add the task's ID to the correct project.

Listing 8.31 Handling CREATE_TASK_SUCCEEDED – src/reducers/index.js

```
...

export function tasks(state = initialTasksState, action) {
  switch (action.type) {
    ...

    case 'CREATE_TASK_SUCCEEDED': {
      const { task } = action.payload;
```

```
        const nextTasks = {
          ...state.items,              Adds the new
          [task.id]: task,             task object
        };

        return {
          ...state,
          items: nextTasks,
        };
      }

      ...

    }
  }

  ...

export function projects(state = initialProjectsState, action) {
  switch (action.type) {
    ...
    case 'CREATE_TASK_SUCCEEDED': {
      const { task } = action.payload;

      const project = state.items[task.projectId];      ◁──┐  Finds the project that
                                                            │  the task belongs to
      return {                                              │  and adds the task's ID
        ...state,
        items: {
          ...state.items,
          [task.projectId]: {
            ...project,
            tasks: project.tasks.concat(task.id),
          },
        }
      };
    }
    ...
  }
}
```

You don't have to dig through nested data anymore, but you do have to handle the same action in multiple reducers. Working in multiple reducers requires complexity overhead, but the benefits of storing data in a flat manner consistently outweigh the costs.

8.4.5 *Summary—normalized data*

Notice how you're not making any major updates to the UI? That's by design! One of the core ideas with Redux is that it allows you to separate state management from UI. Your React components don't know or care what's going on behind the scenes. They expect to receive data that has a certain shape, and that's it. You can make drastic changes to how you store and update application state, and those changes are isolated to Redux. You've successfully separated how Parsnip looks from how it works. This kind of decoupling is a powerful idea and is one of the keys to scaling any application.

8.5 Organizing other types of state

The chapter so far has been devoted to relational data. You had a series of related resources, projects, and tasks, and the goal was to explore different structures and how they affect the way you create and update different resources. Another kind of organization is worth talking about, and that's grouping certain data in Redux in conceptual groups. Up to now, you've stored what we'd call application state.

Assuming you kept developing Parsnip, your store would no doubt grow. You'd add new resources such as users, but you'd also start to see new kinds of state in the store. Here are a few examples of reducers you'll commonly find in Redux apps:

- *Session*—Login state, session duration to handle forced sign-in.
- *UI*—If you store a significant amount of UI state in Redux, it's helpful to give it its own reducer.
- *Features/experiments*—In production apps it's common for the server to define a list of active features or experiments, which a client app uses to know what to render.

8.6 Exercise

One major thing left to update to support normalized data is editing tasks. This is another place where normalized data shines. You can skip the step of finding the task's associated project and update the correct object in the `tasks` reducer. Because the project already has a reference to each of its tasks using IDs, you'll automatically reference the updated task object when you render that project's tasks.

Your mission: modify the code so editing tasks (modifying their statuses) works correctly, given the new normalized state structure from section 8.4.

8.7 Solution

You'll need to do a few things, as shown in listing 8.32:

- Move the `EDIT_TASK_SUCCESS` handler from the `projects` reducer to the `tasks` reducer.
- Update the reducer code to find the object by ID, instead of looping through an array of tasks until the correct object is found. The action's payload has the task object you need to load into the store. Because each task is keyed by ID, you can replace the old task with the new task, and that's it!

Listing 8.32 Updating normalized tasks – src/reducers/index.js

```
export function tasks(state = initialTasksState, action) {
  switch (action.type) {
    ...
```

```
    case 'EDIT_TASK_SUCCEEDED': {
      const { task } = action.payload;

      const nextTasks = {
        ...state.items,
        [task.id]: task,
      };

      return {
        ...state,
        items: nextTasks,
      };
    }
    default: {
      return state;
    }
  }
}
```

Notice any similarities between the CREATE_TASK_SUCCEEDED handler and the EDIT
_TASK_SUCCEEDED handler in the tasks reducer? The code is identical! If you want to
save a few lines of code, you combine the action-handling code, as demonstrated in
the following listing.

Listing 8.33   Refactoring the tasks reducer – src/reducers/index.js

```
export function tasks(state = initialTasksState, action) {
  switch (action.type) {
    ...
    case 'CREATE_TASK_SUCCEEDED':
    case 'EDIT_TASK_SUCCEEDED': {
      const { task } = action.payload;

      const nextTasks = {
        ...state.items,
        [task.id]: task,
      };

      return {
        ...state,
        items: nextTasks,
      };
    }
    default: {
      return state;
    }
  }
}
```

Normalized data is only one strategy for storing application state in Redux. Like all
things programming, no tool is a silver bullet. You won't catch us using the normalizr
package in a quick prototype, for example, but hopefully you can see the value of using

normalized data in appropriate circumstances. At a minimum, you're now aware of more choices available to you when architecting your next Redux application.

The next chapter is fully dedicated to testing Redux applications. You'll finally circle back to how to test components, actions, reducers, sagas, and the rest of the pieces you've assembled over the last eight chapters.

Summary

In this chapter you learned the following:

- Multiple strategies exist for how to store data in Redux.
- Normalizing data helps flatten out deeply nested relationships and removes duplicate resources.
- Selectors can simplify the usage of the normalized data in your application.
- The normalizr package provides helpful abstractions for normalizing data in a Redux application.

Testing Redux applications

9

This chapter covers

- Introducing testing tools
- Strategies for testing Redux building blocks
- Testing advanced Redux features

Instead of testing each Parsnip feature as it was built, our strategy has been to save it all up for one comprehensive chapter. Ideally, this chapter serves as a convenient reference manual for all your Redux testing needs going forward. In the coming sections, we cover common testing tools and strategies for testing action creators, reducers, and components. We also work through examples for testing advanced features: middleware, selectors, and sagas. Feel free to skip around as needed.

Because this chapter is intended to be easily referenced outside the context of the Parsnip application, examples will be inspired by code written for Parsnip but may be pared down to make a clearer point. In the process, you'll gain the knowledge and tools necessary for testing Parsnip code, so the exercise at the end of the chapter asks you to do that. You'll check your understanding by testing a specific feature. As you read through the chapter, consider how the lessons could be extended to test related functionality in Parsnip or your own application.

Good news! Most of this chapter is straightforward and easy to understand and apply. As you'll recall, Redux has the great advantage of decoupling application logic from view rendering. When separated into its constituent parts, each element of the Redux workflow is relatively simple to test in isolation. Where possible, Redux encourages the writing of pure functions, and it doesn't get any easier than testing pure functions.

There will be times where testing becomes unavoidably complex. Think back to each of the points in the workflow where side effects are managed, and you'll have a good idea of where it can get a little hairy. Fortunately, you can keep the testing complexity in one place, just like the implementation.

A note on test-driven development

Before writing Redux full-time, both of us held the steadfast belief that test-driven development (TDD) was the one true path. When it comes to writing Ruby, Go, or a different JavaScript framework, we still advocate using TDD in certain situations. Particularly when working on the back end, having tests sometimes provides the quickest feedback loop for development. The value proposition for TDD in React and Redux applications is dramatically less clear.

Throughout the book, we've practiced and preached the workflow of building the UI before connecting it to Redux. All too often though, the component composition for a new feature will evolve as you're feeling out the feature. Groups of UI elements will get extracted out into new components along the way—that sort of thing. If you took a stab at the component tests before starting their implementation, more often than not, you end up rewriting those tests.

As we hope you can now attest, the development experience in Redux is outstanding. Hot module replacement provides you with immediate visual feedback as you develop, while preserving the application state, and the Redux DevTools spell out every state change coming down the pipeline. Client-side development cycles have never been faster, and for that reason, we prefer not to write component tests in advance of sketching out the components.

More of an argument can be made for writing action creator, reducer, and other tests in advance, though. If those elements are test-driven, you can expect the typical benefits for those domains: better consideration of sad paths, better overall code coverage, and a baseline for code quality. A deeper discussion of the merits of test-driven development is outside the scope of this book, but if it's a value in your organization, our recommendation is to try it with components last, lest you have a bad time and quit before making it to action creators and reducers.

9.1 Introduction to testing tools

You have many options when it comes to JavaScript testing. A common complaint from developers moving to the JavaScript ecosystem from another programming language is a lack of strong conventions. Choice means flexibility, but it also means mental overhead. The React community has attempted to address this concern by including a robust testing utility, Jest, in apps generated by Create React App. When you create a new application with the CLI tool, Jest is installed and configured as a part of that process. You're free to use any test framework you prefer, but in this chapter, you'll run with the default and use Jest as the test runner and assertion library.

As a beginner-friendly convenience, Create React App abstracts many of the application's configuration settings away using the `react-scripts` package. To view the configuration settings requires ejecting from Create React App. Ejecting removes the abstractions and gives you access to the raw configuration files, enabling you to make your own tweaks.

The command for ejecting is `npm run eject`. Once you eject, there's no turning back, so the CLI will give you a final warning before performing the ejection. If you want to look around an ejected application, but don't want to eject your Parsnip application, spin up a new application using `create-react-app new-app` and perform the ejection there.

Within your ejected application, look at the package.json file for the configuration details within the `jest` key. Take a deep breath first, because there's a lot going on. The good news is that you didn't have to write this from scratch, and the settings are straightforward enough to understand. The following listing breaks down the configuration settings.

Listing 9.1   The package.json file after ejecting from Create React App

```
...
"jest": {
    "collectCoverageFrom": [          ⟵── Shows test coverage
                                          for the files that
      "src/**/*.{js,jsx}"                 match this pattern
    ],
    "setupFiles": [                       Executes code before
                                   ⟵── running the test suite
      "<rootDir>/config/polyfills.js"
    ],
    "testMatch": [                        Tests files that match
                                   ⟵── these patterns
      "<rootDir>/src/**/__tests__/**/*.js?(x)",
      "<rootDir>/src/**/?(*.)(spec|test).js?(x)"
    ],
    "testEnvironment": "node",
    "testURL": "http://localhost",        Applies transformers,
    "transform": {                        like Babel, to certain
                                   ⟵── file extensions
      "^.+\\.(js|jsx)$": "<rootDir>/node_modules/babel-jest",
      "^.+\\.css$": "<rootDir>/config/jest/cssTransform.js",
      "^(?!.*\\.(js|jsx|css|json)$)":
     "<rootDir>/config/jest/fileTransform.js"
    },                                    Leaves the node_modules
    "transformIgnorePatterns": [   ⟵── directory alone
      "[/\\\\]node_modules[/\\\\].+\\.(js|jsx)$"
    ],
    "moduleNameMapper": {
      "^react-native$": "react-native-youb"    Jest should handle imports with
    },                                         these filename extensions, even if
    "moduleFileExtensions": [           ⟵── the extension isn't explicitly stated.
      "youb.js",
```

```
      "js",
      "json",
      "youb.jsx",
      "jsx",
      "node"
    ]
  },
...
```

It's not crucial for you to understand what's happening under the hood, and that's exactly why Create React App hides these details by default. What's important is that when you run the test command (npm test), Jest will run any tests in files that are within a __tests__ directory or end in .test.js, .test.jsx, .spec.js, or .spec.jsx. If you prefer to tweak those settings, that's what ejecting is intended for.

If you have experience with the Jasmine testing framework, Jest will look familiar. Jest is a set of features built on top of Jasmine. However, as of May 2017, Jest maintains its own fork of Jasmine. The intention there is to maintain greater control over their own test runner and to add, change, or remove functionality as it meets the needs of Jest.

9.1.1 What does Jasmine provide?

Jasmine (https://jasmine.github.io/) describes itself as a behavior-driven development (BDD) framework for testing JavaScript. Paraphrasing its intention, BDD emphasizes writing human-readable tests focused on the value provided by the feature you're testing. For the purposes of this chapter, that's roughly all you'll need to know about BDD. Among other things, Jasmine provides the syntax to write tests and make assertions. Listing 9.2 provides an example of that syntax.

The describe function exists to group a series of related tests that can be nested to define more nuanced relationships between tests. As an imperfect rule of thumb, each file you test should result in one or more describe blocks.

Within a describe block is one or more test cases declared using the it function. If the describe function defines the noun being tested, the it function defines the verb.

Listing 9.2 Example Jasmine test

The "describe" function provides context for a series of related tests.
The "it" function denotes a unit test.

```
describe('a generic example', () => {
  it('should demonstrate basic syntax', () => {
    expect(5 + 1).toEqual(6);
  });

  it('should also demonstrate inverse assertions', () => {
    expect(true).not.toBe(false);
  });
});
```

Syntax for making assertions

Multiple unit tests reside within a "describe" block.

The tests are easy to read, aren't they? That's the intention of BDD, making test cases readable by even non-technical stakeholders. Jasmine comes packaged with a command-line test runner that uses the `describe` and `it` blocks to generate especially readable output.

If the first test in listing 9.2 were updated to `expect(5 + 3).toEqual(6)`, and you ran the test suite with Jasmine, the abbreviated terminal output would look something like this:

```
Failures:
1) a generic example should demonstrate basic syntax
  Message:
    Expected 8 to equal 6.
```

The friendly test output makes it easy to run a test suite and, in plain English, understand much of what functionality the application has or hasn't implemented.

9.1.2   *What does Jest provide?*

If Jasmine is such a nice tool, why bother with Jest? For one, it works out of the box with React, saving you from having to install and configure something similar to `jsdom`. Jest keeps the syntax and test runner as a foundation but extends Jasmine in many significant ways. The test runner, for example, has been beefed up to provide more detailed output, a watch mode to automatically replay only tests affected by a code change, and a code coverage tool.

Figure 9.1 shows you an example of the watch mode test output. The tests will run every time you save a file, but notice that you can also specify options for running specific tests by file or test name from the runner. This allows you to run only the subset of tests you care about for the feature or bug you're working on.

Beyond the runner, Jest implements performance improvements and has a powerful feature called snapshot testing. This is an optional tool that can come in handy when testing components. We'll look at snapshots later in the chapter.

If you try running the test command (`npm test`) in Parsnip, you'll notice that a single test will run and fail. This is to be expected, because you've paid testing no mind up to this point. Delete the test file found at src/App.test.js.

9.1.3   *Alternatives to Jest*

If you prefer another testing framework, use it! Once you've installed your tool of choice, using it instead of Jest is as simple as changing the test script in the package.json file. Several of the most popular alternatives to Jest include Jasmine proper, Mocha, AVA, and Tape.

The Mocha framework (https://mochajs.org) is among the most popular in the JavaScript community, but doesn't come with "batteries included," as Jasmine likes to tout. As a result, you'll commonly see Mocha paired with an additional assertion library, such as Chai (http://chaijs.com/) or Expect (https://github.com/mjackson/expect), to cover the ground that Mocha doesn't.

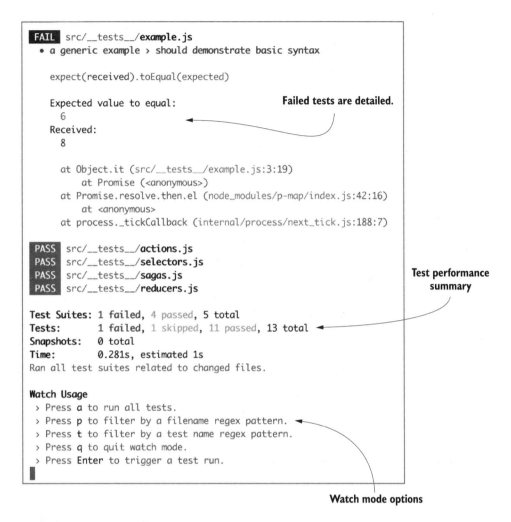

Figure 9.1   Example watch mode output from Jest

AVA (https://github.com/avajs/ava) is newer to the scene. It's received attention for having a slim interface, a slick watch mode, and first-class performance, thanks to tests running concurrently by default.

Finally, Tape (https://github.com/substack/tape) is another newer entrant. It's been embraced for its simplicity, lack of frills, and speed of integration. For these reasons, other open source packages often use Tape for quick examples in their project documentation.

Naturally, this isn't an exhaustive list of testing framework options. By the time this book is published, it's likely you'll have half a dozen more to choose from. Go with whichever makes the best sense for your project and your team. It's outside of the scope of this chapter to provide installation and configuration instructions for these tools, so reference your respective framework's documentation for those details.

9.1.4   *Component testing with Enzyme*

One testing tool that seemingly all React developers can agree on is Enzyme. Enzyme (http://airbnb.io/enzyme/) is a testing tool that makes it dramatically easier to test the output of React components. You can make assertions about the existence of DOM elements, prop values, state values, or callbacks firing on a click event, for example. The syntax is friendly, especially when compared with the utility it wraps, `React-TestUtils` (https://facebook.github.io/react/docs/test-utils.html). If you're interested in testing that three buttons rendered within a component, the syntax looks roughly like this:

```
expect(wrapper.find('button').length).toEqual(3);
```

Enzyme's syntax draws a comparison with jQuery. In this case, the `find` method functions in much the same way it does in jQuery, returning the array of items that match the query. At that point, you're free to use Jest to make the assertion that the number of buttons is equal to three. Later in the chapter, we'll cover more functionality offered by Enzyme.

> **NOTE**   Enzyme underwent a large rewrite between versions 2 and 3, which includes a couple of breaking changes. Version 3 introduces Adapters, meant to make the testing library more extensible for use with React-like libraries, like Preact and Inferno. The examples in this book will use version 3.

9.2   *How does testing Redux differ from React?*

React, of course, includes only the views—the components. If you've tested components in your prior experience with React, you've likely used Enzyme along with one of the frameworks and assertion libraries listed in the previous section. Testing components connected to the Redux store works largely the same way. However, you'll have to account for the augmented functionality of having access to the Redux store in one of two ways, which we'll detail later in the chapter. We'll save component testing for last, to underscore the suggestion not to test-drive development with component tests.

Beyond components, the rest of the elements are newly introduced by Redux and will merit separate test files for each: action creators, reducers, selectors, and sagas. Remember that reducers and selectors are pure functions, so testing them will be straightforward. Pass them data, then make assertions about the results.

Action creator tests must account for both synchronous and asynchronous actions. The former are pure functions as well, so they'll also be easy to knock out, but asynchronous functions will get more involved when you account for side effects such as AJAX requests.

You might be tempted to guess that generators are complicated to test as well, but recall that sagas output only objects called effects, which describe the side effect to be performed by the middleware. Consequently, they're simpler to test than asynchronous action creators.

In the coming sections, you'll walk through test examples for each element in the workflow, starting with the action creators. You'll progress in the sequential order that you'd write the functionality: action creators, sagas, middleware, reducers, and selectors, before circling back to components.

9.3 Testing action creators

This section is broken up into two parts: synchronous and asynchronous action creator tests. As we've mentioned, the latter will account for additional complexity, given the need to manage side effects. You'll start nice and easy with synchronous action creators, though.

9.3.1 Testing synchronous action creators

Synchronous action creators optionally accept arguments and return a plain object, called an action. These are pure functions that produce deterministic results. The following listing introduces a familiar action creator, createTaskSucceeded. Be sure to export the function to make it available to a test file.

Listing 9.3 Example synchronous action

```
export function createTaskSucceeded(task) {       ◁——  Exports the action
  return {                                   ◁—┐          creator for testing
    type: 'CREATE_TASK_SUCCEEDED',            │
    payload: {                                │     The action creator
      task,                                   │     returns an action object.
    },
  };
}
```

When deciding where to write your tests, recall that you have a couple of options provided by the Jest configuration. Jest will run the tests in any file that lives in a __tests__ directory, or is suffixed with .test.js(x) or .spec.js(x). This choice is a matter of style preference, with a couple of practical concerns.

Using a dedicated testing directory makes it easier to view and navigate between all your tests. Another option, co-locating tests alongside the files they're testing, makes it easy to view the tests associated with the feature you're working on at a given time. Co-locating tests also has the advantage of making it obvious when a file doesn't have an associated test file. There's no wrong answer, so try the option that appeals most to you and reorganize if you become dissatisfied with your choice later.

Listing 9.4 offers an example test for the createTaskSucceeded action creator. After importing the function, you'll define the test context, the noun, using a describe block. The it function denotes a unit test—the verb. The goal of the test is to execute the action creator and assert that its result meets your expectation. The example task and expectedAction variables are extracted for readability but aren't a requirement. You can choose to organize your test however you prefer, and it doesn't even necessarily need to have an expect function.

Listing 9.4   Synchronous action creator test

```
                          Imports the action creator to test        Provides the domain noun
                                                                     to the describe function
import { createTaskSucceeded } from './actions/';    ◄─┘

                                                                     Provides the verb to
describe('action creators', () => {                       ◄──────    the it function
  it('should handle successful task creation', () => {    ◄──
    const task = { title: 'Get schwifty', description: 'Show me what you
➥ got' }
    const expectedAction = { type: 'CREATE_TASK_SUCCEEDED', payload: { task
➥ } };
    expect(createTaskSucceeded(task)).toEqual(expectedAction);    ◄─┐
  });                                                    Asserts that the action
});                                                   creator's output is correct
```

If Jest can execute an entire unit test without error, it will consider that a passing test; however, we recommend using the test assertions for greater specificity and confidence that your code is fully tested.

9.3.2   *Testing asynchronous action creators*

Testing asynchronous action creators requires more effort than their synchronous counterparts, but we've found async action tests provide good bang for the buck. Async action creators are these great packages of reusable functionality, and, as a result, any bugs can be felt in multiple places across your application. Generally, the more often a software component is reused, the stronger the case for a unit test. When others who may not have as much context as you want to modify an async action creator, tests ensure they can make changes with confidence.

What do you want to test with async actions? Let's use createTask as an example, one of Parsnip's core action creators. Using createTask is a standard example of async action that makes a network request. Assuming for the sake of this test that you'd get a successful server response, here are createTask's responsibilities:

- Dispatch an action indicating the request has started.
- Make the AJAX request with the correct arguments.
- When the request succeeds, dispatch an action with data from the server response.

These sound an awful lot like things you can translate directly into test assertions, and you'll do that. Before you get to the test, let's look at the implementation of create-Task you'll be using, as shown in the following listing.

Listing 9.5 The createTask async action creator

```
export function createTaskRequested() {
  return {
    type: 'CREATE_TASK_REQUESTED'
  }
}

function createTaskSucceeded(task) {
  return {
    type: 'CREATE_TASK_SUCCEEDED',
    payload: {
      task,
    },
  };
}

export function createTask({ title, description, status = 'Unstarted' }) {
  return dispatch => {
    dispatch(createTaskRequested());
    return api.createTask({ title, description, status }).then(resp => {
      dispatch(createTaskSucceeded(resp.data));
    });
  };
}
```

Makes the request and returns the promise returned by api.createTask

Dispatches an action when the request starts

Dispatches an action when the request succeeds

One thing to note here is that you're returning the promise returned by `api.create-Task` from within the action creator. This wasn't strictly required by your implementation, but as you'll see in a moment, it allows you to make assertions in test. This isn't a code change made based solely on testing requirements; it's often a good practice to return promises from your async action creators because it gives callers the flexibility to respond to the result of the promise.

You know roughly what assertions you need to make, but what kind of setup do you need? You'll need one extra package: `redux-mock-store`. This gives you a convenient interface, `store.getActions()` that returns a list of the actions that have been dispatched to the mock store. You'll use this to assert that the request start/success actions are dispatched properly by `createTask`. The only other thing you'll need is Jest, which you'll use to manually mock the API response. Let's start by configuring the mock store, which you'll eventually use to dispatch `createTask`. Also import and apply the `redux-thunk` middleware, which `createTask` depends on, as shown in the following listing.

Listing 9.6 Configuring a mock Redux store

```
import configureMockStore from 'redux-mock-store'
import thunk from 'redux-thunk';
  import { createTask } from './';

const middlewares = [thunk];
const mockStore = configureMockStore(middlewares);
```

Creates the mock store with the redux-thunk middleware

Next you'll mock `api.createTask`, the function responsible for making the AJAX request. You're using Jest to mock the function out entirely, but you'll commonly see HTTP-mocking libraries such as `nock` used for similar purposes. HTTP mocking has the benefit of being slightly more of an integration test, because an additional component (the API call) is involved directly in the test. The downside is that it can occasionally lead to more overhead in test creation and maintenance. Flat out mocking the function that makes the API call means the action creator test is more focused, but it also means that it won't catch any bugs related to the AJAX call.

For now, you'll mock `api.createTask` directly using Jest's mocking utilities, as shown in the following listing. This ensures `api.createTask` will return a promise that you control directly in the test, and you won't have to worry about anything HTTP related.

Listing 9.7   Mocking api.createTask

Opts out of Jest's auto-mocking   Imports the api module   Explicitly mocks the api.createTask function to return a promise

```
...
jest.unmock('../api');
import * as api from '../api';
api.createTask = jest.fn(
  () => new Promise((resolve, reject) => resolve({ data: 'foo' })),
);
...
```

You've got most of the setup out of the way; now it's time to get into the meat of the test. Use the mock store to dispatch the `createTask` action creator and make assertions about the actions dispatched in the process, as shown in the following listing.

Listing 9.8   Testing createTask

```
import configureMockStore from 'redux-mock-store';
import thunk from 'redux-thunk';
import { createTask } from './';

jest.unmock('../api');
import * as api from '../api';
api.createTask = jest.fn(
  () => new Promise((resolve, reject) => resolve({ data: 'foo' })),
);

const middlewares = [thunk];
const mockStore = configureMockStore(middlewares);

describe('createTask', () => {
  it('works', () => {
    const expectedActions = [
      { type: 'CREATE_TASK_STARTED' },
      { type: 'CREATE_TASK_SUCCEEDED', payload: { task: 'foo' } },
    ];
```

Creates an array of actions you expect to be dispatched by createTask

```
const store = mockStore({          ⊲─┐  Creates the
  tasks: {                            │  mock store
    tasks: [],
  },
});

return store.dispatch(createTask({})).then(() => {  ⊲─
  expect(store.getActions()).toEqual(expectedActions);  ⊲─
  expect(api.createTask).toHaveBeenCalled();  ⊲─
  });
  });
});
```

Creates the mock store

Uses the mock store to dispatch createTask

Uses the store.getActions method, which will return a list of actions that have been dispatched

Asserts that createTask makes the AJAX request

It required a good deal of setup, but all in all this was a reasonable unit test for an async action creator. They tend to have non-trivial functionality and can be difficult to test due to having so many dependencies (for example the Redux store, AJAX). Between redux-mock-store and Jest, the resulting test code isn't over-complicated.

Remember, if the setup starts to become tedious, you can always abstract common work into test utilities.

9.4   Testing sagas

As a quick review, Redux sagas are an alternative pattern to thunks for handling side effects. They're best used for handling more complex side effects, such as long-running processes. In chapter 6, you wrote a saga to manage a timer that kept track of how long a task was in progress. In this section, you'll lean on that saga as an example to test.

Listing 9.9 introduces enough code for the sake of this discussion. You'll see the imports from the root package and the effects helper methods, in addition to the handleProgressTimer generator function. As a refresher, the generator function receives an action, and executes code if the action type is TIMER_STARTED. When that's true, an infinite loop is initiated, and each loop through waits one second before dispatching a TIMER_INCREMENT action, as shown in the following listing.

Listing 9.9   The handleProgressTimer saga

```
import { delay } from 'redux-saga';          │  Imports helper
import { call, put } from 'redux-saga/effects';  │  methods
...
export function* handleProgressTimer({ type, payload }) {  ⊲─  Exports the
  if (type === 'TIMER_STARTED') {                              generator
    while (true) {                          ⊲─  Until the type      function to
      yield call(delay, 1000);                  changes, wait      test it
      yield put({                               one second, then
        type: 'TIMER_INCREMENT',                dispatch an
        payload: { taskId: payload.taskId },    increment action.
      });
    }
  }
}
```

Fortunately, testing generators is simpler than testing most thunks. Remember, the saga middleware is what executes AJAX requests or other side effects. The sagas you write return an effect: an object that describes what the middleware should do. When you test sagas, then, all you need to assert is that the generator function returns the effect object you expect.

After importing the necessary functions, listing 9.10 will test the generator function with a couple of different actions, TIMER_STARTED and TIMER_STOPPED. Keep in mind that each return value of a generator is an object with value and done keys. For the TIMER_STARTED test, you'll want to assert that the value key meets our expectations each time the next function is called on the generator. However, instead of manually typing out the effect object, you can invoke a saga method that produces the expected output.

Context may be helpful to understand the reasoning behind this decision. Effects are generated by the redux-saga helper methods and aren't intended to be pretty. Here's an example of the effect produced by a call of the delay method (for example, call(delay, 1000)):

```
{
  '@@redux-saga/IO': true,
  CALL: { context: null, fn: [(Function: delay)], args: [1000] },
}
```

Instead of writing out this object manually, you can more easily assert that the next value produced by the generator function is equal to the result of executing call(delay, 1000), as shown in the following listing.

Listing 9.10   Testing sagas

```
import { delay } from 'redux-saga';                          Imports the library
import { call, put } from 'redux-saga/effects';             methods and saga
import { handleProgressTimer } from '../sagas';

describe('sagas', () => {
  it('handles the handleProgressTimer happy path', () => {
    const iterator = handleProgressTimer({              Initializes the generator
      type: 'TIMER_STARTED',                            function with a
      payload: { taskId: 12 },                          TIMER_STARTED action
    });

    const expectedAction = {
      type: 'TIMER_INCREMENT',                          Infinitely, the saga waits
      payload: { taskId: 12 },                          for one second, then
    };                                                  dispatches the action.

    expect(iterator.next().value).toEqual(call(delay, 1000));
    expect(iterator.next().value).toEqual(put(expectedAction));
    expect(iterator.next().value).toEqual(call(delay, 1000));
    expect(iterator.next().value).toEqual(put(expectedAction));
    expect(iterator.next().done).toBe(false);           At any point, this saga
  });                                                   will indicate it isn't done.
});
```

```
it('handles the handleProgressTimer sad path', () => {      ◄───  Tests the case
  const iterator = handleProgressTimer({       ◄──┐                that the
    type: 'TIMER_STOPPED',                         │ Initializes the  generator
  });                                              │ saga with a      doesn't receive a
                                                     TIMER_STOPPED    TIMER_STARTED
  expect(iterator.next().done).toBe(true);  ◄──┐  action            action
});                                            │
});                                              Confirms that
                                                 the saga is done
                                                 immediately
```

If there are forks in your logic, be sure to test each of them. In this case, you need to test the saga in the event that an action other than `TIMER_STARTED` comes through. The test proves simple, because the body of the generator function is skipped and the done key immediately returns a `true` value.

Learning to write sagas may not be easy, but happily, testing them is more straightforward. The big idea is to step through the results of the generator function, one next at a time. Assuming there is a conclusion to the saga, eventually you can assert that the value of done is `true`.

A final note on the subject: sagas respond to actions dispatched from somewhere, so don't forget to test that dispatch. Typically, this is a synchronous action creator that requires a simple test of a pure function (section 9.4.1). On to middleware!

9.5 *Testing middleware*

Middleware intercept actions before they reach the reducers. They're written in a peculiar function signature with three nested functions. The goal of middleware tests is to assess that specific actions are being handled appropriately. For this example, you'll reference the analytics middleware written in chapter 5, with slight changes.

Listing 9.11 introduces the middleware. The nested function will check for actions with an analytics key. If the action in question doesn't have any, it gets passed on with the `next` function. Appropriate actions will move on to trigger an analytics AJAX request.

> **Listing 9.11 exampleMiddleware – Analytics middleware**

```
import fakeAnalyticsApi from './exampleService';

const analytics = store => next => action => {
  if (!action || !action.meta || !action.meta.analytics) {   ◄──┐  Passes the action
    return next(action);                                         │  on if no analytics
  }                                                               key exists

  const { event, data } = action.meta.analytics;

  fakeAnalyticsApi(event, data)                  ◄──┐  Performs an
    .then(resp => {                                 │  AJAX request
      console.log('Recorded: ', event, data);
    })
    .catch(err => {
```

```
      console.error(
        'An error occurred while sending analytics: ',
        err.toSting()
      );
    });
```

```
  return next(action);                          Always passes the action
};                                    ◁──┤      to the next middleware
                                               or reducers
```

```
export default analytics;
```

The API service is mocked out for the purposes of testing. See the following listing for that example code. Every call results in a successful promise resolution.

Listing 9.12   exampleService.js – Example fake analytics API service

```
export default function fakeAnalyticsApi(eventName, data) {
  return new Promise((resolve, reject) => {           ◁──
    resolve('Success!');                                      Mocked API call for the
  });                                                         sake of the example
}
```

The mechanics of testing this code are a little cumbersome, but made easier with a helper function provided in the official Redux documentation, found at https://github .com/reactjs/redux/blob/master/docs/recipes/WritingTests.md#middleware. This method is called `create` and can be seen in listing 9.13. The purpose of the `create` function is to mock out all the important functions, while providing a convenient wrapper for executing the middleware.

These tests also require more advanced Jest mocking. The API service gets mocked, so that you can assert whether it was called. In the listing, you can see the mocking and importing of the module. The `mockImplementation` function is used to specify what happens when the mocked function is executed. The mocked value you use is identical to your actual implementation. Your tested version may look like this, but your actual implementation of an API service won't.

Each test will use the `create` method to get running, pass in an object to the middleware, and assert whether it interacts with the API service. Because the service is mocked, it keeps track of whether it was invoked.

Finally, all actions should end up as an argument, executed by the `next` function. This is an important assertion to write for each of the middleware tests.

Listing 9.13   Analytics middleware test

```
import analytics from '../exampleMiddleware';
                                                          Mocks the
jest.mock('../exampleService');                    ◁──   API service
import fakeAnalyticsApi from '../exampleService';
fakeAnalyticsApi.mockImplementation(() => new Promise((resolve, reject) =>
  ➥ resolve('Success')));              ◁──
                                              Determines the mock's response
```

```
const create = () => {
  const store = {                           ⟵  Shows the create helper
    getState: jest.fn(() => ({})),              method from official
    dispatch: jest.fn(),                        documentation
  };
  const next = jest.fn();
  const invoke = (action) => analytics(store)(next)(action);
  return { store, next, invoke };
};

describe('analytics middleware', () => {
  it('should pass on irrelevant keys', () => {     ⟵  Uses the create helper
    const { next, invoke } = create();                to reduce redundancy

    const action = { type: 'IRRELEVANT' };
                                              ⟵  Sends the action through
    invoke(action);                               the middleware

    expect(next).toHaveBeenCalledWith(action);    ⟵  Asserts that the
    expect(fakeAnalyticsApi).not.toHaveBeenCalled();   action was passed
  })                                                    to the next function

  it('should make an analytics API call', () => {
    const { next, invoke } = create();

    const action = {
      type: RELEVANT,          ⟵  Provides an action that
      meta: {                      meets the middleware
        analytics: {               criteria
          event: 'foo',
          data: { extra: 'stuff' }
        },
      },
    };

    invoke(action);

    expect(next).toHaveBeenCalledWith(action);
    expect(fakeAnalyticsApi).toHaveBeenCalled();   ⟵  Asserts that the
  })                                                  service was executed
})
```

That was pretty dense. Revisit the `create` method to make sure you grok what that's doing for you. It's not too magical and does a good job of DRYing up the test suite. Give the quick documentation a read for more details at https://github.com/reactjs/redux/blob/master/docs/recipes/WritingTests.md#middleware.

Mocking functions is another topic that may not come easy the first couple times around the block. Spending time with the related documentation is a good investment. You'll find more than you'll ever need to know at https://facebook.github.io/jest/docs/en/mock-functions.html.

9.6   *Testing reducers*

Testing reducers is pleasantly straightforward. At a high level, you'll test for each case in a `switch` statement. The following listing contains an abbreviated tasks reducer for which you'll write tests. For the sake of example, the reducer won't use normalized data. In the listing, you'll find an initial state object and a tasks reducer with two case clauses and a default clause.

> **Listing 9.14   Tasks reducer**

```
const initialState = {                      Provides initial state
  tasks: [],                                for the reducer
  isLoading: false,
  error: null,
  searchTerm: '',                                      Exports the
};                                                     reducer for
                                                       usage and
export default function tasks(state = initialState, action) {   testing
  switch (action.type) {
    case 'FETCH_TASKS_STARTED': {          A switch statement
      return {                             handles each
        ...state,                          incoming action type.
        isLoading: true,
      };
    }
    case 'FETCH_TASKS_SUCCEEDED': {        Shows one
      return {                             case clause per
        ...state,                          action type
        tasks: action.payload.tasks,
        isLoading: false,
      };
    }
    ...
    default: {                   A default clause is
      return state;              triggered when no
    }                            action type matches.
  }
}
```

Because a reducer is a pure function, testing it requires no special helper methods or any other funny business. Writing reducer tests is a great way to reinforce your understanding of what a reducer does, though. Recall that a reducer takes an existing state and a new action and returns a new state. The signature for that test looks like this:

```
expect(reducer(state, action)).toEqual(newState);
```

For each action type, you'll assert that a new action results in the state you expect. The following listing contains tests for each action type. As demonstrated in the listing, it's also a good idea to test that the default state appears as you expect it to. That test calls the reducer function with no current state value and an empty action object.

Listing 9.15   Tasks reducer test

```
import tasks from '../reducers/';

describe('the tasks reducer', () => {
  const initialState = {
    tasks: [],
    isLoading: false,
    error: null,
    searchTerm: '',
  };

  it('should return the initialState', () => {
    expect(tasks(undefined, {})).toEqual(initialState);
  });

  it('should handle the FETCH_TASKS_STARTED action', () => {
    const action = { type: 'FETCH_TASKS_STARTED' };
    const expectedState = { ...initialState, isLoading: true };

    expect(tasks(initialState, action)).toEqual(expectedState);
  });

  it('should handle the FETCH_TASKS_SUCCEEDED action', () => {
    const taskList = [{ title: 'Test the reducer', description: 'Very meta'
    }];
    const action = {
      type: 'FETCH_TASKS_SUCCEEDED',
      payload: { tasks: taskList },
    };
    const expectedState = { ...initialState, tasks: taskList };

    expect(tasks(initialState, action)).toEqual(expectedState);
  });
});
```

The reducer tests are within one describe block.

Import or declare initial state for all tests.

Tests for the initial state

Defines the action passed into the reducer

Defines the expected state produced by the reducer

In many of the tests, you'll see variables for the action and expected state declared prior to the assertion. This pattern is for the convenience of having more readable assertions.

In these tests, you'll notice that you used initialState as the first argument in the reducer you're testing. You can wander away from this pattern, and will likely need to, to get full test coverage. For example, the FETCH_TASKS_SUCCEEDED test captures the change to tasks in the expected state, but not a change in the isLoading value. This can be tested either by starting with an isLoading value of true or by writing an additional test that captures the functionality.

9.7   *Testing selectors*

Testing selectors is nearly as straightforward as testing reducers. Similar to reducers, selectors can be pure functions. However, selectors created with reselect have additional functionality, namely memoization. Listing 9.16 introduces a couple of generic selectors and one selector created with reselect. Testing the first two generic selectors looks like a test for any other pure function. Given input, they should always produce the same output. The standard test function signature will do. The code is taken directly from the initial task search feature implementation.

Listing 9.16   Example selectors

```
import { createSelector } from 'reselect';

export const getTasks = state => state.tasks.tasks;
export const getSearchTerm = state => state.tasks.searchTerm;

export const getFilteredTasks = createSelector(
  [getTasks, getSearchTerm],
  (tasks, searchTerm) => {
    return tasks.filter(task => task.title.match(new RegExp(searchTerm,
      'i')));
  }
);
```

Exports the generic selectors

Exports the reselect selector

The selector relies on the results of other selectors.

Returns the filtered list of tasks

Selectors written with `reselect` get more interesting, so `reselect` provides additional helper functions. Besides returning the desired output, another key piece of functionality worth testing is that the function is memoizing the correct data and limiting the number of recalculations it performs. A helper method, `recomputations`, is available for this purpose. Again, generic selectors take a state as input and produce a slice of the state as output. `reselect` selectors perform a similar task but avoid extra work if they can help it. If the `getFilteredTasks` function has the same inputs, it won't bother recalculating the output, opting instead to return the last stored output.

In between tests, you can reset the number to zero by using the `reset-Recomputations` method, as shown in the following listing.

Listing 9.17   Testing selectors

```
import { getTasks, getSearchTerm, getFilteredTasks } from '../reducers/';
import cloneDeep from 'lodash/cloneDeep';

describe('tasks selectors', () => {
  const state = {
    tasks: {
      tasks: [
        { title: 'Test selectors', description: 'Very meta' },
        { title: 'Learn Redux', description: 'Oh my!' },
      ],
      searchTerm: 'red',
      isLoading: false,
      error: null,
    },
  };
```

Builds state tree for use by multiple tests

Cleans the test environment after each test

```
afterEach(() => {
  getFilteredTasks.resetRecomputations();
});
```

← The afterEach function executes a callback after each test.

```
it('should retrieve tasks from the getTasks selector', () => {
  expect(getTasks(state)).toEqual(state.tasks.tasks);
});
```

Generic selectors are tested like any other pure function.

```
it('should retrieve the searchTerm from the getSearchTerm selector', ()
⇒ => {
  expect(getSearchTerm(state)).toEqual(state.tasks.searchTerm);
});

it('should return tasks from the getFilteredTasks selector', () => {
  const expectedTasks = [{ title: 'Learn Redux', description: 'Oh my!'
⇒ }];

  expect(getFilteredTasks(state)).toEqual(expectedTasks);
});

it('should minimally recompute the state when getFilteredTasks is
⇒ called', () => {
  const similarSearch = cloneDeep(state);
  similarSearch.tasks.searchTerm = 'redu';
```

← **Prepares new state versions to test selector output**

```
  const uniqueSearch = cloneDeep(state);
  uniqueSearch.tasks.searchTerm = 'selec';

  expect(getFilteredTasks.recomputations()).toEqual(0);
  getFilteredTasks(state);
  getFilteredTasks(similarSearch);
  expect(getFilteredTasks.recomputations()).toEqual(1);
  getFilteredTasks(uniqueSearch);
  expect(getFilteredTasks.recomputations()).toEqual(2);
});
});
```

← **Verifies the selector does the minimum number of recomputations**

Selectors are generally tested in dedicated files or alongside reducers. Having access to a reducer function and using it to produce the next state for your selector to recompute can make for a great integration test. You get to decide how granular of a unit test you'd like.

9.8 *Testing components*

Now, because we discourage TDD with components doesn't mean we're suggesting not testing them. Component tests are valuable for detecting breaking changes to the UI when state is added or removed. This section is broken into a couple of parts: testing presentational components and testing container components.

Again, these tests will make use of the testing tool, Enzyme. If you've any prior React experience, there's a fair chance you've used Enzyme to test common React components already. Enzyme was written to facilitate React testing; however, adding

Redux to the mix doesn't change the equation. You can use still use Enzyme to test presentational and container components.

9.8.1   *Testing presentational components*

Presentational components don't have access to the Redux store. They're standard React components; they accept props, manage local component state, and render DOM elements. Recall that presentational components can either be stateless or stateful. For this first example, you'll examine a stateless presentational component, often referred to as a functional stateless component.

The following listing shows the `TaskList` component. It accepts props, then renders a status and an array of `Task` components.

Listing 9.18   Example presentational component

```
import React from 'react';
import Task from '../components/Task';          The component
                                                accepts props from a
const TaskList = props => {                 ◁── parent component.
  return (
    <div className="task-list">                  Renders a
      <div className="task-list-title">          status prop
        <strong>{props.status}</strong>    ◁──                 Renders a Task
      </div>                                                   component for
      {props.tasks.map(task => (                       ◁──     each task prop
        <Task key={task.id} task={task} onStatusChange={props.onStatusChange}
    />
      ))}
    </div>
  );
}                                          Exports the
                                           component for
export default TaskList;               ◁── usage and testing
```

Testing this type of component is a matter of expecting the important pieces to get rendered to the DOM. Listing 9.19 demonstrates some of the types of things you can test for. The couple examples included check for the text value of a particular element and the number of expected elements rendered as a result of a prop value.

We have an implementation detail worth calling out here. As mentioned in the introduction, Enzyme version 3 introduces the concept of Adapters. Airbnb maintains an adapter for each of the latest versions of React, so you'll configure Enzyme with the React 16 adapter. These adapters are separate installations, so in your case you'll use the package `enzyme-adapter-react-16`.

To traverse the component and make assertions, you need Enzyme to virtually mount the component. The two methods most frequently used to accomplish this are Enzyme's `shallow` and `mount`. Unlike `shallow`, `mount` renders all children components, allows for simulating events (for example, click), and can be used to test React lifecycle callbacks (for example, `componentDidMount`). As a rule of thumb, use `shallow` until your test requires the extra functionality provided by mount, for the sake of performance. Your first examples use `shallow`, as shown in listing 9.19

Components mounted with Enzyme are commonly saved to a variable called `wrapper`. This is a convention perpetuated by examples in the official documentation. Note that the `find` method can locate more than element types. Elements can be selected using class names and IDs, similar to CSS selectors: `wrapper.find('.className')` or `wrapper.find('#id')`.

Listing 9.19 Presentational component tests

```
import React from 'react';
import Enzyme, { shallow } from 'enzyme';            ⟵  Imports shallow from enzyme
import Adapter from 'enzyme-adapter-react-16';           to mount the component
import TaskList from '../components/TaskList';    ⟵
                                                         Imports the        Uses Enzyme
Enzyme.configure({ adapter: new Adapter() });            component         to mount the
                                                         to test           component for
describe('the TaskList component', () => {                                 testing
  it('should render a status', () => {
    const wrapper = shallow(<TaskList status="In Progress" tasks={[]} />);   ⟵

    expect(wrapper.find('strong').text()).toEqual('In Progress');   ⟵  Asserts that the
  });                                                                    DOM contains the
                                                                        right text values
  it('should render a Task component for each task', () => {
    const tasks = [
      { id: 1, title: 'A', description: 'a', status: 'Unstarted', timer: 0 [CA]},
      { id: 2, title: 'B', description: 'b', status: 'Unstarted', timer: 0 [CA]},
      { id: 3, title: 'C', description: 'c', status: 'Unstarted', timer: 0 [CA]}
    ]
    const wrapper = shallow(<TaskList status="Unstarted" tasks={tasks} />);

    expect(wrapper.find('Task').length).toEqual(3);   ⟵  Uses Enzyme to find the
  });                                                     number of expected
});                                                       elements
```

For a long list of additional API methods available to the `wrapper`, reference the documentation at http://airbnb.io/enzyme/docs/api/shallow.html.

9.8.2 *Snapshot testing*

As mentioned in the chapter introduction, Jest comes with a powerful feature called snapshot testing. Snapshot testing can be used to catch any change to your UI at a granular level. It works by capturing a JSON representation of your component the first time the test runs; then each subsequent run of the test compares a fresh rendering of the component to the saved snapshot. If anything in the component has changed since the snapshot, you have the opportunity to either fix the unintentional change or confirm that the update is what you wanted. If the change was desired, the saved snapshot will update.

Snapshot testing diverges in several ways from existing test paradigms. It isn't possible to perform TDD with snapshots. By definition, the component must already be written for the first snapshot to be recorded. This concept jives with our recommendation to test-drive the development of everything except the components.

You'll find that snapshot testing introduces a slightly new workflow, as well. As you'll soon see, writing snapshot tests is tremendously easy and requires nearly zero effort upfront. As such, the speed at which you write tests can accelerate. The other side of the coin is that these new tests provide much output you won't be used to handling. For each tweak you make to the UI, the test suite asks about it. This has the potential to feel obnoxious or overwhelming, until it demonstrates real value and becomes part of the normal workflow.

Jest's well-designed watch mode is the key to making snapshot testing a breeze. If you want to update a snapshot to the most recently tested version of a component, you can do so with a single keystroke. The "u" key will update the saved snapshot, and you're free to carry on. You'll see an example of this output shortly.

One extra package exists that you'll want to leverage to make snapshot testing a seamless process. Install `enzyme-to-json` in your devDependencies by running the following command:

```
npm install -D enzyme-to-json
```

This does exactly what the name implies: converts the component, mounted with Enzyme, to JSON. Without this transform, the component JSON will always include dynamic debugging values, making snapshots fail when they shouldn't.

You're ready to write a snapshot test. You'll continue to use the `TaskList` component from the previous section as our example. In the same `describe` block, you'll add the snapshot test seen in listing 9.20.

As mentioned, these tests are exceptionally simple to write. Once you've mounted the component, you'll expect the JSON-converted version to match the saved snapshot, using the `toMatchSnapshot` method. The first time `toMatchSnapshot` is called, a new snapshot will be saved. Each time thereafter, the component will be compared to the last saved snapshot.

> **Listing 9.20   Example snapshot tests**

```
...
import toJson from 'enzyme-to-json';          ◁┐ Imports toJson
                                                │ to convert the
describe('the TaskList component', () => {      │ enzyme wrapper
  ...

  it('should match the last snapshot without tasks', () => {
    const wrapper = shallow(<TaskList status="In Progress" tasks={[]} />);
    expect(toJson(wrapper)).toMatchSnapshot();  ◁┐ Uses the toMatchSnapshot
  });                                            │ method to create and
                                                 │ compare snapshots
```

```
it('should match the last snapshot with tasks', () => {
  const tasks = [
    { id: 1, title: 'A', description: 'a', status: 'Unstarted', timer: 0 },
    { id: 2, title: 'B', description: 'b', status: 'Unstarted', timer: 0 },
    { id: 3, title: 'C', description: 'c', status: 'Unstarted', timer: 0 }
  ]
  const wrapper = shallow(<TaskList status="In Progress" tasks={tasks} />);
  expect(toJson(wrapper)).toMatchSnapshot();
});
});
```

You may snapshot test a component multiple times with unique props.

The first time around, Jest will output the following message to the console:

```
› 2 snapshots written in 1 test suite.
```

Running the test suite again will produce additional output in the console. You can see that the snapshot tests are running and passing. Figure 9.2 shows the example output.

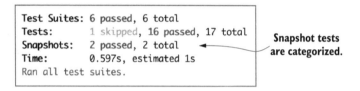

Snapshot tests are categorized.

Figure 9.2   Jest test output with snapshot tests

If you make changes to the UI, you can expect the snapshot tests to let you know about it. Let's add a class to the strong element that renders the status name within the TaskList component:

```
<strong className="example">{props.status}</strong>
```

While the watch mode is running, saving the TaskList file triggers Jest to run the tests again. This time, the snapshot tests will fail, highlighting the differences between the new code and what it expected (figure 9.3).

Further down in the console output, Jest lets you know the outcome: two tests failed, but if the change was intentional, press the "u" key to update the snapshots:

```
› 2 snapshot tests failed in 1 test suite. Inspect your code changes or press
    `u` to update them.
```

If you like the changes, you can hit the "u" key and watch the test suite run again. In the results, all tests are now passing, and you get a confirmation that the snapshots were updated:

```
› 2 snapshots updated in 1 test suite.
```

```
FAIL src/__tests__/components.js
  • the TaskList component > should match the last snapshot without tasks

  expect(value).toMatchSnapshot()

  Received value does not match stored snapshot 1.

  - Snapshot
  + Received

  @@ -2,10 +2,12 @@
     className="task-list"
   >
     <div
       className="task-list-title"
     >
  -     <strong>
  +     <strong
  +       className="example"
  +     >
         In Progress
       </strong>
     </div>
   </div>
```

Diff of component outputs

Figure 9.3   An example snapshot test failure with a file diff of what was received and expected

Snapshot testing with Jest can give you a high degree of confidence that your UI isn't changing unexpectedly. As a rule of thumb, you should use snapshots to unit test individual components. Snapshot tests that encompass the entire application aren't that valuable, because failures will come from distant corners of the app, be exceptionally noisy, and require frequent updates to the snapshots.

The workflow will likely feel unnatural at first. Give yourself time to get a feel for how many snapshot tests are appropriate and how to integrate them into your workflow. Given how easy they are to write, you may have to resist the urge to go overboard with snapshots. Over time, you'll find the right balance.

Note that although Jest was the first framework to introduce and popularize snapshot testing, the functionality isn't exclusive to it. Other frameworks, such as Ava, have since adopted the feature. Remember that the key to snapshots' ease of use is a robust test runner that accommodates them. At the time of writing, Jest is ahead of the pack there, but it may not be long before others catch up and offer similar quality.

9.8.3   *Testing container components*

Container components are components with access to the Redux store. You know that you're working with a container component when you see the connect method, from react-redux, wrapping the component prior to export.

Testing a container component requires accounting for a couple of extra concerns beyond normal components. First, the component will have additional props available to it, between the `dispatch` method and any additional props specified within the `mapStateToProps` function. The second and more tedious concern is the fact that you're exporting not the component you wrote, but instead an enhanced component. Let's examine these ideas using an example.

The following listing contains the `App` component in its state at the resolution of chapter 7. The component is enhanced using the `connect` method. On mount, it uses the `dispatch` function to send an action to the store.

Listing 9.21   Example container component

```
import React, { Component } from 'react';
import Enzyme, { connect } from 'react-redux';         ◁─┐  The connect method
import Adapter from 'enzyme-adapter-react-16';              enables a component to
import TasksPage from './components/TasksPage';             access the Redux store.
import FlashMessage from './components/FlashMessage';
import { createTask, editTask, fetchTasks, filterTasks } from './actions';
import { getGroupedAndFilteredTasks } from './reducers/';

Enzyme.configure({ adapter: new Adapter() });

class App extends Component {
  componentDidMount() {
    this.props.dispatch(fetchTasks());        ◁─┐  When the component
  }                                               mounts, an action
                                                  creator is invoked.
  onCreateTask = ({ title, description }) => {
    this.props.dispatch(createTask({ title, description }));
  };

  onStatusChange = (id, status) => {
    this.props.dispatch(editTask(id, { status }));
  };

  onSearch = searchTerm => {
    this.props.dispatch(filterTasks(searchTerm));
  };

  render() {
    return (
      <div className="container">
        {this.props.error && <FlashMessage message={this.props.error} />}
        <div className="main-content">
          <TasksPage
            tasks={this.props.tasks}
            onCreateTask={this.onCreateTask}
            onSearch={this.onSearch}
            onStatusChange={this.onStatusChange}
            isLoading={this.props.isLoading}
          />
        </div>
```

```
        </div>
      );
    }
  }
}

function mapStateToProps(state) {
  const { isLoading, error } = state.tasks;

  return {
    tasks: getGroupedAndFilteredTasks(state),
    isLoading,
    error
  };
}

export default connect(mapStateToProps)(App);
```

Details which slices of Redux store state the component can read

Uses connect to enhance the App component

Let's try writing the first test. When the Redux store contains an error in the tasks key, you want to render a FlashMessage component with that error message. If you try to test this component the way you tested the presentational component, you'll see that you quickly find trouble. Let's step through it.

The following listing attempts a simple test. You mount the App component, provide an error prop, and make an assertion that the FlashMessage component is rendered.

Listing 9.22   A container test attempt

```
import React from 'react';
import { shallow } from 'enzyme';
import App from '../App';

describe('the App container', () => {
  it('should render a FlashMessage component if there is an error', () => {
    const wrapper = shallow(<App error="Boom!" />);
    expect(wrapper.find('FlashMessage').exists()).toBe(true);
  });
});
```

Imports the component for testing

Mounts the component with an error prop

Asserts that the error message renders

Running this test produces an interesting and descriptive error message:

```
Invariant Violation: Could not find "store" in either the context or props of
"Connect(App)". Either wrap the root component in a <Provider>, or explicitly
pass "store" as a prop to "Connect(App)".
```

This error message reveals much about where you've gone wrong so far. Notably, you're referencing an App component, but what you imported is an enhanced component, Connect(App). Under the hood, that enhanced component expects to interact with a Redux store instance, and when it doesn't find one, it throws an error.

You have at least a couple of ways you can account for the error messages. The easiest route is to export the unconnected `App` component, in addition to the connected one. All this requires is adding the `export` keyword to the class declaration, as follows:

```
export class App extends Component {
```

Once you've exported the unconnected `App` component, you can then import either the enhanced or the plain component. The enhanced component is the default export, so when you want to use it, you can use the default import syntax, the way you already do in the example test. If you want to import the unconnected component, you'll need to specify that using curly braces:

```
import { App } from '../App';
```

With these changes to the component and test file, the test suite should pass. You're free to test the `App` component as if it weren't connected to Redux anymore, because, of course, it isn't. If you want to test any props that `App` should receive from the Redux store, you'll have to pass those in yourself, the same way as the `error` prop in the previous example.

Let's add another test of the unconnected component. Listing 9.23 adds a test to verify that the `dispatch` method is executed when the component mounts. Recall that Enzyme's `mount` function is required to test React lifecycle methods, such as `component-DidMount`. You need to import `mount` and use it instead of `shallow` for this test.

Jest offers a simple way to create spies, using `jest.fn()`. Spies can keep track of whether they've been executed, so you'll use one to verify that `dispatch` is called. Jest supplies the `toHaveBeenCalled` assertion method for this purpose. You'll notice that you've also added an empty array of tasks to the component to prevent a rendering error in the component.

Listing 9.23   Example container test

```
import React from 'react';              Adds mount to the
import { shallow, mount } from 'enzyme';    ⟵ enzyme imports
import { App } from '../App';      ⟵
                                   Imports the unconnected
describe('the App container', () => {     component
  ...
  it('should dispatch fetchTasks on mount', () => {    Creates a spy
    const spy = jest.fn();                      ⟵
    const wrapper = mount(<App dispatch={spy} error="Boom!" tasks={[]} />);   ⟵

    expect(spy).toHaveBeenCalled();    ⟵                          Adds dispatch
  });                              Asserts that the              and tasks props
});                               function was called
```

You find that testing container components in this fashion is usually sufficient for the test coverage you want. However, there may be times that you're interested in testing the Redux functionality as well. The way to accomplish that is to wrap the container in a `Provider` component with a store instance.

Needing a store instance is a common enough need to warrant a utility package. Install `redux-mock-store` to your devDependencies with the following command:

```
npm install -D redux-mock-store
```

You have the rest of the necessary dependencies already installed, so write the test. Listing 9.24 puts it all together to test that the `FETCH_TASKS_STARTED` action is dispatched on mount. A few new imports are required: the `Provider` component, the `configureMockStore` method, any middleware you use in the application, and the connected component.

In the unit test, you'll want to mount the connected component, wrapped by the `Provider` component. Similar to the actual implementation, the `Provider` component needs a `store` instance passed in as a prop. To create the `store` instance, you need to provide the middleware and an initial store state.

Once the mock store is initialized, you can use it to view any actions that it receives. The mock store keeps track of an array of dispatched actions and can be used to make assertions about the content and number of those actions.

Listing 9.24   Container test with a mock store

```
import React from 'react';
import { shallow, mount } from 'enzyme';
import { Provider } from 'react-redux';            ◁── Adds the new imports
import configureMockStore from 'redux-mock-store';      to wrap the connected
import thunk from 'redux-thunk';                         component
import ConnectedApp, { App } from '../App';

describe('the App container', () => {
  ...
  it('should fetch tasks on mount', () => {       ◁── Adds any middleware
    const middlewares = [thunk];                      used in your app
    const initialState = {               ◁┐
      tasks: {                            │  Creates an initial
        tasks: [],                        │  state for the store
        isLoading: false,
        error: null,
        searchTerm: '',
      },
    };
    const mockStore = configureMockStore(middlewares)(initialState);   ◁── Creates the
    const wrapper = mount(<Provider store={mockStore}><ConnectedApp       mock store
 ➥ /></Provider>);                                        ◁──┐ Mounts the
    const expectedAction = { type: 'FETCH_TASKS_STARTED' };       wrapped
                                                                  container
    expect(mockStore.getActions()[0]).toEqual(expectedAction);  ◁── component
  });
});                              Tests that the action was
                                 dispatched to the mock store
```

Although this strategy is definitely more labor-intensive than testing the unconnected component, you get something for the extra effort. This flavor of test integrates more pieces of the puzzle, and therefore makes for a higher-quality integration test.

> **TIP** We recommend you write most component unit tests in the unconnected fashion and write a smaller number of integration-style tests using mock stores.

Before we move on from component testing, there's one debugging strategy we can't leave out. If you're ever stumped as to why a test is passing or failing unexpectedly, you can log the contents of a component to the console. The debug method allows you to visualize each element in the virtual DOM:

```
console.log(wrapper.debug());
```

Use this line within any test to compare the actual DOM elements with your expectations. More often than not, this will keep you moving forward.

9.9 *Exercise*

To practice testing each component, you can write additional tests for any of Parsnip's functionality that we haven't covered so far in the chapter. Use this chapter's examples as a guide and adjust each individual test to fit your needs.

For now, try writing another async action test, this time for the editTask action creator. The following listing shows a simple implementation of editTask you can work from so we're all on the same page.

Listing 9.25 The editTask action creator

```
function editTaskStarted() {
  return {
    type: 'EDIT_TASK_STARTED',
  };
}

function editTaskSucceeded(task) {
  return {
    type: 'EDIT_TASK_SUCCEEDED',
    payload: {
      task,
    },
  };
}

export function editTask(task, params = {}) {
  return (dispatch, getState) => {
    dispatch(editTaskStarted());

    return api.editTask(task.id, params).then(resp => {
      dispatch(editTaskSucceeded(resp.data));
    });
  };
}
```

Given that `editTask` is a standard request-based async action creator, here are a few good things to test:

- The `EDIT_TASK_STARTED` action is dispatched.
- The API call is made with the correct arguments.
- The `EDIT_TASK_SUCCEEDED` action is dispatched.

9.10 *Solution*

Here's how to approach this:

- Create the mock store with `redux-thunk` middleware.
- Mock the `api.editTask` function.
- Create the mock store.
- Dispatch the action creator, `editTask`.
- Assert that the right actions are dispatched by `editTask`, and that the request is made.

Keep in mind this is much like the test for `createTask` you wrote earlier in the chapter. Generally, a testing strategy like this will work well with any thunk-based async action. The following listing shows the solution.

Listing 9.26 Testing the editTask action creator

```
import configureMockStore from 'redux-mock-store';
import thunk from 'redux-thunk';                       ◁── Imports the async
import { editTask } from './';                              action you want to test

jest.unmock('../api');
import * as api from '../api';
api.editTask = jest.fn(() => new Promise((resolve, reject) => resolve({
⮑ data: 'foo' })));
                                                       ┐ Adds the redux-
const middlewares = [thunk];                           │ thunk middleware
const mockStore = configureMockStore(middlewares);     ◁─┘ to the mock store

describe('editTask', () => {                            ┐ Creates a list of expected
  it('dispatches the right actions', () => {            │ actions you'll use in an
    const expectedActions = [                           ◁─┘ assertion later in the test
      { type: 'EDIT_TASK_STARTED' },
      { type: 'EDIT_TASK_SUCCEEDED', payload: { task: 'foo' } }
    ];

    const store = mockStore({ tasks: {       ◁── Creates the
      tasks: [                                    mock store
        {id: 1, title: 'old' }
      ]
                                                       ┐ Dispatches the
    }});                                               │ editTask action

    return store.dispatch(editTask({id: 1, title: 'old'}, { title: 'new'
⮑ })).then(() => {                                      ◁──────────┘
```

Mocks the API call with a resolved promise (annotation pointing to the `jest.unmock` / `api.editTask` lines)

```
      expect(store.getActions()).toEqual(expectedActions);
      expect(api.editTask).toHaveBeenCalledWith(1, { title: 'new' });
    });
  });
});
```

**Asserts the API request is made
with the correct arguments**

**Asserts the correct
actions are dispatched**

Of note, you're continuing to mock the `api.editTask` method directly, meaning you totally bypass any test setup related to handling HTTP requests. HTTP-mocking libraries such as nock are always an option and may give you more bang for your buck, as you can also exercise making the HTTP request.

JavaScript developers have left code untested for years! Why start now? That's a joke, of course, but testing JavaScript has earned a reputation for been notoriously difficult. That difficulty largely stems from the deeply coupled, "spaghetti" code that too often characterized client-side applications of the past. Without a robust test suite, however, it's difficult to have any confidence that new code isn't introducing breaking changes.

Fortunately, Redux moves us a large step toward sanity by decoupling many of the moving pieces into small, testable units. Are there still confusing parts? You bet. Are we headed in the right direction, though? We sure think so.

In the next chapter, we'll move on to discuss topics related to performance in Redux. You'll find several ideas for how to optimize React and Redux applications for scale.

Summary

- Jest builds upon Jasmine's test runner and assertion library and comes standard within apps generated by Create React App.
- Testing pure functions, such as reducers or synchronous action creators, is simplest.
- Testing sagas is a matter of testing the effect object that gets sent to the middleware.
- The two ways to test connected components are to import and wrap a `Provider` component or to export the unconnected component.

Performance

10

This chapter covers

- Measuring Redux/React performance with tools
- Using `connect` and `mapStateToProps` effectively
- Working with memoization
- Batching actions

Redux is "fast" out of the gate. It's an extremely lightweight library, so Redux dragging performance down isn't an issue, even at scale. Remember, all Redux provides is a way to store state and broadcast changes. Fear not, you have plenty of opportunities to squander your app's performance. Whether it's using Redux features in non-optimal ways or allowing changes in the store to re-render views such as React components too often, as a user of Redux you need to ensure you're doing what it takes to keep your apps running smoothly.

This chapter focuses on strategies for keeping Redux applications fast. Consistent with the rest of the book, we'll address Redux within a React context. The key to maintaining a performant React/Redux application is reducing or eliminating unnecessary computation and rendering.

Coming up, you'll first look at tools to profile performance in a React application. Spotting the waste is the first step in cleaning it up. Then you'll dig into the

Redux-specific performance strategies, such as using `connect` to prevent unnecessary re-renders, memoizing with selectors, batching actions, and caching.

If you aren't interested in React-specific optimizations, feel free to skip to the Redux optimizations in section 10.3. Please note, though, that optimizing Redux can only do so much for your application's performance if the underlying stack implementation is inefficient.

10.1 Performance-assessment tools

To address any inefficiencies, you must first identify them. A few different tools exist to do the job. One important thing to note before you jump in: in development mode, React does additional work to produce helpful warnings. For a genuine performance assessment, you'll want to profile a minified production build.

> **NOTE** Generally, the tools in this section are to be used in development, so they serve to identify relatively expensive renders rather than definitive measurements.

10.1.1 Performance timeline

The first tool you'll look at it is the performance timeline feature. It leverages a User Timing API feature implemented by many browsers to visualize the component lifecycle of React components. Using this tool couldn't be any simpler, requiring you add `?react_perf` to the end of your URL. While looking at the Parsnip app in development, you need only plug `localhost:3000/?react_perf` as the URL, then check the Performance tab within the Google Chrome developer tools.

This tool is particularly useful for visually identifying components that are egregiously re-rendering. In figure 10.1, you can see the timeline of react-redux's `Provider` component, the connected `App` component, and each additional component mounting. Each orange-colored bar represents a component process. You'll find the component name, as well as the lifecycle method taking place, listed within each of the bars. A stacked list of bars indicates one component tree's sequence of updates.

The depth of the graph is often a dead giveaway for unnecessary rendering. Each time a component renders, a new row is added to the graph. If something caused a component to re-render multiple times, this graphical representation makes it much easier to diagnose. It also keeps an eye on how long each component needs to render. The longer the row, the longer a component takes to render. Use this feature to profile different pages of your application and see if anything stands out as particularly problematic.

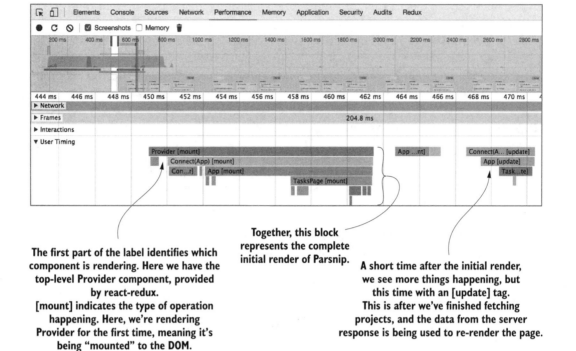

The first part of the label identifies which
component is rendering. Here we have the
top-level Provider component, provided
by react-redux.
[mount] indicates the type of operation
happening. Here, we're rendering
Provider for the first time, meaning it's
being "mounted" to the DOM.

Together, this block
represents the complete
initial render of Parsnip.

A short time after the initial render,
we see more things happening, but
this time with an [update] tag.
This is after we've finished fetching
projects, and the data from the server
response is being used to re-render the page.

Figure 10.1   The performance timeline feature

10.1.2 *react-addons-perf*

The react-addons-perf package is from the React team and provides an alternate
window of similar data found in the performance timeline. Please note that React 16
isn't supported by this tool at the time of writing. Using react-addons-perf involves
more manual configuration to specify what you'd like to benchmark, but with it
comes more control over what you'd like to measure.

Once you've imported the Perf object, you can wrap what you want to measure in
Perf.start() and Perf.stop(). You have several choices for how you want to print
the outcome of the measurement, but one of the more interesting options is the
printWasted method, which reveals the number of unnecessary renders made and
the amount of time that took. See the documentation for a more detailed look at the
API and several implementation articles at https://facebook.github.io/react/docs/
perf.html.

10.1.3 *why-did-you-update*

The why-did-you-update package is a diagnostic tool that provides actionable feedback. This tool is specifically valuable for identifying unnecessary component renders.
Once it's installed, console logs will alert you to components that are re-rendered

despite having identical props. With that information, you can take appropriate action. Figure 10.2 provides an annotated version of the example in the package's README.

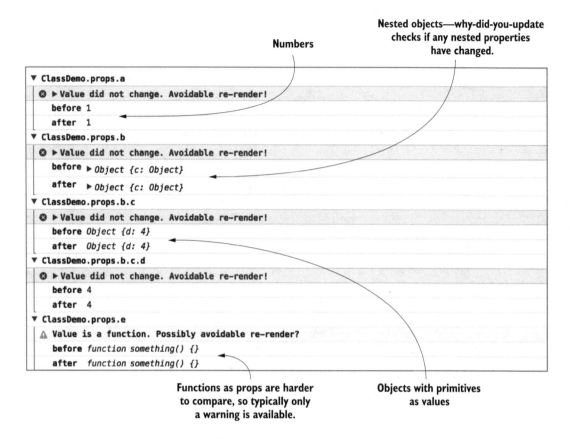

Figure 10.2 Example output from why-did-you-update

The `why-did-you-update` option performs a diff of the props passed to a given component and lets you know if those props are identical or potentially identical. As you can see in figure 10.2, this works for primitives, such as numbers and strings, and objects (including nested objects!). Functions, on the other hand, can't be diffed with as much confidence, and instead produce a warning. The tool can check each individual property of an object to see if two objects have identical values, but functions, even with identical bound arguments using `Function.prototype.bind`, will fail an equality check. For installation and usage instructions, see the package README at https://github.com/maicki/why-did-you-update. If this doesn't do exactly what you're looking for, Mark Erikson maintains a list of similar tools at https://github.com/markerikson/redux-ecosystem-links/blob/master/devtools.md#component-update-monitoring.

10.1.4 *React developer tools*

The React developer tools come packaged in a Chrome or Firefox extension and provide insight into the data each component uses to render. Clicking a component reveals its prop values and allows you to edit those props directly in the browser to aid in your bug hunting. One useful performance feature is "Highlight Updates," which can help you see which components re-render most often.

With the developer tools open, select the "Highlight Updates" option. Now, whenever you interact with the application, colored boxes will appear around each component. The color ranges from a light green to a dark red and indicates the relative frequency that the component is updating; the redder the box, the more frequently it re-renders.

Note that because something is red doesn't necessarily indicate a problem. In Parsnip, for example, when you type quickly into the search box, it and several other components go from green to red in a hurry. This is expected, though, because you want each character typed into the text field to update the list of tasks instantly. See figure 10.3 for an example display.

This figure was produced by typing several characters in the search field, then taking a screenshot after rapidly deleting them. You'll notice that the orange coloring isn't around the tasks themselves, because they update infrequently by design.

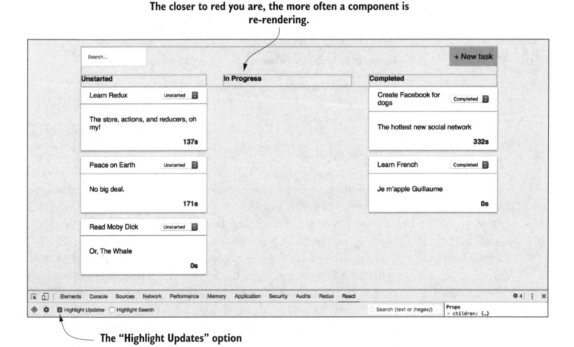

Figure 10.3   The "Highlight Updates" option provides a color-coded indication of how frequently updates are made.

10.2   *React optimizations*

Now that you have tools to identify problematic components, let's look at how to address them. Before Redux even enters the picture, though, there are always ways to get more out of your view library. In your case, that happens to be React. In this section, we'll quickly cover tips for optimizing React components. Again, React is plenty performant if you stick to best practices and keep the number of re-renders to a minimum.

10.2.1   *shouldComponentUpdate*

The `shouldComponentUpdate` lifecycle method is one of your first lines of defense against unnecessary component renders. The default behavior of React components is to re-render when `setState` has been called, or a parent component has rendered; you can use this lifecycle callback to prevent that from happening more than is necessary. It's common for a parent component to re-render, but to pass the same props to a child as the previous render. Without intervention on your part, the child component will re-render with the same data.

When a re-render is triggered, there are a handful of lifecycle methods that get called: `componentWillReceiveProps`, `shouldComponentUpdate`, `componentWillUpdate`, `render`, and `componentDidUpdate`. Once the component becomes aware of the incoming props using `componentWillReceiveProps`, `shouldComponentUpdate` is where you're given an opportunity to cancel the rest of the update cycle. The component has access to the potential next props and state, giving you the opportunity to make custom comparisons with current props or state, and ultimately returning a boolean to indicate whether to continue with the re-render.

As a semi-contrived example, let's say you want to prevent a re-render of a component for as long as an ID in the URL remains unchanged. The code for accomplishing this might look like listing 10.1. In this snippet, the return value evaluates to a boolean after comparing the present and future values of the parameter, `id`. If the values are the same, the buck stops here, and the re-render is avoided. If the values are unique, the component proceeds with the rest of the update cycle, eventually re-rendering the component.

Listing 10.1   shouldComponentUpdate example

```
shouldComponentUpdate(nextProps, nextState) {
 return nextProps.params.id !== this.props.params.id;
}
```

React's diffing algorithm handles most component updates efficiently, but it won't catch all the optimization opportunities that are unique to your use cases. This technique is a great strategy for manually fine-tuning your application.

10.2.2 *PureComponent*

`React.PureComponent` was introduced with React 15.3 and is an alternative to `React.Component`. You can use `PureComponent` to get a simple `shouldComponentUpdate` implementation for free. Using `PureComponent` gives you a shallow equality check of state and props between renders, and bails out of the update cycle if there are no perceived changes.

When should you use `PureComponent`? Our research produced conflicting answers. Certain teams prefer to write functional stateless components as often as possible, citing the simplicity of pure functions as most valuable. Others stand by writing `PureComponents` as often as possible, swearing by the performance implications. Functional stateless components don't have lifecycle callbacks, so they'll render each time their parent does. But you don't need all components to implement `shouldComponentUpdate`; a few strategically placed higher in the component tree will do the trick.

In practice, you'll likely find bigger fish to fry. The choice between a `PureComponent` and functional stateless component usually won't make a noticeable difference, but for the rare case that it does, consider `PureComponent`. Make sure not to mutate state or props in a `PureComponent`, or you'll end up bug hunting. See the official documentation for more details on `PureComponent` at https://reactjs.org/docs/react-api.html#reactpurecomponent.

10.2.3 *Pagination and other strategies*

Pagination—the process of displaying content (usually lists) as separate pages—isn't unique to React or Redux, but it's a useful tool you'll want to use if you're rendering potentially large amounts of content. Generally, if you're rendering a list and you have a sense that the list could be large, use pagination. After all, the best way to improve rendering performance is to render fewer things.

If you're working with large enough datasets, at a certain point you'll find that the standard optimization techniques won't be enough. This problem isn't unique to React, but there are multiple React-specific approaches to handling large datasets.

Certain React packages, such as `react-paginate`, provide logic and components to facilitate pagination. You can view the demos and implementation details on the project's GitHub page at https://github.com/AdeleD/react-paginate. Alternatively, an example project within the Redux documentation contains a more manual, Redux-specific pagination implementation at https://github.com/reactjs/redux/tree/master/examples/real-world.

A more recent spin on pagination is the infinite scroll technique. Infinite scroll, used, for example, in most apps with an activity feed, is a popular feature where more items are loaded as you scroll to the end of the current list. A couple popular packages make writing the feature simpler, but `react-infinite` is most popular by GitHub stars (see https://github.com/seatgeek/react-infinite).

If pagination and infinite scrolling won't cut it for your use case, maybe `react-virtualized` will. This package is as good as it gets for rendering massive lists and tabular data. It supports tables, grids, lists, and other formats. If you need your large dataset rendered up front, read more about the project on its GitHub page at https://github.com/bvaughn/react-virtualized.

10.3 Redux optimizations

Using tools such as PureComponent can take you far, but there's a good deal you can do in Redux-land that can help. In fact, connect has a similar feature and can help save you from having to use shouldComponentUpdate in the first place. Both accomplish something similar, but with connect, the bulk of the work is done for you. Instead of comparing old and new props, you define the data a component needs in mapStateToProps, and connect will put the right checks in place.

You can also dispatch fewer actions unnecessarily, which will cause connected components to try to re-render. We'll look, too, at caching in the next section, which can greatly help reduce load on your server by re-using data already stored in the browser.

10.3.1 Connecting the right components

The Parsnip example application didn't get large enough to merit a thoughtful discussion about which components should be connected, but your production application inevitably will. Earlier in the book, we described a simple strategy for deciding when to connect components: start with presentational components by default, and wrap them with connect once they become too cumbersome to maintain without access to the Redux store. Again, the description is intentionally vague to give teams the freedom to decide where to draw the line of "too cumbersome."

We'll provide one more guiding principle now: if it saves you costly re-renders, connect the component. Use the foundational React knowledge learned in or refreshed by this chapter; by default, an updated React component will re-render its children, unless the children guard against re-renders with a custom shouldComponent-Update method or by using PureComponent.

10.3.2 A top-down approach

One of the benefits of Redux is that data is potentially available to all components, which means you have a lot of flexibility in how you want data to flow through the application. Up to now, you've used a simple strategy of connecting a single component, App, which passes down any data its children may need. Here's a refresher in figure 10.4.

This approach, although simple, has held up well so far. The main advantage of having a single point of entry, meaning using connect in one top-level component, is simplicity. The bindings between Redux and React have a small footprint, and the rest of the app gets to function as any React application would, by receiving props.

But there are at least two major downsides. First, as applications grow they inevitably stand to benefit more and more from connecting additional components, mainly

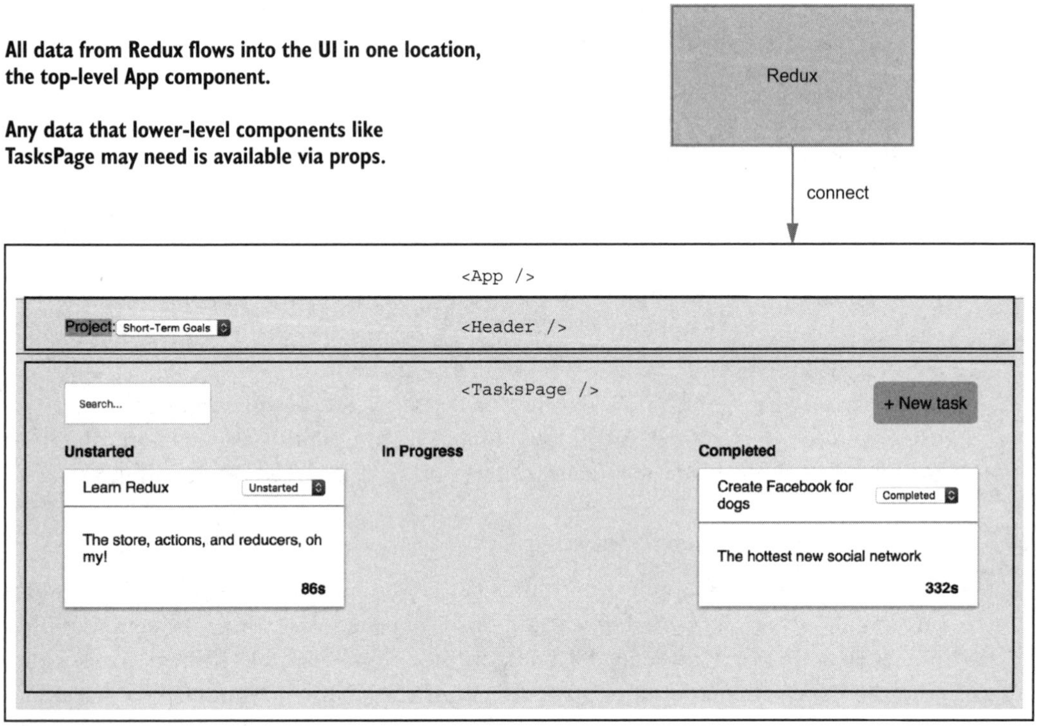

All data from Redux flows into the UI in one location, the top-level App component.

Any data that lower-level components like TasksPage may need is available via props.

Redux

connect

<App />

Project: Short-Term Goals

<Header />

<TasksPage />

Search...

+ New task

Unstarted

In Progress

Completed

Learn Redux   Unstarted

The store, actions, and reducers, oh my!

86s

Create Facebook for dogs   Completed

The hottest new social network

332s

Figure 10.4   Parsnip's main React/Redux configuration

to avoid giant prop-passing chains between components that become difficult to maintain and understand.

More importantly for the purposes of this chapter, it also has a performance cost. Because you have a single point of entry, whenever data from Redux changes, such as projects or tasks being updated, the entire app will attempt to re-render. Take the two major components from figure 10.4, for example. Because they're both children of App, any time App re-renders (after an action is dispatched), both Header and Tasks-Page will attempt to re-render as well. Let's look at one specific interaction: updating a task. Figure 10.5 demonstrates what a single "cycle" might look like, as data flows from React via a user interaction, through Redux, and then back into the component tree. Think about the Header and TasksPage components and what they require to successfully fulfill their responsibilities. Header needs to render a list of projects in a drop-down. TasksPage needs to render tasks.

The main problem is that Header attempts to re-render when unrelated data changes. Header doesn't need tasks to fulfill its responsibilities, but because it's a child of App, it will re-render whenever tasks are updated, unless you add a shouldComponent-Update check. This problem isn't something that's unique to Redux: it's a fundamental part of React. As mentioned, one way to solve this is by using shouldComponentUpdate

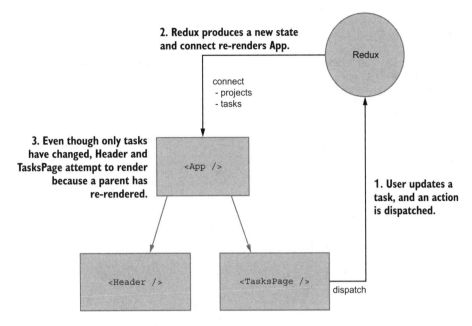

Figure 10.5 A single "cycle" after a user updates a task

to tell React not to complete a render when non-Header related data changes. This is a perfectly fine solution, but what if you could solve this upstream with Redux?

10.3.3 *Connecting additional components to Redux*

Under the hood, like shouldComponentUpdate, connect and mapStateToProps will do a shallow comparison of old and new props, bypassing a render if no relevant data has changed. Proper usage of connect can save you from having to write your own shouldComponentUpdate logic. What if you connect Header and TasksPage directly to Redux? Each component will use selectors to get only the data they need—no more, no less.

You'll write the code to do this in a moment, but first let's update the diagram from figure 10.5 to match the setup you're going for (see figure 10.6). We like to think in terms of data dependencies—what data does a component need to fulfill its intended role? Take note that Header and TasksPage are connected only to data they specifically require. Restricting components to only the data they need with connect is a powerful idea: you can use connect for performance over custom shouldComponent-Updates, and it's also great for organizing and decoupling growing apps.

When tasks in the state tree are modified, Header won't re-render because 1) no parents re-rendered because of the change, and 2) Header isn't subscribed to the tasks portion of the Redux store. Adding connect will run Header's mapStateToProps

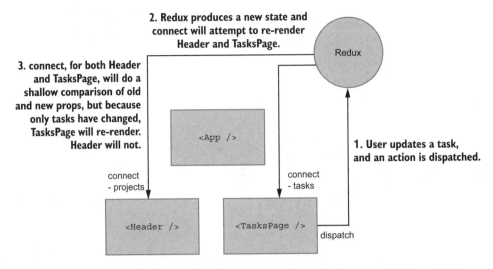

Figure 10.6   Instead of connecting one top-level component, you'll connect multiple lower-level components.

function, see that the old and new results are equal using a shallow comparison, and bail out, preventing an unnecessary re-render.

Performance work is all about measuring and improving, so you need something to measure. Your goal is to change how you use `connect` to prevent unnecessary re-renders, so let's add a few logging statements so you know when both `Header` and `TasksPage` are rendering, as shown in the following listings. Many tools can help with render debugging, but plain old `console.log` will do fine here.

Listing 10.2   Log renders in TasksPage – src/components/TasksPage.js

```
...
class TasksPage extends Component {
  ...
  render() {
    console.log('rendering TasksPage')

    if (this.props.isLoading) {
      return <div className="tasks-loading">Loading...</div>;
    }

    return (
      <div className="tasks">
        ...
      </div>
    );
  }
}
```

```
...
class Header extends Component {
  render() {
    console.log('rendering Header')
    ...
  }
}
```

Refresh your browser, and you should see both components rendering. Update a task by moving it to "In Progress" or "Completed." Only the tasks portion of the state tree changed, but your highly advanced log debugging confirms that both components re-rendered. Let's see what you can do about that.

10.3.4   Adding connect to Header and TasksPage

You'll need to make a few major changes:

- Removing most of the functionality from `App`
- Moving `Header`-specific data and actions to `Header`
- Moving `TasksPage`-specific data and actions to `TasksPage`

Makes sense, right? The changes were motivated by performance, but this also starts to make more sense from a separation-of-responsibilities perspective. As your applications grow over time, connecting additional components the way you're about to do can keep any one module from becoming too bloated and tangled.

Start with `App` by removing most of the code having to do with `Header` and `Tasks-Page`, as shown in listing 10.4. For imports, you'll remove all the action/selector imports except for one. Later, you'll move those imports to their respective components. You'll leave one action, `fetchProjects`, which is responsible for fetching data for the initial page load.

As far as `Header` and `TasksPage`, you'll remove all props. They'll still require the same data, but instead of props being passed by the parent `App`, you'll inject the data directly from Redux with `connect`, as shown in the following listing.

```
import React, { Component } from 'react';
import { connect } from 'react-redux';
import Header from './components/Header';              Remove most of
import TasksPage from './components/TasksPage';         the action/selector
import FlashMessage from './components/FlashMessage';   imports.
import { fetchProjects } from './actions';

class App extends Component {
  componentDidMount() {                       Continues to do the
    this.props.dispatch(fetchProjects());  ◁─ initial projects fetch
  }
```

```
  render() {
    return (
      <div className="container">
        {this.props.error && <FlashMessage message={this.props.error} />}
        <div className="main-content">
          <Header />                              Updates props for
          <TasksPage />                           Header/TasksPage
        </div>
      </div>
    );
  }
}

function mapStateToProps(state) {
  const { error } = state.projects;
                                        Radically simplifies
  return { error };          ◁┘        mapStateToProps
}

export default connect(mapStateToProps)(App);
```

Header is currently the only component that renders anything projects-related, so it
makes sense to migrate its major functionality out of App: querying projects from the
store and dispatching an action when the user selects a new project, as shown in the following listing.

Listing 10.5   Adding connect to Header – src/components/Header.js

```
import React, { Component } from 'react';
import { connect } from 'react-redux';
import { setCurrentProjectId } from '../actions';    Adds the imports you
import { getProjects } from '../reducers/';          extracted out of App

class Header extends Component {
  onCurrentProjectChange = e => {                                              ◁─┐
    this.props.setCurrentProjectId(Number(e.target.value));
  };

  render() {
    console.log('rendering Header');
    const projectOptions = this.props.projects.map(project => (    Dispatches
      <option key={project.id} value={project.id}>                 an action
        {project.name}                                            when a new
      </option>                                                  project is
    ));                                                             selected

    return (
      <div className="project-item">
        Project:
        <select onChange={this.onCurrentProjectChange} className="project-
➡ menu">                                                                      ◁─┘
          {projectOptions}
        </select>
      </div>
```

```
    );
  }
}

function mapStateToProps(state) {            Uses a selector
  return {                                   to get the list of
    projects: getProjects(state),    ◁──     projects
  };
}                                                       Passes any required
                                                          actions to connect
export default connect(mapStateToProps, { setCurrentProjectId })(Header);  ◁─┘
```

The Header is now responsible for dispatching the SET_CURRENT_PROJECT_ID action, when previously that was App's responsibility. You've now transitioned Header away from being a presentational component that accepted props to a container component that's fully aware of Redux. Container components are typically hooked up to data directly from Redux, instead of relying on a parent component passing props, and are where the bulk of the action handling logic is.

You'll follow a similar set of changes for TasksPage. To do its job, TasksPage needs at least tasks from the store and behavior for creating, editing, and filtering tasks in the form of Redux actions. Using App, previously the main container component and hub of functionality within Parsnip, used to take care of passing TasksPage the right props, including callback functions that would dispatch actions. The same way you did with Header, now you'll convert TasksPage into a container component that deals with Redux-specific tasks logic, including selectors and actions. Like you did with Header, you'll add connect and mapStateToProps, which uses selectors to retrieve the right data from the Redux store. And you'll also move any task-related action handling out of App and in to TasksPage.

Two notable additions are bindActionCreators and mapDispatchToProps, which together allow you to conveniently bind dispatch to the actions you imported. Instead of using dispatch directly in a component, this.props.dispatch(createTask(...)), connect accepts a second argument, a function conventionally named mapDispatch-ToProps. connect will pass dispatch as an argument to the mapDispatchToProps function, where you can bind it directly, allowing components to use more generic prop names. See the following listing.

> **Listing 10.6 Adding connect to TasksPage – src/components/TasksPage.js**

```
import React, { Component } from 'react';          Imports bindActionCreators,
import { connect } from 'react-redux';             a helper for binding dispatch
import { bindActionCreators } from 'redux';   ◁──  to actions
import TaskList from './TaskList';
import { createTask, editTask, filterTasks } from '../actions';
import { getGroupedAndFilteredTasks } from '../reducers/';

                                          Adds task-specific imports
                                          you extracted out of App
```

```
class TasksPage extends Component {
  ...
  onCreateTask = e => {                              ◁───┐
    e.preventDefault();

    this.props.createTask({
      title: this.state.title,
      description: this.state.description,
      projectId: this.props.currentProjectId,
    });

    this.resetForm();
  };

  onStatusChange = (task, status) => {              ◁───┘
    this.props.editTask(task, { status });
  };

  onSearch = e => {
    this.props.onSearch(e.target.value);
  };

  renderTaskLists() {
    const { tasks } = this.props;

    return Object.keys(tasks).map(status => {
      const tasksByStatus = tasks[status];

      return (
        <TaskList
          key={status}
          status={status}
          tasks={tasksByStatus}
          onStatusChange={this.onStatusChange}
        />
      );
    });
  }

  render() {
    ...
  }
}

function mapStateToProps(state) {
  const { isLoading }  = state.projects;

  return {
    tasks: getGroupedAndFilteredTasks(state),
    currentProjectId: state.page.currentProjectId,
    isLoading,
  };
}

function mapDispatchToProps(dispatch) {          ◁───┐
```

Updates create/edit handlers

Defines a mapStateToProps function that accepts the store's dispatch function as an argument

```
    return bindActionCreators(
      {
        onSearch: filterTasks,
        createTask,
        editTask,
      },
      dispatch,
    );
}
```

Passes any actions
you need as an object
and dispatch to
bindActionCreators

```
export default connect(mapStateToProps, mapDispatchToProps)(TasksPage);
```

10.3.5 *mapStateToProps and memoized selectors*

After all this code, did you achieve your goal of preventing `Header` from re-rendering when updating a task? If you check the browser console and look for `console.log` statements from each component's render method after updating a task, you'll still see `Header` re-rendering after updating a task. Ugh.

You've successfully split out the projects and tasks portions of state in the store, and `Header` and `TasksPage` are now successfully self-contained. That part seems to work properly, so the answer lies in something more fundamental—reference checks in JavaScript and `connect`'s shallow comparison. Listing 10.7 shows the `getProjects` selector, which you use in `Header` to find and prepare project state. This is a simple selector, where you translate the projects object, which is keyed by ID in the Redux store, into an array that's friendlier for components to render.

Listing 10.7   getProjects selector - src/reducers/index.js

```
...
export const getProjects = state => {
  return Object.keys(state.projects.items).map(id => {
    return projects.items[id];
  });
}
...
```

The trouble comes when you consider how `connect` checks whether any props have changed. Using `connect` stores the return value of `mapStateToProps` and compares against new props when a render is triggered. This is a shallow equality check, meaning it will go over each field and check if `oldPropA === newPropA`, without diving deeper into any nested objects should they exist.

Value types in JavaScript, primitives such as numbers and strings, work as you expect with the `===` operator. `2 === 2` and `"foo" === "foo"` both return `true`. Reference types, such as objects, are different. Try running `{} === {}` in your preferred JavaScript console. You should see `false` returned, because each new copy of an object has a totally separate object reference.

How does this relate to `Header` and why the component is still unnecessarily re-rendering? `getProjects` runs after every state change in Redux, but it's return value isn't memoized. Every time you call `getProjects`, regardless of whether the data has changed or not, a new object will be returned. As a result, `connect`'s shallow equality check will never pass, and react-redux will think that `Header` has new data to render.

The solution is to use reselect to change `getProjects` to be a memoized selector, as demonstrated in listing 10.8. The bulk of the logic for retrieving projects from the store is the same, but now you're going to memoize the return value. Reselect will memoize, or cache, return values based on given arguments. If `getProjects` sees for the first time a set of arguments, it will compute a return value, store it in the cache, and return it. When `getProjects` is called again with the same arguments, reselect will check the cache first and return the existing value. You'll return the same object reference instead of returning a new object for every call.

Listing 10.8   Making getProjects a memoized selector – src/reducers/index.js

```
export const getProjects = createSelector(          Uses reselect's
  [state => state.projects],                        createSelector to
  projects => {                                     create a memoized
    return Object.keys(projects.items).map(id => {  selector
      return projects.items[id];
    });
  },
);
```

Give updating tasks another go. The most effective performance optimization out there is "do less stuff," and that's what you achieved here. You should now see only `Header` renders on initial page load, but not on subsequent task updates. With `Header`, by adding `connect` and returning only the data you need using `mapStateToProps`, you let react-redux do the heavy lifting and `Header` only re-renders when relevant data has changed. Using `connect`/`mapStateToProps` lets you be more declarative about what data should cause a component to re-render. You don't need to check old and new props manually; you declare what data matters and let the framework handle the rest.

10.3.6 *Rules of thumb for advanced connect usage*

We've covered much ground with `connect`, so here are a few general rules of thumb:

- The `connect` command gives you `shouldComponentUpdate` for free. Using `connect` to try to provide components with only the data they require can help eliminate the need for manual `shouldComponentUpdate` usage.
- Use `connect` in a more granular way than you did with `Header/TasksPage`; this works best with normalized data. Due to Redux's immutability restrictions, if projects and tasks were nested, updates to tasks would cause all ancestors (projects) in the tree to be updated. New object references mean shallow comparisons (such as `shouldComponentUpdate`) will fail. Even if you used `connect` more frequently the way you did here, updates to nested data would still result in unwanted renders.

- Using `connect` like this is an architectural choice, and it's one that could bite you under certain circumstances. Having `App` be the only entry point for data from Redux meant that you were potentially free to make changes to major page sections without too much of a refactoring cost. The more stable an app is, typically the easier it is to introduce `connect` optimizations like this.

10.3.7 *Batching actions*

As you've seen, one of the central goals in optimizing Redux is trying to minimize unnecessary renders. We've looked at strategies such as using `shouldComponentUpdate` to check whether props changed before going through with a render, and using `connect` effectively to make sure components aren't dependent on unrelated data, which may cause them to re-render when given data that won't affect their output in any way.

Another case we haven't covered is multiple actions being dispatched close together timewise. Take the initial page fetch, for example, where you dispatch two actions, one to load the tasks from the response into the store and another to choose a default project. Remember that each dispatch will trigger a re-render in any connected components. Here when you dispatch `RECEIVE_ENTITIES` and `SET_CURRENT_PROJECT_ID` one after another, you trigger two renders within fractions of a second of each other. It won't have a noticeable difference here because Parsnip is still small, but it's worth always keeping an eye on too many actions being dispatched within a short span of time. This can happen anywhere, but one place it tends to happen often is when handling successful requests, like you are in the following listing. For example, you could do any or all of loading data in to multiple reducers, setting error states, and making decisions based on the server response.

> **Listing 10.9   fetchProjects action – src/actions/index.js**

```
export function fetchProjects() {
  return (dispatch, getState) => {
    dispatch(fetchProjectsStarted());

    return api
      .fetchProjects()
      .then(resp => {
        const projects = resp.data;

        const normalizedData = normalize(projects, [projectSchema]);

        dispatch(receiveEntities(normalizedData));        ◁─┐ Dispatches an
                                                            │ action with the
                                                            │ response body
        // Pick a board to show on initial page load
        if (!getState().page.currentProjectId) {
          const defaultProjectId = projects[0].id;
          dispatch(setCurrentProjectId(defaultProjectId));  ◁─┐ Picks a default
        }                                                     │ project
      })
```

```
      .catch(err => {
        fetchProjectsFailed(err);
      });
  };
}
```

Batching actions is something you could implement on your own, but to keep things simple you'll use a small package named redux-batched-actions. Listing 10.10 shows how you can batch action dispatches in the fetchProjects async action creator to cut down on an unnecessary re-render. In src/index.js where you handle most of Parsnip's configuration, import enableBatching from redux-batched-actions and wrap the rootReducer when configuring the store.

Listing 10.10   Configuration for batching actions – src/index.js

```
...
import { enableBatching } from 'redux-batched-actions';        <── Imports the
                                                                   enableBatching
...                                             Wraps the          higher order
                                                rootReducer to    reducer
const store = createStore(                      support batch
  enableBatching(rootReducer),        <──       dispatches
  composeWithDevTools(applyMiddleware(thunk, sagaMiddleware)),
);
```

The enableBatching function wraps your rootReducer, enabling you to use the batchActions method, which you'll import and use in fetchProjects. Note that in the previous example you're batching two synchronous actions; not having to worry about async flow control greatly simplifies things. Batching here is as straightforward as taking each action object, getting new state from the reducers, and dispatching an action with the combined results, as shown in the following listing.

Listing 10.11   Batching fetchProjects dispatches – src/actions/index.js

```
    import { batchActions } from 'redux-batched-actions';        <── Imports
                                                                     batchActions,
                                                                     which accepts
...                                                                  an array of
                                                                     actions
export function fetchProjects() {
  return (dispatch, getState) => {
    dispatch(fetchProjectsStarted());

    return api
      .fetchProjects()
      .then(resp => {
        const projects = resp.data;

        const normalizedData = normalize(projects, [projectSchema]);
```

```
            dispatch(
              batchActions([                                Calls batchActions
                receiveEntities(normalizedData),            with an array of
                setCurrentProjectId(projects[0].id),        synchronous actions
              ]),
            );
        })
        .catch(err => {
          fetchProjectsFailed(err);
        });
    };
}
```

Figure 10.7 is a look at the final payload generated by batchActions. It combines the
result of dispatching both RECEIVE_ENTITIES and SET_CURRENT_PROJECT_ID and dispatches a single BATCHING_REDUCER.BATCH action.

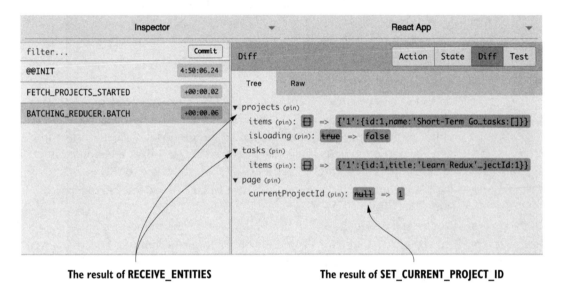

The result of RECEIVE_ENTITIES   **The result of SET_CURRENT_PROJECT_ID**

Figure 10.7   A look at how batched actions have state changes rolled into a single dispatch

One small downside here is that you lose part of the benefits of the Redux DevTools,
because individual actions will no longer be logged—a small price to pay. Batching
actions is certainly not a requirement for Redux and may not be necessary at all for
use cases that don't run into these kinds of frequent dispatch issues. When it is an
issue, simple batching strategies such as the one provided by redux-batched-actions
are more than sufficient.

10.4   Caching

Network requests are one of the big bottlenecks in web applications. Data travels fast,
but the most noticeable delays for your users will happen while a network request is in

progress. Typically, this is when you're fetching data to populate the page, and no one likes loading times. They're expected and tolerated by users to a certain degree, but too much too often means your app will be perceived as unresponsive. One surefire way to mitigate this is to not make extraneous requests in the first place. By determining which pieces of data are cacheable, meaning the possibility of showing stale data to users is OK, you can greatly reduce server load and make the experience feel more responsive by fetching data less frequently.

How you determine which data is cacheable is up to you and your use case. Take financial data for example—probably not a great idea to rely on a cache because accuracy is what matters. You'll take waiting an extra second over seeing a stale bank balance. It's something you access infrequently, and you won't mind the extra wait.

But what about something like a newsfeed for a social network like Facebook? That kind of content can be expensive to generate, and though elements of it are likely cached at the server level, you can still improve performance by caching data on the client with Redux.

Here's one approach to caching data on the client, based on how long ago the resource was fetched from the server:

- Fetch a resource such as `tasks`.
- Add a `lastUpdated` field to store when tasks were last fetched from the server.
- Define a "time to live," or TTL, which could be anything from 1 second to 1 minute, which represents how long you can comfortably cache tasks without them becoming too stale. What exactly you set this to will depend on context. Is the data important? Is it OK to potentially show stale data to users?
- When subsequent calls to fetch tasks are made, check the `lastUpdated` field against the TTL.
- If you're still inside the TTL bounds, don't make the request.
- If it's been too long (for example with TTL of one minute, and you haven't fetched tasks in 70 seconds), fetch fresh data from the server.

10.5 *Exercise*

Earlier in the chapter, we looked at a few different ways to reduce unnecessary re-renders, such as using `connect` and adding `shouldComponentUpdate` lifecycle methods where appropriate. Another popular strategy for cutting down on extra work that's specific to lists is connecting each list item instead of connecting a common parent. Currently, tasks data enters the UI through the `App` component and is passed down through props to each individual `Task`. Instead, you'll pass only task IDs as props, and allow each `Task` to fetch its own data using `connect` and `mapStateToProps`.

Take the list of tasks in Parsnip as an example. Any time a single item in the list is updated, the entire list will have to reconcile. Add more logging and see for yourself. Add the `console.log` from the following listing to the `Task` component.

Listing 10.12 Logging Task renders – src/components/Task.js

```
import React from 'react';

import { TASK_STATUSES } from '../constants';

const Task = props => {
  console.log('rendering Task: ', props.task.id)
  ...
}
```

You're looking for which `Task` components render and how often. Refresh Parsnip in the browser, where you'll see output for each `Task` from the initial mount. Update an object by updating its status and look back at the console. You should see every `Task` re-render, even though data from only a single task changed. This is a result of the component hierarchy and how data from Redux connects to React. `TasksPage`, through `connect`, receives a new list of tasks (including the task object you updated), and renders `TaskList`, which renders each `Task`.

How can you fix it? Instead of passing the task object as a prop to `Task`, you can pass only the task's ID. Then you can add `connect` to `Task` and use the task's ID to pull the correct task out of the store. As a result, when a list item changes, only that one list item will re-render.

Figure 10.8 is what you have now. Because data flows from the `TasksPage` down, each `Task` component will try to re-render whenever any task changes.

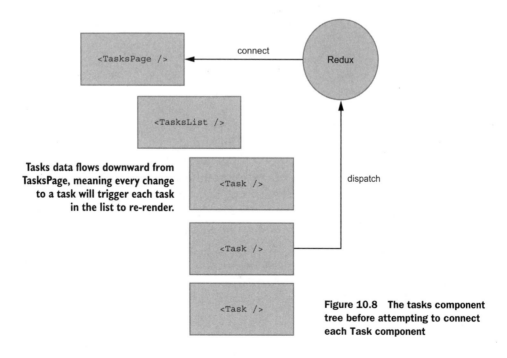

Figure 10.8 The tasks component tree before attempting to connect each Task component

A structure like this isn't necessarily a bad thing. In fact, most React/Redux apps render lists in this way. It's the most straightforward, simple way to approach lists. Redux offers a unique opportunity to highly optimize lists, with little in the way of wasted renders.

Figure 10.9 is what you're going for. To summarize, you want to

- Stop passing tasks from Redux into `TasksPage`.
- Have `TasksPage` take a list of IDs and pass them to children as props.
- Add `connect` to each `Task`, where `mapStateToProps` will take the task ID passed in as a prop and find the right task from the Redux store.

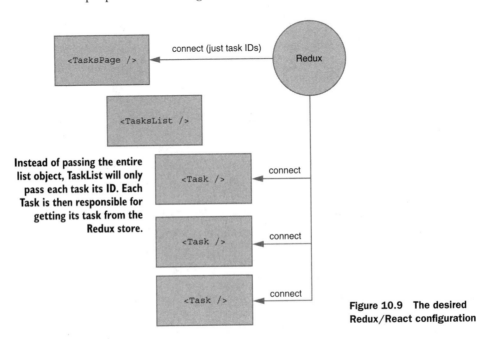

Figure 10.9 The desired Redux/React configuration

10.6 *Solution*

You won't need major changes to each individual component, but you'll need to make significant changes around how data flows through the component tree. First, make the big change in `Task` and work your way up from there. Listing 10.13 adds `connect` to the `Task` component. You'll take two pieces of data, the task ID provided as a prop by `TaskList` (which you'll take care of in a moment), and the list of tasks from the state tree. You'll then use the ID to get the right task in `mapStateToProps`.

Listing 10.13 Connecting the Task component – src/components/Task.js

```
import React from 'react';
import { connect } from 'react-redux';          ⟵——— Imports connect

import { TASK_STATUSES } from '../constants';
```

```
const Task = props => {
  return (
    <div className="task">
      <div className="task-header">
        <div>
          {props.task.title}
        </div>
        <select value={props.task.status} onChange={onStatusChange}>
          {TASK_STATUSES.map(status => (
            <option key={status} value={status}>
              {status}
            </option>
          ))}
        </select>
      </div>
      <hr />
      <div className="task-body">
        <p>
          {props.task.description}
        </p>
        <div className="task-timer">
          {props.task.timer}s
        </div>
      </div>
    </div>
  );

  function onStatusChange(e) {
    props.onStatusChange(props.task, e.target.value);
  }
};

function mapStateToProps(state, ownProps) {         ◁─┐  **Accepts state, but also
  return {                                               accepts ownProps as
    task: state.tasks.items[ownProps.taskId]     ◁─┐    an argument**
  };                                                  **Uses the ID provided as a
}                                                      prop to find the correct
                                                       task in the Redux store**

export default connect(mapStateToProps)(Task);   ◁────── **Applies connect**
```

Notice anything interesting about the markup? It didn't have to change! You've seen this several times so far in the book, and it's one of the benefits of using Redux to handle the bulk of the logic around state and behavior. You can adjust the plumbing by using connect to get the right task instead of passing the object using props, but Task doesn't need to know or care where that data comes from. The backbone of your UI can be made up of these data-agnostic components. And because they're decoupled from Redux, experimenting with new data patterns is easy.

Many of the concepts here are familiar, such as connect and mapStateToProps. The ownProps as an argument to mapStateToProps is new, which is an object of any props passed to the component by a parent. In this case, you have TaskList pass the task's taskId.

Now you need to go up the component tree and make sure TaskList and Tasks-Page are passing the correct props. Starting with TaskList, listing 10.14 makes two changes:

- TaskList should now expect a taskIds prop instead of tasks.
- Instead of passing the entire task object to each Task component, now you'll pass only the ID.

The general theme here is that where you were previously passing full task objects between components, now you'll only pass IDs.

Listing 10.14   Updating TaskList – src/components/TaskList.js

```
import React from 'react';
import Task from './Task';

const TaskList = props => {
  return (
    <div className="task-list">
      <div className="task-list-title">
        <strong>{props.status}</strong>              Instead of mapping over
      </div>                                         tasks, now map over taskIds.
      {props.taskIds.map(id => (
        <Task key={id} taskId={id} onStatusChange={props.onStatusChange} />
      ))}
    </div>                                                   Passes IDs to
  );                                                            each Task
};

export default TaskList;
```

You have Task and TaskList covered, so the final changes will be one step higher in the component tree, with TasksPage. The major change in listing 10.15 involves importing a new getGroupedAndFilteredTaskIds selector, which functions identically to the existing getGroupedAndFilteredTasks. The only difference is that you'll return an array of IDs, instead of an array of task objects. In TasksPage, import the selector, apply it in mapStateToProps, and then replace the tasks prop with taskIds when rendering TaskList.

Listing 10.15   Updating TasksPage – src/components/TasksPage.js

```
...
import { getGroupedAndFilteredTaskIds } from '../reducers';     Imports the
                                                                selector
class TasksPage extends Component {
  ...
  renderTaskLists() {
    const { taskIds } = this.props;              Operates on taskIds
                                                 instead of tasks when
    return Object.keys(taskIds).map(status => {  rendering TaskList
      const idsByStatus = taskIds[status];
```

```
      return (
        <TaskList
          key={status}
          status={status}
          taskIds={idsByStatus}                          Operates on taskIds
          onStatusChange={this.onStatusChange}           instead of tasks when
        />                                                rendering TaskList
      );
    });
  }

  render() {
    ...
  }
}

function mapStateToProps(state) {
  const { isLoading } = state.projects;

  return {                                               Applies the
    taskIds: getGroupedAndFilteredTaskIds(state),        selector
    currentProjectId: state.page.currentProjectId,
    isLoading,
  };
}
...

export default connect(mapStateToProps, mapDispatchToProps)(TasksPage);
```

You still need to implement the selector, so the final change will be in your main reducers file, as shown in the following listing. The only difference between the existing getGroupedAndFilteredTasks selector is returning IDs versus raw task objects.

Listing 10.16 Adding the new selector – src/reducers/index.js

```
...
export const getGroupedAndFilteredTaskIds = createSelector(
  [getFilteredTasks],
  tasks => {
    const grouped = {};

    TASK_STATUSES.forEach(status => {
      grouped[status] = tasks
        .filter(task => task.status === status)
        .map(task => task.id);        ◁
    });                                     After applying a search filter
                                            to the raw list of objects,
    return grouped;                         map to return only the IDs.
  }
);
...
```

To quickly recap the changes, we went with another outside-in approach, starting with the last component to be rendered, `Task`, and working our way up the tree to `Task-List` and `TasksPage`:

- In `Task`, accept an ID as a prop, and use `connect` to get the correct task from Redux.
- In `TaskList`, accept `taskIds` as a prop instead of `tasks`, and pass each ID down to `Task`.
- In `TasksPage`, use a new `getGroupedAndFilteredTaskIds` selector to pass a list of raw IDs down to `TasksPage`.
- In src/reducers/index.js, implement the new ID-only selector.

With everything in place, refresh your browser and keep an eye on how often `Task` renders in the console. Previously, after updating a task you'd see every `Task` re-render, effectively meaning an update to a single list element would cause the entire list to reconcile and re-render. By connecting each `Task` component, and passing only the ID as a prop, you ensure that when any one task changes, only its corresponding `Task` component will re-render. The key takeaways here are the potential performance and maintainability improvements from being picky about only making components aware of the data they need. By using `connect` effectively, you can eliminate the need for manual `shouldComponentUpdate` checks.

One of the great things about React and Redux is the conceptual refresh whenever state changes occur. You don't have to worry about finding and updating individual UI elements when data in Redux changes; you only need to define templates and the dynamics they require, declaratively. Data in, UI out.

It's now up to you as the developer to prevent too much rendering from happening. Your main goal in optimizing Redux with React is to "do less stuff," or, prevent components from re-rendering when unrelated data has changed.

Summary

- Rendering performance in the browser can be measured.
- Best practices for general front end performance.
- How to control the flow of data to prevent unnecessary rendering.

Structuring
Redux code

This chapter covers

- Understanding popular options for organizing
  Redux code
- Scaling the structure of a Redux application

If you remember one thing from this chapter, let it be this: Redux couldn't care less where you put its constituent parts. The package has a curious dynamic; Redux comes with a tiny API for storing and updating state, but it introduces a comprehensive design pattern into an application. Looking at the Redux architecture diagram, there are few methods provided by Redux to connect all the pieces. Figure 11.1 highlights the location of those methods. As you know, React Redux provides an important role in exposing some of that functionality to the web application.

The takeaway here is that Redux doesn't have any reason or ability to dictate how your code is structured. If an action object makes it back to the store, a Redux workflow is satisfied. Whatever mousetrap you build to facilitate this is completely up to you.

The documentation and official examples offer one simple option, but this chapter will explore the most popular code structure alternatives. We won't say there are

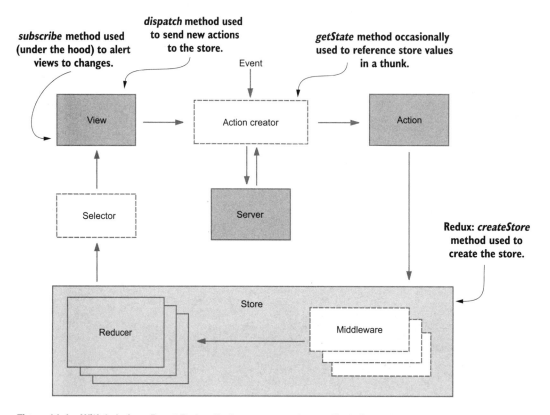

Figure 11.1   With help from React Redux, Redux exposes a few methods for state management.

no wrong answers for how you should organize your code, but there could be multiple right answers. Ultimately, the right decision for your projects depends on what you're building. A prototype, a small mobile app, and a large-scale web app each have distinct needs and probably deserve unique project layouts.

11.1   Rails-style pattern

The default organization found in the documentation, example projects, and many tutorials (including this book) is sometimes referred to as Rails-style. Rails, a popular web framework for the Ruby programming language, has a well-defined directory layout in which each file type is grouped within a corresponding directory. For example, you'll find every model within the `model` directory, each controller within the `controller` directory, and so on.

You'll recall that there are no models or controllers written in Parsnip, but each file type similarly resides in an appropriately named directory: actions, reducers, components, containers, and sagas. Figure 11.2 illustrates this structure, as it's found in the Parsnip application.

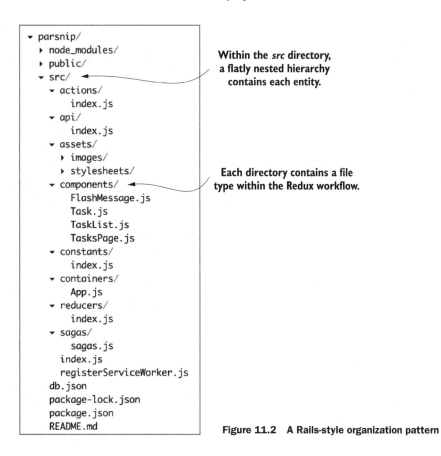

Within the *src* directory, a flatly nested hierarchy contains each entity.

Each directory contains a file type within the Redux workflow.

Figure 11.2 A Rails-style organization pattern

This is the default strategy, because of its simplicity. No explanation is required when a new Redux-familiar developer joins the team; the actions are in the `actions` directory.

11.1.1 Pros

The strengths of the Rails-style approach are clear enough. First, it's the simplest strategy to teach. If it's your job to ramp up a developer who's joined your team, you explain that a container component can be found in the `containers` directory. The container dispatches an action, which can be found in the `actions` directory, and so on. The simplicity reduces the onboarding time for new developers.

The second strength of choosing this pattern is its familiarity. Any Redux developer brought onto the team likely has learned Redux using the same pattern. Again, this boils down to minimal onboarding time for new developers. The Rails-style pattern is a great choice for prototypes, hackathon projects, training initiatives, and any application of a similar scope.

A final thought that will make more sense as the chapter progresses: actions and reducers have a many-to-many relationship. It's common practice for an action to be handled by multiple reducers. The Rails-style organization pattern arguably does the best job of representing that relationship, by keeping actions and reducers in separate peer directories.

11.1.2 Cons

The cost of this approach is scalability. On the extreme end of examples, Facebook consists of more than 30,000 components, as of April 2017. Can you image having all those components within a `components` or `containers` directory? To be fair, it would be difficult to find anything in an application that large without Facebook's serious investment in tooling, regardless of how thoughtful the architecture is.

The fact remains, you won't need to come anywhere close to Facebook's scale to experience growing pains with this pattern. In our experience, the Rails-style approach pushes its limits around the 50–100 component range, but every team will find its own breaking point. At the heart of this complaint is how frequently you'll end up in half a dozen different directories when adding one small feature.

From the directory structure, it's nearly impossible to tell which files interact with one another. The next pattern alternative attempts to address this concern.

11.2 *Domain-style pattern*

You'll find many variations of domain-style, or feature-based, organizations. Generally, the goal of each of these variations is to group related code together. Let's say your application has a subscription workflow to sign up new customers. Instead of spreading related components, actions, and reducers across several directories, the domain-based pattern advocates for putting them all in one `subscription` directory, for example.

One possible implementation of this pattern is to loosely label each container component as a feature. See figure 11.3 for an example using Parsnip again. Within the `containers` directory, you might find a list of feature directories, such as `task`. Each directory may contain the component, actions, reducers, and more related to the feature.

This pattern works great for some applications. It certainly scales better, because each new feature produces one new directory. The problem, however, is that actions and state are commonly shared across domains. In the case of an e-commerce application, products, the shopping cart, and the rest of the checkout workflow are unique features, but they are heavily dependent on one another's state.

It's not unusual that a single container component might pull state from several of these domains to render a page in the checkout process. If, for example, the user adds an item to their shopping cart, you may see updates in the product page, the header, and a shopping cart sidebar. Is there something you can do to better organize shared data?

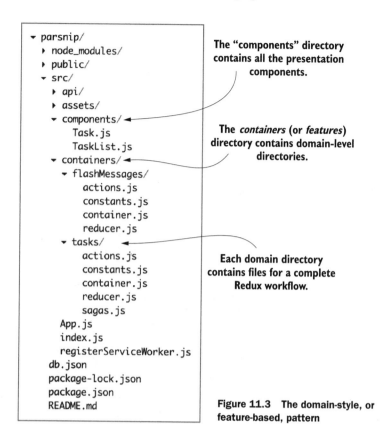

```
▾ parsnip/
  ▸ node_modules/
  ▸ public/
  ▾ src/
    ▸ api/
    ▸ assets/
    ▾ components/ ◀
        Task.js
        TaskList.js
    ▾ containers/ ◀
      ▾ flashMessages/
          actions.js
          constants.js
          container.js
          reducer.js
      ▾ tasks/     ◀
          actions.js
          constants.js
          container.js
          reducer.js
          sagas.js
      App.js
      index.js
      registerServiceWorker.js
    db.json
    package-lock.json
    package.json
    README.md
```

The "components" directory contains all the presentation components.

The *containers* (or *features*) directory contains domain-level directories.

Each domain directory contains files for a complete Redux workflow.

Figure 11.3   The domain-style, or feature-based, pattern

One alternative domain-style pattern is to leave containers and components in the Rails-style pattern, but organize actions and reducers by domain. Figure 11.4 refactors the last example to demonstrate this pattern. With this alteration, containers no longer live within one specific domain, while they import state from several others.

If you prefer, the domain-specific files may live within a data directory instead of within store. Several projects you'll work on will have minor variations of this nature. These tweaks are the natural result of teams of developers reaching consensus on what makes the most sense for their project (or trying something and running with it.)

11.2.1 Pros

The biggest win is the ability to find more of what you need in one place. If you've picked up a ticket to add a new feature to a Header component, you may expect to find everything you need within a Header directory, for example. Whenever you need to add a new feature, you need add only one directory. If you choose to separate the components and containers from your domain directories, that decoupling serves as a good reminder to keep those components reusable.

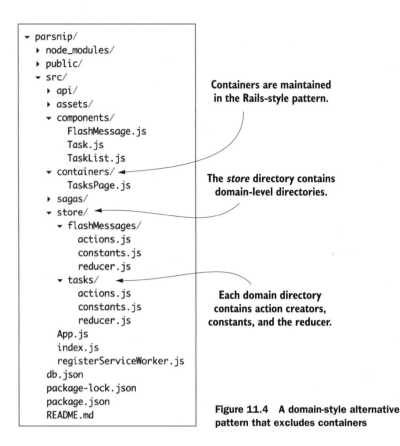

```
▾ parsnip/
   ▸ node_modules/
   ▸ public/
   ▾ src/
      ▸ api/
      ▸ assets/
      ▾ components/
         FlashMessage.js
         Task.js
         TaskList.js
      ▾ containers/  ◀
         TasksPage.js
      ▸ sagas/
      ▾ store/  ◀
         ▾ flashMessages/
            actions.js
            constants.js
            reducer.js
         ▾ tasks/  ◀
            actions.js
            constants.js
            reducer.js
      App.js
      index.js
      registerServiceWorker.js
   db.json
   package-lock.json
   package.json
   README.md
```

Containers are maintained in the Rails-style pattern.

The *store* directory contains domain-level directories.

Each domain directory contains action creators, constants, and the reducer.

Figure 11.4   A domain-style alternative pattern that excludes containers

One nice aspect of maintaining domains within a `store` directory is that the file structure reflects the top-level keys in your store. When specifying the `mapStateToProps` function within container components, the slice of Redux store you specify will mirror your file structure.

11.2.2   Cons

You'll find there are still many tradeoffs to this approach, and you should understand that there's not a single answer for every application. One of the potential weaknesses in this pattern is the lack of certainty or clarity around what constitutes a domain or feature. There will be times when you'll debate whether some new functionality belongs in an existing directory or merits the creation of a new one. Adding more decisions and overhead like this to a developer's work isn't ideal.

With a domain-style pattern, each project tends to take on at least a few nuances of its own. Introducing new developers to the project will require passing on the tribal knowledge of how your team likes to introduce new features and where lines have been drawn already. Consider that there's at least a small amount of overhead here.

One concern that isn't addressed by any discussed variation of this pattern is the idea that actions may be handled by multiple reducers. One domain directory generally contains a single actions file and a single reducer file. Watching for actions in a different domain's reducer can be a source of confusion. That comes with the territory and should be considered when weighing the tradeoffs in your application. One option you have is to create a domain directory for shared actions.

11.3 *Ducks pattern*

Before you ask, the name "ducks" is a riff on the last syllable of Redux. The intent of the ducks pattern is to take domain-style organization a step further. The pattern's author, Erik Rasmussen, observed that the same groupings of imports repeatedly appeared across an application. Instead of keeping a feature's constants, actions, and reducers in one directory, why not keep them all in a single file?

Does keeping all those entities in one file leave a bad taste in your mouth? The first question many developers ask is whether the file bloat is manageable. Fortunately, you shave off a little boilerplate code with this pattern. The first to go are the import statements required across the action and reducer files. In general, though, it's helpful to keep each slice of your store fairly flat. If you notice that a ducks file is getting especially large, take the hint and ask yourself if the file can be broken into two feature files.

Going back to Erik's original proposal, there are a few rules to follow when using this pattern. A module

- Must have the reducer be the default export
- Must export its action creators as functions
- Must have action types in the form `npm-module-or-app/reducer/ACTION_TYPE`
- May export its action types as `UPPER_SNAKE_CASE`

When keeping all these elements in one file, it's important to have consistency in how you export the various pieces. This rule set was designed for that purpose. The default export of a ducks module should always be the reducer. This frees up the ability to import all the action creators for use in containers with the syntax `import * as taskActions from './modules/tasks'`, for example.

What does a ducks file look like? Listing 11.1 is an abbreviated example based on Parsnip. You'll see all your old friends in one place: constants, action creators, and a reducer. Because they're used only locally, the action type constants can be shortened to remove redundant context. You'll notice that covering the standard CRUD operations for a resource can be done in a modest number of lines of code.

> **Listing 11.1 An example ducks file**

```
const FETCH_STARTED = 'parsnip/tasks/FETCH_STARTED';
const FETCH_SUCCEEDED = 'parsnip/tasks/FETCH_SUCCEEDED';
const FETCH_FAILED = 'parsnip/tasks/FETCH_FAILED';
const CREATE_SUCCEEDED = 'parsnip/tasks/CREATE_SUCCEEDED';
const FILTER = 'parsnip/tasks/FILTER';
```

Action-type constants can be shortened, given the context of the single file.

```
const initialState = {
  tasks: [],
  isLoading: false,
  error: null,
  searchTerm: '',
};

export default function reducer(state = initialState, action) {
  switch (action.type) {
    case FETCH_STARTED:
      return { ...state, isLoading: true };
    case FETCH_SUCCEEDED:
      return { ...state, tasks: action.payload.tasks, isLoading: false };
    case FETCH_FAILED:
      return { ...state, isLoading: false, error: action.payload.error };
    case CREATE_SUCCEEDED:
      return { ...state, tasks: state.tasks.concat(action.payload.task) };
    case FILTER:
      return { ...state, searchTerm: action.searchTerm };
    default:
      return state;
  }
}

export function fetchTasks() {
  return { type: FETCH_STARTED };
}

export function createTask({ title, description, status = 'Unstarted' }) {
  return dispatch => {
    api.createTask({ title, description, status }).then(resp => {
      dispatch(createTaskSucceeded(resp.data));
    });
  };
}

export function createTaskSucceeded(task) {
  return { type: CREATE_SUCCEEDED, payload: { task } };
}

export function filterTasks(searchTerm) {
  return { type: FILTER, searchTerm };
}
```

The reducer is the module's default export.

Exports each action creator for use in containers

You don't have to be quite this dogmatic when writing your own ducks files. For example, the lengthy naming convention of the action types, such as parsnip/tasks/FILTER, are meant to accommodate modules that may be packaged as npm modules and imported for use in other projects. At the risk of making assumptions, this likely doesn't apply to your application.

Across various apps, these files go by more than a few names. In our experience, ducks and modules seem to be the most popular. We prefer modules, if only because the name is more intuitive, particularly for newcomers to the codebase; seeing ducks is sure to raise an eyebrow.

Let's look at an example ducks project layout, shown in figure 11.5. Each file within the modules directory is a ducks file.

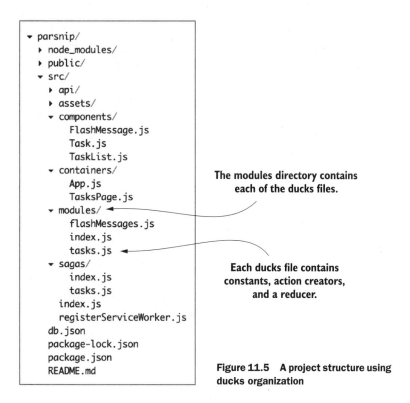

The modules directory contains each of the ducks files.

Each ducks file contains constants, action creators, and a reducer.

Figure 11.5 A project structure using ducks organization

Within that modules directory, the index.js file is a good location to handle importing each of the individual reducers and apply combineReducers.

11.3.1 Pros

The ducks pattern is a big win for scalability for a few reasons, not the least of which is the meaningful reduction in the number of files created. Whereas several of the domain-style patterns produce a file for each of the constants, reducers, and action creators, the ducks pattern results in one.

The ducks pattern also shares the domain-style pattern advantage of being able to find more feature-specific code in one place. Again, ducks go one step further, allowing you to find the relationships between action creators and reducers in a single file. Adding a feature is potentially as easy as changing a single file.

As mentioned, this pattern has the additional advantage of removing a small amount of boilerplate code, but more importantly, it lowers the mental overhead required to engage with a feature or absorb the context around a bug. When sagas are used to manage side effects, the action creators can become simplified to synchronous functions and make for more concise modules.

11.3.2 Cons

You'll find tradeoffs for the advantages. The most obvious of which is that these module files will, by definition, become larger than any of the individual files they replace. Larger files go against the JavaScript trend toward greater modularity, and this will no doubt get under certain developers' skin.

Like the domain-style pattern, if your application shares much state between domains, you may run into the same frustrations. Deciding where to draw lines between domains relies on tribal knowledge, which must be passed on to newcomers to the codebase. If you have actions being handled by multiple reducers, you have the same option to create a module for shared actions.

11.4 Selectors

Selector placement seems to be one item most of us can agree on: they belong either in the same file as their corresponding reducer or in a separate file in the same directory. Redux creator Dan Abramov encourages using this pattern to decouple views and action creators from the state shape. In other words, your container components shouldn't have to know how to efficiently calculate the state they need, but they can instead import a function that does. Keeping selectors alongside reducers will also help you remember to update them if your reducer state changes.

11.5 Sagas

Sagas are useful for managing complex side effects and are covered in detail in chapter 6. When it comes to sagas, you'll find a couple of commonly used organizational patterns. The first is to create a `sagas` directory within the `src` directory, as you did in chapter 6. This falls in line with the Rails-style organization pattern and shares the same advantages: predictability and familiarity.

A second option for handling sagas is to store them within the domain directories of a domain-style organizational pattern. This generally works well anywhere that the domain-style pattern is already a good fit. Earlier in the chapter, figure 11.3 demonstrated this pattern. You'll find a saga.js file within the `tasks` directory.

In all our travels, we've never seen sagas implemented within a `ducks` module. It's certainly possible, but by that point, there's too much going on in one file. As mentioned in the earlier section, sagas are a popular way to slim down a `ducks` module. When all side effects are handled by sagas, the action creators typically become simple synchronous functions, keeping the ducks file nice and tidy.

11.6 Styles

Stylesheet location tradeoffs are similar to sagas. For the most part, your choices boil down to either co-locating them alongside the files they style or to stick them in a dedicated, Rails-like directory. Stylesheets co-located with their respective components are convenient to reference and import, but effectively double the size of a `components` or `container` directory. Only a couple scenarios exist in which you'd consider co-locating stylesheets: small prototypes or domain-style patterns that include components within the domain directory.

11.7 Tests

Tests have roughly the same options as sagas and selectors: either co-locate them alongside the files they test or stick them in a dedicated test directory. Frankly, there are great reasons to do either.

When storing tests in a dedicated directory, you're free to creatively organize them as you see fit. The most popular options are to group them by file type (for example, reducers), test type (for example, unit tests), by feature (for example, tasks), or some nested combination.

Co-locating tests is an increasingly popular option. Like other co-located files, the boon is the convenience of referencing and importing a file in a peer directory. Beyond that, there's significant value communicated by the absence of a co-located file: it's quite clear that the component, action file, or reducer is untested.

11.8 Exercise and solutions

For this chapter's exercise, take the time to refactor the Parsnip application from the Rails-style organization to a variation of the domain-style pattern or the ducks pattern. The "solution" to each of these options has been partially presented in the figures throughout the chapter. The goal of this exercise is to gain experience with, and to form stronger, more-informed opinions about, your available patterns.

You're close but you haven't stayed exactly true to the Rails-style pattern. You've left the `App` container in the root of the `src` directory and never circled back to address it. Let's file that away in a `containers` directory and make sure to update the file paths of import statements in related files.

A couple of stylesheets are lying around in the `src` directory. Make the call whether they belong alongside their components or in a dedicated `stylesheets` directory. If you're interested in co-location, move the `App.css` file into the container directory alongside `App.js`. If you'd rather clean up the root of the `src` directory a little more, go for the Rails-style directory captured in figure 11.2 earlier in the chapter.

Take a moment to weigh the resulting code structure. Is it an appropriate fit for this application? If you add a couple more features, will it still be? Which stress points would you be concerned about?

After the thought experiment, take a pass implementing a domain-style code pattern. Use figures 11.3 and 11.4 as guidelines. When you've completed the exercise, answer the following:

- Does the application feel more intuitively structured?
- If you were to add a new feature to bookmark or "favorite" tasks, is it clear where the new logic should end up?
- How about if you wanted to add a feature to login or create a user account?

When you're ready, give the ducks pattern a try. It's not a far stretch from the domain-style pattern with containers abstracted out (figure 11.4). Move each of the domain-specific actions, constants, and reducers into a module, or ducks file.

- Is the size of the file overwhelming or manageable?
- Can you reduce the size of the file if it's troublesome?
- What are your early impressions of each strategy?

Admittedly, the number of decisions that you can make on this topic is exhausting. It merits a chapter, after all. This flexibility of Redux is a double-edged sword; you have the freedom and the burden to structure your application however you please. Fortunately, you only have to make most of these decisions once per application. If you want to dig deeper into this topic, check out the list of articles and resources found in the official documentation at http://redux.js.org/docs/faq/CodeStructure .html#code-structure.

In the next chapter, you'll explore the use of Redux in other mediums outside of React in a web application.

Summary

- Redux makes no demands on how you organize your code.
- Several popular patterns exist for structuring code and files with a Redux application, each with their own tradeoffs.
- Organizing code by domain or using the ducks pattern can improve your application's ability to scale.

Redux beyond React

This chapter covers

- Using Redux outside of a React web application
- Implementing Redux in mobile and desktop applications
- Using Redux in other web frameworks

JavaScript spaghetti code doesn't discriminate against which frameworks it appears in. That's one ailment applications across the framework spectrum have in common. Redux is most often billed as the cure to messy state management in React applications, but one of its major selling points is its compatibility with many JavaScript frameworks and environments. As long as bindings exist between Redux and the framework, you're good to go.

Because of its value and flexibility, Redux bindings have appeared for many of the major JavaScript frameworks. Where Redux isn't compatible, you'll often find that Redux-inspired packages have been written to make the ideas and patterns accessible in that environment. Given the small size of the Redux API, writing the bindings for a new framework is a manageable workload.

To iterate an idea espoused throughout this book, it may be helpful to think of Redux as a design pattern first. The package you import from npm merely contains a few helpful methods to facilitate that design pattern in your application. You'll be hard-pressed to find a client-side application where the design pattern can't be applied.

Libraries such as React are a natural fit for Redux because the surface area is small; it has few opinions about how state should be managed on a macro scale. More opinionated frameworks usually require more consideration of how the Redux pattern fits into their paradigm, but as evidenced by all the binding packages, it can be done and often brings with it an improved quality of life.

In this chapter, we'll explore using Redux in development environments outside of React web applications. React's sibling mobile-development framework, React Native, is covered first. It's a relatively simple transition for Redux from the web and the source of countless questions on developer forums. After that, we'll explore Redux within desktop applications, using the Electron framework. Finally, we'll break into other JavaScript web frameworks.

12.1   *Mobile Redux: React Native*

React Native is a popular mobile development framework maintained by Facebook and community contributors. The open source tool allows you to build native Android and iOS applications using JavaScript, and React, specifically. React DOM and React Native are alternative renderers that leverage the same diffing algorithm under the hood: React's reconciliation algorithm. The role of that algorithm is to monitor changes to component state, then stingily trigger updates only to those elements that require them.

Because they share the same underlying mechanisms, React Native development feels similar to development of React for the web. Instead of HTML tags, React Native makes native mobile components available from both platforms. Conveniently, most React web development skills translate to React Native development skills, and that includes the use of Redux. What luck!

Within a React Native application, a top-level entry-point file may look similar to the analogous index.js file within a web app. Within that file, you should expect to see the `Provider` component, imported from react-redux and used to wrap the body of the application. Similar to a web application, the `Provider` component accepts a `store` as a parameter, so that it may make its contents available to specific children components within. The key takeaway here is that there are no specific, additional packages required to make Redux compatible with React Native applications. Just install redux, react-redux, and any middleware you require, then get to work!

12.1.1   *Handling side-effects*

Developing for mobile devices comes with unique concerns, but Redux doesn't get in the way of handling those concerns. Let's say you want to interact with the hardware of a device, such as the camera or accelerometer. These are side effects, like any other, and can be handled in a similar fashion to side effects within a React web application.

Action creators, sagas, and middleware can be used to keep application logic out of your components.

Like a web application, many mobile apps interact with a remote server and local storage. Similar to when you employed the use of an API service in Parsnip, you can do the same within your React Native application. You may find it useful to have a separate service for each domain or side-effect type: remote server calls, local storage getters and setters, and hardware interactions. These abstractions are optional and subject to organizational preferences.

12.1.2 *Network connectivity*

When it comes to mobile apps, network connectivity cannot be guaranteed. As a result, mobile developers generally need to be more conscious of the offline user experience of their applications than web developers. Strategies for building a seamless offline experience vary based on the app, but one popular pattern is to store a minimal amount of data in the device's local storage to reference if a network is unavailable. This way, the application can pull cached data to populate the app until a connection is restored.

Drawing on discussions from way back in chapter 2, can you recall a way to initialize a Redux store with data retrieved from local storage? Remember that the `create-Store` method takes up to three arguments. The second argument is an optional `initialState` value:

```
const store = createStore(reducers, initialState, enhancers);
```

This `initialState` value can be retrieved from local storage on the device on startup. As the application is used, relevant data can be synced with local storage, so that it's available next time the app is opened. If you're developing a calendar app, for example, the user's favorite events can be stored in local storage and viewed later, even if not connected to a network.

12.1.3 *Performance*

Mobile development comes with heightened concerns for performance. Although mobile devices become more powerful every week, their performance will naturally lag behind larger devices, such as laptops and desktop machines. The same way the size of the hardware plays a role in performance, so too will the wireless network connectivity, as discussed in the previous section.

The priority on performance makes following React and Redux best practices even more crucial. Chapter 10 of this book is dedicated to those best practices. If you're working on a React Native app, pay special attention to opportunities where you can limit the number of unnecessary computations. As you might imagine, React Native applications are also subject to some performance concerns that are unique to the framework. You can read more about performance in the official documentation at https://facebook.github.io/react-native/docs/performance.html.

12.2 Desktop Redux: Electron

Adding to the idea of JavaScript taking over the world, Electron is a framework that enables you to write native desktop applications in JavaScript. The team at GitHub created the framework to facilitate the writing of their text editor, Atom (https://atom.io/). Fortunately for the community, both Atom and Electron are open source projects that anyone can learn from, fork, or contribute to.

12.2.1 Why native desktop?

Before you dive into implementation details, a quick aside: Why bother writing a native desktop application? Chances are a web application will be sufficient for your needs. With exceptions, you can expect to write the application once and have it work on any browser, operating system, or device. Beyond that, there's a huge pool of web development talent to pull from for building and maintaining the system.

You have several excellent reasons to write desktop applications, however. Native apps are closer to the user. Once opened, they occupy prime real estate in the operating system's menu, dock, or tray. They may always be visible or a keystroke away. Access to the native notification system allows you to alert users of important events and keep them engaged with your application. If your app requires frequent or frictionless use to provide value, this quality of a native application can't be understated. Messaging, timers, to-do, and calendar applications are all typical examples, well-suited for a native environment, but a creative use of the same tools could set your product apart from competitors.

12.2.2 How Electron works

In the first chapter of *Electron in Action*, author Steve Kinney gives an excellent high-level introduction to the framework (https://livebook.manning.com#!/book/electron-in-action/chapter-1/v-11/point-452-75-83-0). From the app developer's perspective, *Electron* starts with the main process: a Node.js application. Complete with a package.json file, you're free to import whatever modules your application will need. Within that main process, you can create, hide, and show the application's windows as well as the tray or menu icon.

For security reasons, each window you render is something of a sandbox environment. Naturally, you don't want to give the user any permissions to interact with API keys or other sensitive variables that the main process needs to track. As a result, a separate client-side application is typically maintained in its own directory within the Electron app. You could, for example, move the contents of the Parsnip application into such a directory and expect it to function within an Electron window with minimal modifications.

Under the hood, Electron leverages Chromium, Google's open source web browser, to render the contents of those windows. This is a massive boon for the developer experience. The Chrome Developer Tools are available within each window, and, consequently, so are the Redux DevTools. Even hot-loading with webpack is possible.

The main process and each renderer process need to have a way to communicate if the application is going to provide any real value. Electron's system for communication across main and renderer processes is fittingly named IPC, or inter-process communication. IPC methods allow you to emit events from one process, while listening and responding to those events in another process.

Let's say, for example, that a user wanted to upload a video in an Electron application. When the user selected their video file and clicked the submit button, an IPC message with the path of the video would be emitted. The code would look something like the following:

```
ipcRenderer.send('upload-video', '/path/to/video');
```

On the other side, the main process would watch for this event type and respond accordingly:

```
ipcMain.on('upload-video', (event, path) => {
    // handle the upload and return a success or failure response
}
```

Figure 12.1 illustrates this communication between processes.

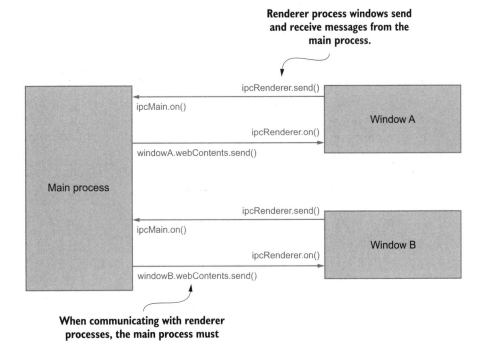

Figure 12.1 IPC communication between Electron processes

This is as deep as we'll take the discussion of Electron internals in this book. For full details, we recommend digging into a sister title in the Manning library: *Electron in Action*.

12.2.3 *Introducing Redux to Electron*

The client side of an Electron application can be written in any framework. The code running in each of the windows, or renderer process, can leverage any view library you want. React happens to be a popular option due to the architecture of Electron apps. Given that React handles the view layer, it fits well within a renderer process. Again, the role of the renderer process is to communicate with the main process, where the bulk of the business logic resides. The separation of concerns fits the React paradigm well.

Within the renderer process, the Redux store plays the same role it does in a web application: it decouples application logic from the view layer and organizes interactions with side effects. In terms of implementation, there's no difference from the setup required in a web application. You may have differences in the types of side effects managed, but they're still handled in the same locations you're used to. Instead of interacting with local storage in an action creator, you may instead use IPC methods to kick off computation in the main process.

One detail worth revisiting is that the Redux store for a renderer process is isolated to that context. Multiple windows could have a separate Redux store, each operating completely independently of one another. While you're at it, the main process can use a separate Redux store, too. On their own, each store has some value, but you have to imagine that it would be more valuable to keep each store in sync. Good news! A couple of open source packages provide that functionality.

Packages electron-redux and electron-redux-store offer two similar implementations for keeping multiple sandboxed stores in sync. Under the hood, both leverage IPC to communicate between the processes. Each provides a way for dispatched actions in one process to feed through the reducers of another process.

The electron-redux package declares the Redux store in the main process as the source of truth. Other process stores act as proxies. When creating renderer stores, they'll need to get their initial state from the main store using a `getInitialState-Renderer` function. When using this package, all actions are required to be Flux Standard Action (FSA)-compliant.

We covered FSAs in an earlier chapter, but as a quick reminder, they require all actions to use a standard set of keys: payload, error, metadata, and type. electron-redux uses the meta key to determine if an action should be kept within a local renderer's store or dispatched to the main process as well. For more implementation details, see the official documentation at https://github.com/hardchor/electron-redux.

We'd argue that the `electron-redux-store` is the simpler of the two packages to use. Installation requires fewer steps and dispatched actions need not be Flux Standard Actions. When updates are made to the main Redux store, you can subscribe renderer processes to subsets of store value changes using filters. For more details, reference the official documentation at https://github.com/samiskin/redux-electron-store.

12.3 *Other Redux bindings*

As you've learned, Redux bindings come in many flavors. Up to this point, this book has introduced only the react-redux package, providing the means to connect React components with the Redux store. In this section, we'll take a quick tour of several of the most popular alternatives. If you're interested in a more complete list, see Mark Erikson's list at https://github.com/markerikson/redux-ecosystem-links/blob/master/library-integration.md.

12.3.1 *Angular*

Angular is one of the most popular JavaScript frameworks on the block. With its backing by Google and level of maturity as a project, it's a regular choice for applications in the enterprise space. More recently, Angular overcame a great deal of churn when it released a rewrite of the framework for version 2.0.0. It's possible to use Redux in an Angular v1 application and, if that's the boat you find yourself in, you can view the corresponding Redux binding library here: https://github.com/angular-redux/ng-redux. We won't cover the implementation details in this section, given that it's unlikely a new project will choose Angular v1.

Angular 2 introduced components that more closely resemble React components. Between these new Angular components and other application-logic decoupling, Angular has become a more welcoming environment for introducing Redux. Welcoming is a relative term, however.

If you're coming to Angular with only React experience, you'll experience a mildly intimidating learning curve. Angular applications are written in TypeScript (https://www.typescriptlang.org/), a superset of JavaScript that adds optional static typing. The framework also leverages observables with RxJS and implements its own change detector, analogous to React's reconciliation algorithm.

Angular was also written with the intention to cover more ground than React. Instead of only the view layer, Angular accounts for an application's models and controllers in the MVC framework terminology. For these architecture-related reasons, the Redux bindings for Angular look and operate differently than react-redux.

Usage of Redux within an Angular app requires installation of the redux package, but additionally you'll need to install @angular-redux/store. Similarly to React, you'll need to make one of your top-level components aware of the Redux store. From there, you can inject NgRedux into the components you want connected with Redux functionality. The dispatch method is available on the object you inject, typically called ngRedux:

```
this.ngRedux.dispatch({ type: 'FETCH_TASKS' });
```

As for displaying Redux store data, the bindings are implemented using a method or a decorator, called `select`. `select` leverages Observables to make changes to the DOM when the store updates. As described in the RxJS documentation, "Observables are lazy Push collections of multiple values." André Staltz, creator of Cycle.js, encourages you to think of them as "asynchronous immutable array[s]."

Angular makes regular use of Observables to handle asynchronous events. If this is foreign territory and you'd like more context on Observables, we recommend the RxJS documentation at http://reactivex.io/rxjs/manual/overview.html#observable. For detailed implementation instructions, reference the `angular-redux` bindings codebase here: https://github.com/angular-redux/store.

12.3.2 *Ember*

Ember is another popular JavaScript framework, regularly compared to and contrasted with Angular and React in blog posts and conference talks. Ember is similar in scope to Angular, offering models, views, and controllers. Drawing inspiration from Ruby's Rails framework, Ember offers an opinionated take on a client-side application structure, baking in many common configuration choices, so you don't have to.

The Redux bindings for Ember are used in a similar fashion to the bindings for React. You'll need to install the ember-redux add-on. Installation of this add-on also installs redux, redux-thunk, and other dependencies. In Ember, components consist of two files, a Handlebars template for the HTML and a JavaScript file for deriving the data that gets rendered in the template. The goal in introducing Redux is to simplify the logic required in those component JavaScript files.

The method for connecting a component will look very familiar. Import connect from ember-redux and pass it the slices of state required by your component. You'll find that `stateToComputed` is an Ember-friendly function name, but it's implemented identically to `mapStateToProps`:

```
connect(stateToComputed, dispatchToActions)(Component);
```

Many of the other Redux elements will also look roughly the same as their react-redux counterparts. Once you've injected the Redux service into a route, it can be used to return an action following a successful API call:

```
redux.dispatch({ type: 'FETCH_TASKS', payload });
```

From there, reducers work like what you're accustomed to. Reselect selector functions are available with a shim. The `combineReducers` package is used from the redux package, too. One method you won't find in an Ember app, however, is `createStore`. Under the hood, ember-redux is taking care of it.

Ready to dive in? The codebase (https://github.com/ember-redux/ember-redux) and official documentation (http://www.ember-redux.com/) are a wealth of information. The documentation site contains a video tutorial and several example applications with advanced features. Check out the Redux Saga demo for an example middleware configuration. The use of sagas is identical to a React context, but because `ember-redux` hides the store creation from you, middleware initialization has a new home.

12.4 Redux without a framework

Though a bit unorthodox, there's nothing stopping you from introducing Redux to a plain old JavaScript application. As you know, Redux bindings make it easy to use Redux within popular frameworks, but aren't a requirement for its use. If you have a hand-rolled JavaScript codebase, Redux can, at a minimum, handle all updates in one predictable location, improving your ability to debug and test the application.

Within JavaScript applications suffering from closely coupled modules, breaking down your business logic into smaller, organized units (for example, action creators and reducers), can introduce a great deal of clarity. As you learned in chapter 9, there are clear paths for unit testing these components of the application.

Another argument for introducing Redux into this type of application is the potential insight offered by the Redux DevTools. Dispatching and monitoring actions are low-hanging fruit for an application that's difficult to debug. Using the DevTools as a log aggregator can prove more timely and convenient than existing options.

Because this isn't a conventional or popular option, you won't find many playbooks online in the form of tutorials or official documentation. One example use case is within the main process of an Electron app, but again, documentation is hard to come by. We should also note that adding Redux to an application doesn't guarantee that your state management woes will vaporize. When applied thoughtfully, though, Redux can help untangle "spaghetti" code without the use of bindings.

12.5 Exercise and solutions

As an exercise to expand your understanding of how Redux fits into other technology stacks, look at one or more of the starter kits described in this section. Your goal should be to read through the existing code to identify how and where the Redux stores are configured. Next, compare the usage patterns you see with those covered in this book while building Parsnip, the React web application. You should answer the following questions:

- In this environment, does the creation of a Redux store differ from that of React web applications? If so, how?
- What data is kept in the store?
- Where are side effects handled and by what means?
- What file organization patterns are used?

If you're stumped while tracking down the Redux store initialization in any of the mentioned repositories, try using the global search functionality within GitHub to look for the `createStore` method.

If you're interested in exploring Redux within a React Native application, look at one of the following starter kits. Both are robust options for getting a jump on a production-quality application and include many features beyond Redux. Do your best to focus exclusively on the Redux implementations the first time through the codebases. Your options are the starter kit by Matt Mcnmee, https://github.com/mcnamee/react-native-starter-app, and the Snowflake application by Barton Hammond, https://github.com/bartonhammond/snowflake.

Is Electron more your style? Try the starter kit created by C. T. Lin at https://github.com/chentsulin/electron-react-boilerplate. Again, you'll find many features beyond Redux within this repository, so do your best to ignore those while you attempt to answer the previous questions.

Those looking for Angular 2+ implementations of Redux will be happy to find an officially supported example repository at https://github.com/angular-redux/example-app. This is one case where you won't find the `createStore` method. Instead, search for `store.configureStore` to find one entry point into the Redux workflow.

Looking for Ember instead? Try this TodoMVC implementation at https://ember-twiddle.com/4bb9c326a7e54c739b1f5a5023ccc805. Again, you won't find the `create-Store` method here, as `ember-redux` takes care of store initialization under the hood.

You'll notice there are few limits to where Redux can be applied within JavaScript applications. Many times, it's the perfect tool for the job of taming a messy application state. You'll find joy in breaking down state management into a predictable, testable, unidirectional data flow. A gentle reminder, though, for the road ahead: if Redux is a hammer, not every application is a nail.

If you'd like to dig deeper into the available Redux bindings, or countless other rabbit holes, check out the official ecosystem documentation page at http://redux.js.org/docs/introduction/Ecosystem.html.

Summary

- Redux is flexible and generic enough for use in all kinds of applications.
- React Native applications have unique constraints but can leverage Redux without any additional dependencies.
- Electron applications can use Redux like a web application in the renderer processes, but each store is sandboxed. Open source options exist for synchronizing several Redux stores.
- In addition to React, Redux bindings exist for many of the major web frameworks.
- It's possible to enjoy the benefits of Redux without bindings at all.

appendix
Installation

This appendix covers

- Setting up a server
- Installing axios
- Configuring Redux Thunk
- Updating the Redux DevTools

Setting up a server

Before you can start dispatching async actions, you need to do a few things:

- Install and configure json-server, a popular tool for generating REST APIs quickly. This is a Redux book after all, so you don't want to expend too much energy writing a fully featured back end. json-server allows you to specify a set of resources (such as tasks) and creates a standard set of endpoints to use.
- Install axios, a popular AJAX library. There's no shortage of popular AJAX libraries, including the new native browser API window.fetch, but axios is our choice due to a solid feature set and a straightforward API.
- Install and configure Redux Thunk. You'll have to add middleware to the Redux store, which is simpler than it might sound.

Installing and configuring json-server

First things first, install json-server globally by running the following command in a terminal window:

```
npm install --global json-server
```

Next create a db.json file in the root directory and add the contents shown in the following listing.

Listing 1   db.json

```
{
  "tasks": [
    {
      "id": 1,
      "title": "Learn Redux",
      "description": "The store, actions, and reducers, oh my!",
      "status": "Unstarted"
    },
    {
      "id": 2,
      "title": "Peace on Earth",
      "description": "No big deal.",
      "status": "Unstarted"
    },
    {
      "id": 3,
      "title": "Create Facebook for dogs",
      "description": "The hottest new social network",
      "status": "Completed"
    }
  ]
}
```

Finally, start the server with the following command. Note that you're specifying the server to run on port 3001, because the Create React App development server is already running on port 3000:

```
json-server --watch db.json --port 3001
```

That's it! You'll start to use each of the newly available endpoints as you add more functionality to Parsnip.

Installing axios

With a server configured, you need to install one more package, axios. axios is one of the many options for making AJAX work a bit more pleasant, and it will be your tool for making HTTP requests from the browser throughout the book. Make sure you're in the parsnip directory and install axios using npm:

```
npm install axios
```

If you see the standard npm success output, you're all set!

Redux Thunk

Install Redux Thunk using npm from the terminal by running the following command:

```
npm install redux-thunk
```

Add the middleware via the `applyMiddleware` function exported by Redux, as shown in the following listing.

Listing 2   src/index.js

```
import React from 'react';
import ReactDOM from 'react-dom';
import { createStore, applyMiddleware } from 'redux';      ← Imports applyMiddleware from Redux
import { Provider } from 'react-redux';
import thunk from 'redux-thunk';                           ← Imports the middleware from Redux Thunk
import { tasks } from './reducers';
import App from './App';
import './index.css';

const store = createStore(
  tasks,
  applyMiddleware(thunk)     ← Applies the middleware during store creation
);

ReactDOM.render(
  <Provider store={store}>
    <App />
  </Provider>,
  document.getElementById('root')
)
```

Before you get off to the races, there's one more important update to make regarding the Redux DevTools.

Configuring the Redux DevTools

Now that we've introduced middleware, the old `devToolsEnhancer` function will no longer do the trick. You'll import another method from the same DevTools library that can accommodate middleware, called `composeWithDevTools`, as shown in the following listing.

Listing 3   src/index.js

```
import { composeWithDevTools } from 'redux-devtools-extension';    ← Imports composeWithDevTools
...
const store = createStore(
  tasks,
  composeWithDevTools(applyMiddleware(thunk))     ← Wraps the applyMiddleware function
);
```

Now you're ready to return to the action! Don't forget to use the DevTools Chrome extension to see each action come through the system. The API story resumes in chapter 4.

Installing lodash

Install lodash, a popular functional programming library, by running the follow command:

```
npm install lodash
```

Installing Enzyme

Enzyme is a testing tool that mainly helps with React component testing. Enzyme used to require special configuration to use with Jest, but since Jest version 15, no additional configuration is required. Install Enzyme using npm:

```
npm install -D enzyme
```

Installation script

Included with the book's source code is a bash script to get you up and running quickly. It requires you to have a few pieces of software installed before you run it:

- *Git*—https://git-scm.com/book/en/v2/Getting-Started-Installing-Git
- *Node/npm*—https://nodejs.org/en/

For OS X and Linux, download the install.sh script, and run the following commands:

```
chmod +x install.sh
./install.sh
```

For Windows, download the install.ps1 script and look at the instructions for running PowerShell scripts (https://docs.microsoft.com/powershell/scripting/core-powershell/ise/how-to-write-and-run-scripts-in-the-windows-powershell-ise).

That's it! The script will clone the book's repository from GitHub, install json-server (which you'll use beginning with chapter 4), and start a local development server from a fresh Create React App installation. This should set you up perfectly to begin coding with chapter 2.

index